WAR AND WAR CRIMES

JAMES GOW

War and War Crimes

The Military, Legitimacy and Success in Armed Conflict

HURST & COMPANY, LONDON

First published in the United Kingdom in 2013 by
C. Hurst & Co. (Publishers) Ltd.,
41 Great Russell Street, London, WC1B 3PL
© James Gow, 2013
All rights reserved.
Printed in India

A Cataloguing-in-Publication data record for this book
is available from the British Library.

ISBNs: 978-1849040938 (hardback)
       978-1849040945 (paperback)

This book is printed using paper from registered sustainable
and managed sources.

www.hurstpublishers.com

CONTENTS

Preface   vii

1. Strategy, War and Law   1
2. Strategy and the Multidimensional Trinity   23
3. Prosecuting War Crimes   45
4. Strategy and Justice   67
5. Conduct and Cases   91
6. War and War Crimes   115

Annexes
Selected Extracts from International Criminal Statutes

Annex A: Statute of the International Criminal Tribunal for the
             Former Yugoslavia (Extract)   145
Annex B: Statute of the International Criminal Tribunal for
             Rwanda   149
Annex C: Rome Statute of the International Criminal Court   153

Notes   161
Index   203

PREFACE

The seed of this book was sown in a conversation in late 1994 or early 1995 in the corridors of the Office of the Prosecutor at the United Nations' International Criminal Tribunal for the former Yugoslavia, in the The Hague. That conversation was with Bill Fenrick. He was an experienced Canadian military lawyer, who had become a legal advisor in the Office of the Prosecutor. At that time, I was a consultant expert advisor to the OTP, assisting it—and ultimately that court—as an expert witness, to establish jurisdiction for the crimes to be charged.

Bill and I seemed to share two perceptions, although the expression of the issues here is entirely my own, as I never consciously confirmed his thinking. The first was that discussions were circulating in the corridors of the OTP that would mean charges of unlawful attack being brought for the first time ever, in any international context. That in turn would mean military personnel being investigated and charged for offences that were clearly about professional competence—rather than conduct, such as massacring civilians, that was clearly outside any bounds of acceptability. This was an intriguing intellectual (primarily) and legal problem for anyone with an interest in both the armed forces and war crimes. It was evident at that stage, and to a great extent since, that those most interested in questions of war crimes are lawyers and human rights activists who, broadly speaking, seem to lack any understanding of the nature of military operations or the armed forces. This was confirmation for the second perception, viz. that an understanding of the nature of warfare and the perspective of military professionals was largely lacking in discussion of suspected and alleged war crimes at that time.

This idea was a long time germinating, but I continued to give it much thought and it eventually became the basis for research with military professionals, both directly and more contingently as part of other research. That

PREFACE

work, from 2003 onwards, mainly between 2005 and 2011, was variously funded by grants from the ESRC and the AHRC (twice), with the latter responsible for the majority of the directly related research. That research was made possible, not only by the funding available, but crucially by the strong links between King's College London, as the primary academic provider to the UK Defence Academy, and so to education at both the Royal College of Defence Studies in London, and the Joint Services Command and Staff College in Shrivenham. Of course, strong links are not enough. So, it is also important to note the good will of the relevant directing staff and colleagues, and, above all, the members who volunteered to take part in the focus group research that informs key parts of this volume. Indeed, thanks are due also to all those who participated in the research elsewhere. The institutional cooperation of others also requires acknowledgement, in particular the Humanitarian Law Center, Belgrade, the Humanitarian Law Center, Priština, and the Center for Interdisciplinary Postgraduate Studies, University of Sarajevo.

The long journey from idea, to research, to book has benefited from the views of two sets of anonymous peer reviewers, the first of which, pointed out that really I had been writing at least two books, which was a sound judgement and led to my revisiting the whole project to identify and separate the 'joint' parts of the project, where the two books overlapped, and starting again, this time to write two books. The present volume is one of those books, also read twice by anonymous readers and greatly enhanced by the input of Gordon Burck, who read the whole manuscript and commented extensively and critically. Of the two later readers, one was clearly a strategist who 'got' the essence of the book and the other was a lawyer, who also provided wise counsel in questioning and challenging parts of the book with a view to making it 'lawyer proof.' By which I mean that the reader recognised that the book was not a 'law' book, as such, and thought 'the $Trinity^3(+)$ concept... genuinely interesting and innovative', but that, as an interdisciplinary study, it was important that aspects of law were 'dealt with well.' I hope and trust that I have managed to make the work pass legal muster, at least to the extent that lawyers will not simply dismiss it, but pay attention to the ethical, strategic and social research encompassed herein. In this respect, I am particularly grateful to my colleague Guglielmo Verdirame, Professor of International Law at King's, who read key chapters in the final version of the manuscript, to my former colleague Professor Rein Müllerson and to Professor Zoran Pajić. Zoran Pajić also deserves thanks for a wider role on the last of the funded research projects.

PREFACE

It is impossible to do this kind of work alone, so my thanks also go to the others who worked with me, one way or another: Marie Gillespie, Andrew Hoskins, Ben O'Loughlin, Ivan Zveržhanovski, Dave Whetham, Ann Lane, Ernst Dijxhoorn, Inara Khan, Rachel Kerr and Milena Michalski, as well as all the other members, across the years, of the War Crimes Research Group at King's College London.

The list of those who have helped any book to print is always longer than the names that actually appear in it. For those whose names do not appear here, my apologies for forgetfulness or poor judgement in not including you. Those of whom I am aware include Jan Willem Honig, (Professor Sir) Lawry Freedman, (Professor Sir) Michael Howard, and Professor Martin Edmonds, all of whom have shaped my thinking and conceptualisation concerning war and war crimes. Thanks to: Air Vice Marshall Steve Chisnall, who was especially important in facilitating research; Philip Bobbitt; Sir Adam Roberts; Huw Strachan; Theo Farrell; Chiyuki Aoi; General Jim Mattis; Dick Kohn; Lt. Gen. Paul Newton; Rear Admiral Bob Shepherd; Jack Spence; Christopher Dandeker; Gavin Ruxton; Minna Schrag; Sir Geoffrey Nice; Rodney Dixon; David Gowan; Bojan Zrnić; Iva Vukušić; Wolfgang Danspeckgrüber, and Mervyn Frost. Thanks also to Michael Dwyer for his patience and support, as well as Daisy Leitch, Holly Catling and Jonathan de Peyer for their editorial input.

Although mentioned already, it is entirely appropriate to acknowledge some people again, a little more fully. First, thanks go to Bill Fenrick for engaging me in such interesting discussion and, in so doing, helping to stimulate the research reflected here. Thanks are also due in a broader sense to Rachel Kerr, who has been an inspiration and font of support, as well as counsellor, and a model colleague. Despite the various contributions of all these wonderful people, in the end, as interpreter of the material and author of this book, the responsibility for any failings lies with me alone. Finally, thanks to my late father, Donald, a constant guide in thinking about wrong and right; to Baka and Deka, for their support and putting up with academics, and bridging the gaps; Milena, another inspiration and font of support, and so much more as well, without whom, quite literally, there would probably have been nothing (ever) finished, and most things never started; and our miraculous, playful, wise young man, Gabriel, who already knows more about war and war crimes, and research and writing, than most people will discover in a lifetime.

AJWG, London, August 2012

1

STRATEGY, WAR AND LAW

War is a social phenomenon involving specific, dedicated social organisations (armed forces) in the management of restrained coercive violence for political purpose, governed by rules and conventions.*

---

* My definition draws on three decades of reflection, discussion and reading. It has been particularly influenced by Martin Edmonds, Lawrence Freedman, Jan Willem Honig and Michael Howard, in all cases, both in person and in writing. I offer developed discussion of the definition, its reasoning and the sources underpinning it in a forthcoming book on aspects of war (to be published in 2012–13, all being well). It is important to note that 'war' is a political phenomenon, involving armed forces, in some sense, and the use of armed force, or the threat to use armed force (the threat being a use of that force). These aspects of the definition draw on Carl von Clausewitz, who linked the use of armed force to political purpose (Clausewitz, *On War*, trans. J. J. Graham, Introduction and Notes by Colonel F. N. Maude, C. B. (Later R. E.), 'Introduction to the New Edition' by Jan Willem Honig, New York: Barnes and Noble, 2004). War is a social phenomenon in two senses: it involves whole human groups, not just two individuals, which means it is subject to social dynamics; and it is man-made, not some kind of natural disaster or natural phenomenon—although it often seems as though people regard it in this way. Each social group has a particular sub-group (in time of war, at least, and usually outside it), a dedicated social organisation—the military—disciplined and skilled in the application and management of violence on behalf of the wider social group and for its political purposes (Morris Janowitz, *The Professional Soldier: A Scoial and Political Portrait*, Glencoe, Ill: The Free Press, 1960). It is subject to rules and conventions that set its boundaries as a legitimate activity: politics creates a condition (war) in which normal rules and conventions cease to apply, so that, for

1

However, war is not what it used to be. Or rather, warfare—the conduct of militaries, distinct from war as a whole—is not what it used to be. While certain essentials of definition are eternal, specifics change. In the twenty-first century, the rules at the heart of warfare are changing, or they are in need of change. Change is necessary to match the shifting issues, demands and nature of contemporary warfare. This applies not just to the rules of conduct—how battle is practised—but also to those of undertaking the use of destructive armed force in the first place. The flux surrounding war in a time of change has meant increasing debate since the end of the Cold War surrounding the legitimacy of using armed force. That discussion has focused on the question of legality, particularly among advanced industrial

---

example, killing human beings is permitted where this would normally not be the case. Yet, there are still limits, there are still always rules and conventions that dictate the circumstances in which killing human beings is made legitimate by the peculiar political condition of war, and those in which it remains unacceptable, even taking this peculiar political condition into account. (See Michael Howard *et al.*, eds, *Restraints on War: Studies in the Limitation of Armed Conflict*, Oxford: Oxford University Press, 1979). War is not the same as 'battle', nor, crucially, the same as 'armed conflict'. These are important points because I have found over the years that students tend initially (and perhaps beyond that) to think of war as battle and while battle involves the engagement of armed forces against each other, which is a contingency of war, it lacks the political purpose that defines war. I have also found that among those who accept that the rules of war limit and delimit it, framing its definition, many assume that 'war' and 'armed conflict' are interchangeable terms. This is especially true of international humanitarian lawyers, whose concern is provisionally with applying the laws of armed conflict. However, war, as a political phenomenon involving the use of armed forces, does not absolutely and necessarily have to involve the application of coercive violence—the use of armed force—in such a sustained manner that the laws of armed conflict would come into play. Indeed, it should be recognised that all great warriors have worked on the presumption that the ideal victory is the one where the mere threat of armed force secures the desired political goals without ever having to use actual force.

This book is informed by research from three major projects, noted in the preface and elsewhere in the text as appropriate: 'Pictures of Peace and Justice: Documentation, Evident and Impact of Visual Material in Relation to International War Crimes Prosecutions' (with Dr. R. C. Kerr), Beyond Text Programme, Arts and Humanities Research Council, Award AH/H015566/1; 'Shifting Securities: Television News Cultures Before and After Iraq 2003' (with Dr. M. L Gillespie, Professor A. J. W. Gow and Dr. A. D. Hoskins), New Security Challenges Programme, Economic and Social Research Council, ESRC Award RES-223–25–0063; and 'War and War Crimes', Arts and Humanities Research Council, AHRC Award No. RL/111925.

liberal democracies and among transnational communities and wider international publics. Discourse has been driven, to a large extent, by accusations of war crimes, both in the context of complex regional conflicts and in that of engagement by international forces in areas of crisis, conflict and threat.

In January 2004, a panel of international lawyers called on the International Criminal Court (ICC) to investigate the British government for alleged war crimes in Iraq.[1] This discourse inevitably added to existing pressure to avoid any incidents that might be alleged as war crimes. Similarly, US conduct in the Global War on Terror was surrounded with accusations of war crimes and abuse, with the Abu Ghraib prison in Baghdad and the detention facility at Guantanamo attracting particular attention.[2] The atmosphere of accusation was not helped by Washington's insistence in this phase on getting parties to the Rome Statute of the ICC to sign agreements excluding US personnel from prosecution. Thus, the changing character of war opened up questions of lawfulness and legitimacy, regarding what constituted legitimate warfare, and what constituted a war crime. The very notion of war crimes shows that warfare is subject to rules, and these rules, when cast as laws, define war crimes. Legality and other rules separate war, as an awful but legitimate political process, from that which would otherwise be criminality, pure and simple. To understand war crimes, it is necessary to understand war and its enduring relationship with that which is understood as right, as well as that which is seen as wrong.

Ancient questions of wrong and right concerning the conduct of war gained new currency and were challenged by new circumstances. The eternally relevant key notions of the 'Just War' tradition—*jus ad bellum* (just cause) and *jus in bello* (just conduct)—were cast into the crucible of the changing character of warfare.[3] While the essence of war is unchanging, the character of its conduct changes periodically in relation to social and technical conditions.[4] The contemporary era is characterised by a continuing process of change, which will last years, probably decades.[5] Yet, the dominant understanding of the laws of war derives from the preceding phase of what can be termed 'conventional' warfare, understood as the mode of armed combat made familiar by the tumultuous world wars of the twentieth century. This created tension between the existing law and the new phase of armed conflict. There were attempts to apply these existing laws but they were not entirely appropriate for the new context. In this new context there was increasing pressure on those involved in decisions about using force and applying it.

The Yugoslav War was an important marker of change during the 1990s. That war, especially in Bosnia and Hercegovina and in Kosovo, epitomised the changing character of warfare. It was also the mainspring for concern about gross abuse of human rights, international crimes and war crimes. This was particularly because, as I have noted previously, this war was defined by the Serbian strategy of war crimes at its core.[6] Similar allegations of atrocity and crime emerged elsewhere, notably in Africa, with the Rwandan genocide and the horrors of Liberia and Sierra Leone.[7] However, while these conflicts were key examples of what was dubbed 'new war',[8] accusations of war crimes and abuse were not restricted to the parties to those murderous agendas. Human Rights Watch produced influential studies regarding the NATO operations over Kosovo, in 1999.[9] Amnesty International produced similar reports.[10] Under pressure from these and other NGOs and human rights activists, NATO action in Kosovo even attracted the attention of the Prosecutor at the UN International Criminal Tribunal for the former Yugoslavia (ICTY). While the Prosecutor's preliminary review concluded that there was not sufficient evidence to warrant devoting resources to further investigations, the issue had already made an impact through media and public discourse (this is discussed in Chapter 5, in particular, in connection with the use of cluster munitions).

A big concern for Western governments and soldiers is that in many of these instances, and others, they have come under scrutiny, not for having committed acts outside legitimate military activity (such as Crimes Against Humanity or genocide), but in relation to allegations of war crimes involving the normal conduct of operations. This happened in the cases of Kosovo and Iraq, and such allegations seem more easily and readily made each time there is an instance of genuine wrongdoing. Indeed, the Yugoslavia Tribunal, for the first time, raised charges that may impinge on the normal conduct of warfare, such as disproportionate artillery bombardment.[11] Away from the criminal courtroom, civil proceedings have also added to the pressure: for example, the Netherlands Appeal Court found that the Dutch government was responsible for the deaths of three Muslim men who were forced to leave a compound near Srebrenica under Dutch military UN control, and were subsequently murdered in the course of the massacre of over 8,000 Muslim men by Serbian forces commanded by General Ratko Mladić.[12] This pattern of accusation combined with the increasing scrutiny of the actions of Western armed forces and political leaders, and the emergence of new mechanisms for prosecution, has been described as the 'judicialisation of armed conflict',[13] or the 'juridification of war'.[14] With activists and news media keen to allege wrong-doing, and with visual material of overriding importance to these allegations,[15] governments and military alike faced serious challenges in the securing of necessary public support for the use of force. As discussed in Chapter 2, support—various publics' 'hearts and minds'—lies at the centre of gravity for success in contemporary armed conflict. In this context, accusations of wrongdoing can undermine the quest for success. This is the case even where circumstances are ambiguous or contested, but is all the more so when actions are evidently beyond the pale. The remainder of this first chapter will consider both actions that can be deemed to be war crimes, and then, having signalled the problems that can surround apparent war crimes, it will address the difficulties associated with discussions where matters such as context are essential, confirming the intrinsic and mutually defining relationship between war and war crimes.

We Know a War Crime When We See It

Some war crimes are incontestable. Indeed, this judgement applies to the vast majority of those matters considered as war crimes historically. This is because it has generally only been matters that so clearly exceed the bounds of any form of acceptability that have generated attention in this way—such as the mass murder of civilian non-combatants. Some matters have always been more ambiguous—for example, the killing of prisoners of war by England's King Henry V in Shakespeare's eponymous treatment, where the justice of the King's orders to kill the prisoners is discussed by those ordered to commission the deed.[16] Other events stand outside their context as crimes. These egregious acts tend to be patently obvious and observers from almost any perspective have little problem recognising them. Among the most lucid examples are those recorded for all to witness—once non-existent, then rare, with the advent of handheld digital image capture devices visual evidence of the actual commission of crimes is becoming ever more common.[17] Examples of clear-cut war crimes have come to the fore with the increasing availability of dense moving-image capture and dissemination. As discussed in the remainder of this section, that which is seen on screen is not always as it might seem. But, for the most part, it is just that. Generally, when we see a war crime, we just know that it is one, as the examples below show.

The first example, and one of the most shocking pieces of evidence, concerns a film recording shown during the last days of the never-completed war crimes trial of Slobodan Milošević at the International Criminal Tribunal for the Former Yugoslavia (ICTY).[18] During the prosecution's cross examination of Obrad Stevanović (former head of the Serbian MUP—the interior ministry special police forces), a witness for the defence, the prosecutor played an extract that showed six young males in civilian clothing, four of whom were shown being murdered. One at a time they were pushed and made to walk forward, hands bound behind their back, and shot from behind. The remaining two then had their hands freed and were ordered to move the four corpses to another location. There, these last two were also shot dead. Although this was powerful visual material of the kind that almost required no words of explanation, Geoffrey Nice, the lead prosecutor in the case, read a description into the trial record:

This video, which is potentially distressing viewing and I'm only going to play very small parts of it, reveals, Mr. Stevanovic [sic], if the evidence is in due course admitted, and that's why I want your assistance, reveals that men were brought from Srebrenica in batches to this group of Skorpions [sic] to be executed and they were executed, and what you see here is a lorry load of six young men. This is the same truck with the men in the back. And you can see the red berets…. The lorry leaves. The men are eventually taken up into the hills. It may be difficult to move it, but I don't need to linger on this. Here they are taken up into the surrounding countryside. Two remaining not shot are untied. [sic] I needn't go into the detail, or we needn't view the detail. They're untied, they move the four bodies, and then they are themselves shot, and I'll leave it there.[19]

The extract shown came from several hours of film recorded by a member of the Scorpions unit and started two hours and thirty-five minutes into the footage, with scenes of the Scorpions being blessed by a priest. This astonishing film had come into the hands of the prosecution and those of the Humanitarian Law Center in Belgrade, run by Nataša Kandić, who had received it from a member of the unit. This was remarkable, unusual and unequivocal evidence of illegal action by Serbian forces. It did not have material weight in the trial of the Serbian leader during a decade of war marked by war crimes. The court decided neither to admit the evidence as it was, nor to permit the prosecutor the chance to bring supporting testimony to confirm its authenticity and true character.[20] Yet, despite not being admitted into evidence in court, this was universally recognised as evidence of the commission of war crimes. Its status as historical and social evidence was unchallenged, despite its not being adopted formally as criminal evidence in court. This applied even in Serbia, where there had largely been denial concerning Serbia's role in the war and the atrocities that defined it, but now there had to be acknowledgement of the kind of crime that Serbian forces had perpetrated.[21] It was unchallenged in Serbia and everywhere else because anyone caring to consider this evidence could see the crime being committed with their own eyes: the murder of civilian captives.

The second historic example of visually recorded war crimes concerns the case of *R v. Payne and others*. This landmark case, otherwise referred to as the 'Baha Mousa' case, in reference to the Iraqi civilian who was killed while in UK custody, involved the first conviction of a British soldier for war crimes under the International Criminal Court Act. To avoid any issues of friction or manipulation with the nascent International Criminal Court (ICC) in The Hague, which the UK had strongly supported and assisted, the Rome Statute of the ICC had almost entirely been absorbed into British law (and entirely so far as any matters of criminal substance were concerned)[22] before the ICC Statute itself had even formally come into force.

The Baha Mousa case was one of several allegations made against UK forces in the context of the Iraq expedition; six of these resulted in judicial proceedings after they were investigated in 2003.[23] The other five cases involved shooting incidents of some kind, all in combat situations and with degrees of ambiguity surrounding them. Baha Mousa was quite different. It involved the alleged abuse of Iraqi civilians in British hands. Although several Iraqis were involved in the incidents that prompted charges, the focus was on Mousa, who died while in British custody, having, according to the autopsy report, been the victim of numerous assaults over a period of thirty six hours. Mousa and the others were detained after the First Queen's Lancashire Regiment (1st QLR) raided a hotel in Basra on 14 September 2003. The raid discovered various pieces of weaponry and appeared to confirm the information that had prompted the raid: the hotel was one of several being used as an insurgent base. The hotel's employees were taken to a temporary detention facility to determine whether or not they posed a threat to Coalition forces. In the process of being detained and more markedly while in detention, the Iraqis were subject to abuse and inhumane treatment. In addition to the apparent beatings that occurred, all detainees were forced into a position with their knees bent so that their thighs were parallel to the ground (as they would be while sitting on a chair—but there was no chair) while their backs were against the wall and their arms were stretched out straight in front of them. This 'stress' position was part of the 'conditioning' process formally set out by 1st QLR in its procedure for handling detainees. While the precise cause of Mousa's death could not be diagnosed, this stress position was closely linked to one of the two possible causes of death—postural asphyxia. The other possible cause was the multiple injuries received as a result of the beatings he received—Mousa had ninety-three externally visible injuries, evidence of strangulation, broken ribs and a broken nose.[24] There was no doubt about the effects and the crime. The only issue was to identify the perpetrators.

In the end, only Corporal Donald Payne was convicted in the case. He was convicted for abuse, having admitted guilt on one count of inhumane treatment. He was acquitted on charges of manslaughter and perverting the course of justice, with the Judge Advocate, Justice McKinnon's ruling that there was no case to answer on either count. Justice McKinnon reached the same conclusion with respect to all charges against the six other accused.[25] Payne was the only convict in the case, in all probability, because he had no alternative to pleading guilty, as he was captured on film abusing the detainees. The film was also shown at the inquiry into Baha Mousa's death, where it formed part of the inquiry's evidence.[26] The film was a souvenir recorded by one member of the regiment and it clearly depicted Payne forcing the Iraqi detainees into the stress position described above and beating them. The reason for Payne's admission of guilt regarding inhumane treatment was the clear evidence. On that basis, he became the first British soldier convicted of a war crime under the International Criminal Court Act. This was a war crime that all who viewed the film evidence could see.[27]

The images of a US Marine shooting dead an Iraqi civilian in a Mosque in Fallujah provide a third example for discussion here. This fits the pattern of seeing war crimes and recognising them—on the surface, at least. Yet, actually, this example makes recognition of a war crime, possibly even when we might be witnessing its commission, more problematic. What doubt could there be that this moving image was evidence of a war crime? In practice, the doubt is quite extensive, even though *prima facie* the incident is shocking and appears to be murder.

Kevin Sites, an NBC journalist embedded with the Marines' unit, filmed the incident. Sites had simply captured what he had witnessed. Then it was broadcast with his personal commentary by NBC, and later re-broadcast in different versions by other broadcasters.[28] The perception of the snapshot coverage suggesting atrocity and war crime was at odds with the context, as a subsequent criminal investigation proved.[29] Professionally, this was a combat situation. It was a difficult room clearing operation, where the troops were ensuring that there was no continuing threat from that source (a Mosque, which had been used by the insurgents). The man had apparently been feigning death, lying on the ground. He was not a prisoner who had surrendered. He was, in the circumstances, a potential threat, who could have been about to detonate an explosive device, for example. In this scenario, or a similar one, the apparently cold-blooded murder that the snapshot images conveyed was potentially a serious misrepresentation, or misunderstanding, of what actually occurred.

The Fallujah image illustrates the problems that arise when discussing war crimes out of context, though this is rarely evident when such accusations are lodged. As with the Scorpion images, and those of Corporal Payne, the Fallujah shooting seems to be moving image evidence, which confirms the crime. We know when something is wrong. We know when we see it. Often this is the case, of course. Yet, Fallujah raises the awkward possibility that there might be events where the context makes a particular action justifiable and necessary. This possibility is what lies at the core of this book. Without doubt, as the Srebrenica and Basra cases attest, there are certain matters, even within the testing circumstances of war, that are, beyond any reasonable doubt, clear-cut instances of war crimes. These have historically constituted the caseloads of war crimes prosecutors. Fallujah, however, points to two significant features of the contemporary era. First, the prevalence of image-capture devices in the twenty-first century means that, more than ever, there will be a visual record (whole or partial) of incidents. Secondly, even where there is a visual record, there will be cases where ambiguity surrounds allegations of war crimes, and context will define final judgements. If this is true in cases involving one action and visual evidence, it is even more so in complex situations that lack the apparent clarity of a case such as Fallujah. Certain events in the context of armed conflict are indubitably war crimes and recognised as such. This confirms that war and war crimes are mutually constitutive. The following section will explore this relationship and discuss the problem of alleging war crimes in another, even more ambiguous, historical example that has been a focus for deeply controversial debate.

From War to War Crimes and Back

In the 1990s, the creation of *ad hoc* international judicial bodies and the development of the International Criminal Court brought new focus to the laws of war. However, despite the crucial relationship between war and war crimes, lexically and conceptually, there has been little contemporary effort to consider war crimes issues in the context of war itself.[30] As noted above, some matters are unequivocally war crimes and can be seen as such. Historically, though, these have involved issues well outside the scope of normal military conduct, such as the mass murder of civilians, or the physical abuse of civilian prisoners (as discussed above) to say nothing of the best known case: the Holocaust conducted in Nazi Germany. This has certainly been the case in recent debate and scholarship, as well as the advent of international war crimes prosecutions in the twentieth century.[31]

In an atmosphere of growing concerns about, and allegations of, the commission of war crimes, arguments about war and war crimes have also had re-invigorated retrospective application, with longstanding knotty canards given fresh life. A key example is A. C. Grayling's interpretation of the Allied bombing of Hamburg (and, by extension, all other cases) in the Second World War as a 'crime'.[32] However, there are two aspects of Grayling's argument that are problematic.

The first concerns the law. Telford Taylor efficiently handled this question at a far earlier stage, but only on one level. The simple approach is to point out that there was no applicable law governing the use of air power at the time the alleged action took place.[33] *Ergo*, no crime, in law, could have been committed.[34] However, this response is not necessarily adequate,[35] given the reality that categories of crimes were invented *ex post facto* and retrospectively applied regarding Nazi suspects. This was a process of which Taylor not only approved, but in which he participated as a prosecutor at the Nuremberg trial of senior Nazis for war crimes. A category, such as 'Crimes Against Humanity' might perhaps (politics notwithstanding) have been applied. Or, another entirely novel category might have been plucked from the air. More likely, threads on which to draw might have been found, for example, in the Regulations attached to the Hague Convention of 1907.

In addition, Taylor's summary dismissal of the allegation that area bombing constituted a crime is not accepted by all commentators. Markusen and Kopf, for example, argue on a variety of fronts that Allied strategic bombing was criminal, asserting scientific, technical and psychological parallels between this campaign and the commission of the Holocaust through the mass shooting or industrial gassing of civilians. The fact that in both cases civilians were killed leads them to infer that, while the two phenomena are discrete, they each constitute criminal activity: 'the most important fact for the purposes of this study is the fact that both projects entailed the slaughter of masses of helpless, innocent civilians'.[36] They continue by stating that both 'violated international law', citing war crimes 'which include "murder, ill-treatment or deportation or slave labour or for any other purpose of civilian population of or in occupied territory"' and Crimes Against Humanity, 'which include "murder, extermination, enslavement, deportation and other inhumane acts committed against any civilian population, before or during the war"'.[37] The first of these could never apply technically, as suggested here, because the strategic bombing campaign was not an action on occupied territory. This small and pedantic point is significant in any serious consideration of criminality, where there would need to be applicable law. There might be a case to consider regarding the latter, given that there are interpretations, such as Grayling's, which focus on the inhumane effects of the bombing. However, this is not necessarily so clear-cut. While no one would approve of the incineration of tens of thousands of people, the questions of intention and neglect must be reviewed. On the first of these, even where Markusen and Kopf claim to identify an 'explicitly anticivilian plan' by US air forces against Japan, known as Project Clarion, they undermine this claim by stating that: 'Ostensibly, the targets for Clarion were transportation facilities, but the real victims were civilians'.[38] Even though they cite the view of one officer that the plan was unethical and report criticism by others, this does not take the argument further, in terms of criminality and intent—their account concludes that the intention was not to kill civilians, as such. Any allegation of criminality, as far as these issues can be treated in the limited context of this text, would therefore need to rest on some form of negligence: the intention was not to kill, but it was disregard of that which would occur contingently that is wrong. But, as noted below, this assumes that unrealistic degrees of accuracy were available, or that the costs did not justify the action. In a sense, the discussion remains, therefore, in the realm of the moral, not the legal.

This leads to Grayling's main line of argument, in the ethical domain, which is that the raids on Hamburg constituted a 'moral crime'.[39] The morality of this 'saturation bombing' certainly raised questions for others. Bradley F. Smith's 'Conclusion' to his seminal study on the judgements on major Nazi War Criminals at the Nuremberg International Military Tribunal offers telling reflection on similar lines (although his reference points are Nuremberg itself and Dresden—showing that the issues surrounding the Allied bombing campaign had a broad character). Smith also had qualms about the bombing campaign, thirty years before Grayling raised his concerns. Reflecting on the Tribunal and its relationship to the war, he writes that a range of actions, including Dresden and the bombing campaign, 'went a long way toward forfeiting the claim of righteousness on which the Allies based this trial of their enemies'. He continues by referring to a 'breathtaking' moment in a letter from one of the American prosecutors to his wife, recounting a walk through Nuremberg, which gives 'a long and sensitive description of the mass destruction in the city and the helpless confusion and suffering of the German civilians'. Smith 'waits almost breathlessly' for the author 'to ask himself whether the Allies had not lost the right to sit in judgement because of the fact that they had used such patently inhumane methods of warfare'.[40] Smith concludes that the Allies had little if any moral authority, as they 'lost the moral triumph over Nazism with a double-edged quid pro quo [sic] of saturation bombing and of a trial'.[41] There is not space, and indeed this is not the place, to engage with Smith's verdict on the morality of the Tribunal (even though he notes its positive work)—but it is worth noting that the unequalled character of Nazi crimes created an ethical context in which the application of criminal justice, while problematic, was a more measured and responsible step than mass revenge would have been. This makes it hard to concur completely with the judgement Smith offers, and it is important to stress the relative aspect in his expression of moral concerns: actions 'went a long way' towards losing any claim to 'righteousness'. A long way is not all the way. There can be no complete moral equivalence in the contexts of 'total war' and icy-blooded industrial mass murder: the Allies were justified in actions necessary to stop (and stop as soon as possible) the Nazi German campaign of evil. Purist judgements are not possible. And quite reasonably, it might be suggested that Smith's effort to find a sense of self-doubt in the 'sensitive' account of Nuremberg's devastation that he cites, misses the ethical truth perhaps grasped intuitively by the individual: it is possible, in the complex patterns of negotiating notions of wrong and right that constitute ethics, to recognise and feel sorry for those who suffered dreadfully in the bombing, but also to have the conviction reinforced that the cause was ultimately just and both the bombing and the trials were necessary. Saturation bombing was awful. No one with any normal degree of humanity would decide to operate in that way in the abstract, or out of the blue, on a regular Sunday afternoon. But it was a means morally justified, in the clumsy environment of war and mass murder, given the depths of Nazi iniquity.[42] In the end, as

Smith acknowledges, without completely linking it to this point or understanding its significance for his discussion of morality: 'Total war, as we can now see more clearly, has a momentum of its own and what may appear as an atrocity by one side at the beginning of hostilities looks like civilised reticence when viewed from the crescendo of carnage that develops at the end'.[43] In other words, most things are relative and defined entirely by context in the conduct of war. Some, however, such as the pre-meditated mass murder of whole civilian population groups, will never be justifiable—at least so far as the bounds of humane imagination permit.

This sense of how important context is in making assessments regarding war and war crimes, such as that found in Smith's questioning of Allied bombing in the context of his focus on the Nuremberg process, is barely apparent or felt in Grayling's lodging the 'moral crime' charge. Smith's discussion gives us some context for appreciating the kinds of moral concern that drive Grayling, but also allows for nuances of understanding and, perhaps despite itself, in the end, encloses the need to understand the importance of the context that is war. However, despite a chapter on the bomber's mind—which seems unduly driven by the impression that Air Marshall Arthur 'Bomber' Harris 'was not a man of culture', his account is wanting in understanding of warfare and the use of force, that blunt, destructive, largely imprecise instrument of politics.

The condemnation of 'area bombing' over the attempt at 'precision bombing', to begin with, rests on presumptions about the relationship of precision (closely bunched impact, contradicted by the very sense of 'area') to accuracy (closeness to intended target, bull's eye) that are unfounded, not giving due recognition to the problems of accuracy and the nature of area weapons (although it must be conceded that these aspects are not completely overlooked),[44] and that 'area' and then 'saturation' bombing were far from simply questions of killing people on the ground.[45] Grayling adds a fallacious extension of his opposition to 'area bombing' to the employment of nuclear weapons at Hiroshima and Nagasaki, which were qualitatively and empirically different—and where his arguments might conceivably have more merit, if properly situated, as, it could be argued, Michael Walzer's were.[46] Apart from the basic problem with this approach, it also fails to understand how area munitions work—and hence why they are called area munitions—and lacks an acceptance of the consequences of using such devices. These consequences entail so-called collateral damage, the inevitable contingent destruction of life and property that most types of weapons 'by-produce' in warfare. This is a reality, even if it is a reality that is generally subject to efforts to limit unintended damage. The failure to understand this aspect of using force is complemented by the failure to understand the importance of human character and morale in all types of war, but above all in the sort of 'total war' exemplified by the Second World War.

It is hard to avoid the inference that Grayling, and the thinking that his book typifies, does not fully understand war—although it can also be said that his interpretation reflects the liberal conscience and culture of the societies that spawn Western militaries and which, therefore, shape and form the environment in which those armed forces have to succeed. To be clear, this is not to question Grayling's quality as a philosopher. It is certainly not to promote war or, even less so, indiscriminate aerial area bombardment. Nor, emphatically, is this discussion an attempt to suggest anything like a charter for military indulgence in wrongdoing. Understanding of warfare and its context might mean considering the benefit of the doubt in the most marginal cases. But, it absolutely cannot be seen to condone unethical behaviour and abuse in war. However, if there is to be serious consideration of war crimes, it is important to understand them in the context of war and so to exercise discrimination between that which is a war crime, and that which is merely the awful consequence of war.

The Book

If there is contestation and challenging discussion of war crimes surrounding aerial bombing in the context of 'total war' and Nazi atrocities, where much in the situation was incontestable—major countries engaged in armed conflict, with matters of high morality and statehood—then the early twenty-first century and the decade preceding it provides an even more challenging set of circumstances. As is well-recognised by scholars and practitioners—and is discussed in Chapter 2—the character of warfare began to change, along with international order, statehood, and law, in the late twentieth century. A state such as Nazi Germany invading a country such as Poland was no longer the real challenge for those dealing with matters of international peace and security; Iraq's invasion of Kuwait in August 1990 was the exception that proved the rule. The real threats to peace and security emerged from other sources and involved not only states, but, predominantly, sets of non-state actors. These threats were often linked to weak and fragile states, or changing global conditions.[47] These changes were recognised by scholars and practitioners alike. The first ever Summit Meeting of the Heads of State and Government in January 1992 recognised these changes by giving a new interpretation to the meaning of threats to international peace and security, clarifying that the threats stemmed not from confrontations between states, but from issues lying within and across their boundaries.[48]

Indeed, the question was perhaps not so much one of direct threats, but risks and uncertainties. It had become a question of what Philip Bobbitt labelled 'vulnerability', tackling this issue head on, in his magisterial *Shield of Achilles*.[49] This darker, more complex and dangerous world of vulnerabilities was also recognised by the Field Marshall Lord Inge, who linked them to the problems of judging wrong and right in the conduct of war and invoked the founding thinkers of the Christian and Western 'Just War' tradition: St. Augustine and Thomas Aquinas. In the Lord Inge's words:

The moral challenges faced have a new context. The tradition of St. Augustine and Aquinas, including the charges against Axis leaders for initiating aggressive war, encounters new challenges in the contemporary age. Technical means permit highly sophisticated weapons. These weapons can be very effective in the hands of unstable, unreliable regimes. Yet, it has become increasingly hard to take effective military action because of the moral questions involved.[50]

As well as the moral questions, he might well have mentioned legal ones, as laws of war had emerged from the Petri dish of the 'Just War' tradition to which he referred.[51] These legal questions, with their moral sources and contexts, lay at the heart of questions of legitimacy in the context of contemporary warfare.

General Klaus Naumann might well have posed the key question for legitimacy. He asked: 'Will the use of force become a means not of "last" resort, but first resort?' This recognised the needs of the contemporary world. 'And if so', he continued, 'how will it be legalised?'[52] His understanding of 'last' resort was more chronological than conceptual. What he might have more accurately asked is whether the chronological sense of 'last resort' (to some extent, always a fallacy) should be superseded by increasing focus on identifying the 'last resort' conceptually sooner and sooner. That is, the moment when it is clear that 'no other means will do' will become a matter of ever-earlier decisions. It is the early decision-making points—those at which the issue is to act before it is too late—that will raise the question of law. That question of legality, coupled with strategy, political context and communication of images, constitutes the heart of the legitimacy issue. Fragile legitimacy makes it harder to make necessary decisions and to undertake necessary action. But fragile, contested legitimacy is what we can expect in the years ahead. Faced with accusations of war crimes that might jeopardise success, it is the armed forces that have the greatest interest in the re-alignment of strategy law and war. The law-politics nexus will form the exposed core of legitimacy as the West wages war, in new ways, in a changing world. That world entails a changing international order that requires new law, new interpretations of the law, and new approaches to the law. As the views of defence practitioners are vital to addressing issues of wrong and right in warfare, they must significantly inform that realignment, even if they cannot—and should not—exclusively define it. Those views are crucial to delineation of the changing character and content of both war and war crimes.

The core challenge has to be re-establishing the intrinsic relationship of war crimes to war. This focuses the problem of defining precise boundaries for military conduct where, in all but a few cases, the interpretation of the law has to be subject to the interpretation of military necessity and proportionality. International judicial developments, coupled with advances in communications, have changed the landscape for the future conduct of warfare. This has clearly been the case, from Bosnia to al-Qa'ida terrorists, Afghanistan, Iraq and Libya, and will be wherever else action has to be taken. No future war will be conducted, it seems to me, without intense public—particularly media—scrutiny and attention to potential war crimes.

The majority of matters historically treated as war crimes have involved issues clearly outside the scope of normal military conduct, such as mass murder of civilians (as noted above). However, the International Criminal Tribunal for the former Yugoslavia shifted the historical pattern, for the first time raising charges that might impinge on the conduct of warfare, such as disproportionate artillery bombardment.[53] At the same time, it has become a concern for Western governments and armed forces that politicians and soldiers have come under scrutiny, not for having committed acts undoubtedly outside legitimate military activity (such as Crimes Against Humanity or genocide), but in relation to allegations of war crimes involving the normal conduct of operations, as happened in the cases of Kosovo and Iraq. Allegations are increasingly made against Western forces, often deployed to prevent, or limit, gross abuses of human rights and war crimes.[54] These allegations are based on interpretations of necessity and proportionality that might differ from those employed by the armed forces and their military lawyers. As one writer and cultural commentator wisely reflected, '[T]here is a very fine line in modern warfare between being a murderer and being a hero'.[55] The nature of contemporary warfare has increased the pressures on those making and implementing strategy, as approaches to the law and its implementation have been changing.

To return to the views of the Field Marshall Lord Inge, '[T]he conduct of those involved in war will be under constant scrutiny'. In this context, he complains, 'It is easy for governments and lawyers sitting remote from the battlefield to set restrictions without regard for soldiers and situations on the battlefield'. In the Field Marshall's words, 'The way our servicemen and women conduct themselves in war is vital to their sense of integrity, as well as the support of their nation'.[56] This is the core of the law-politics nexus that shapes legitimacy. It affects the way that military personnel think of themselves and crucially affects their relationship with their parent societies. It means that strategy and the conduct of operations are shaped and constrained by the political debate surrounding legality—all the more so in terms of conduct and the *jus in bello*, because the contemporary idea of legality regarding the right to use force, the *jus ad bellum*, is so frail. The rules are more important than ever, lying at the core of the competition for legitimacy. But there is a mismatch between the new context and the prevailing law: Marco Roscini asks if this is a case of 'Old Law, New Targets?' in identifying a 'Legal Framework Under Stress'.[57] The rules and the context in which they are invoked are becoming increasingly difficult to align.

The only proper way in which to understand the concept of war is by reference to rules, but war crimes, the markers of those rules, can only properly be comprehended and addressed if there is a developed understanding of what war is—its nature and the realities of using force. The use of force has to be understood not only in terms of its impact, but also of decisions on employing armed force. This, then, is my purpose in this study: to explore the concepts of war and war crimes in their mutuality and in the early stages of a period of change, where critical issues surround each of these linked concepts. The rules of war define war, but they remain rules of war—and familiarity with the phenomenon that is war is essential to proper interpretation and application of those rules. In the pages that follow, the mission is: to explore the concepts of war and war crimes (broadly cast); to consider how the latter are essential to defining the former; and to understand how awareness of the mutual relationship between them is central to understanding each of them as they undergo rapid change in the contemporary era—change affecting the character and outcome of war.[58]

Strategy, politics and law are changing simultaneously, where, previously, change has been in more sequenced steps.[59] Laws of war have always been concerned with issues of necessity and proportionality, the bedrock concepts of both the *jus ad bellum* and the *jus in bello*. How are these principles applied in modern warfare? What are the pressures on practitioners in this changing context with increasing emphasis on legality? Where do the boundaries of proportionality and necessity lie in the contexts, means and methods of contemporary war? Can they apply at all in the context of operations labelled 'humanitarian?'[60] What is wrong or right, in the view of military-political practitioners, as those concepts relate to contemporary means and methods of war?

While purely independent judgement and analysis contribute to answering some of these questions, a fuller understanding of how further questions should be judged, or of the impact change has on warfare, can emerge through investigation involving military practitioners. In most cases to date, opinions and judgements were informed by the views of human rights activist groups and international humanitarian lawyers,[61] or by individual views on proportionality and necessity.[62] In the view of one legal commentator, military judgement should be eschewed unless it is 'civilianised'. Michael Bothe has suggested that when questions of war crimes are posed, 'the answers may differ depending on the background and values of the decision-maker', which 'simple truth', he continues, 'underlies the debates between human-rights-oriented NGOs and military circles', before adding that the judgement of a '"reasonable military commander"' is 'not really a satisfactory solution' unless the commander 'is defined in more civilian terms'.[63] The value of considering military views as matters of fact relating to the law on this matter is argued in this volume. War crimes, conceptually, are placed in the context of warfare. The boundaries and content of certain potentially criminal actions are explored through empirical investigation with defence professionals, encouraging understanding of that which defence professionals regard as acceptable and unacceptable, or 'right' and 'wrong' in contemporary operations.

All too often, the voice of those who really understand warfare, the armed forces, is absent from discussion. This book begins to address this lacuna. Key parts of the following analysis draw on empirical focus-group research, carried out with defence professionals, allowing their voices to be heard on issues of wrong and right in contemporary warfare. These parts of the book consider soldiers' views both on that which is acceptable and that which is questionable, and also on how their work as managers of restrained coercive violence is affected, or not, in a context where the boundaries of law and war are changing. This analysis is informed by data from focus-group research and supplemented by semi-structured interviews with senior defence practitioners, as well as critical examination of written and visual material. This was part of a wider program of research, involving the War Crimes Research Group at King's College London and including specific research projects funded by two UK research councils—the Arts and Humanities Research Council (AHRC) and the Economic and Social Research Council (ESRC).[64] Although this research has involved focus-group research in Belgrade, Sarajevo and Priština (which will inform later work more significantly), much of the empirical research presented in this volume was conducted at the Royal College of Defence Studies (RCDS) and the Joint Services Command and Staff College (JSCSC), both in the UK. The JSCSC runs a range of programs at different levels of officer career development, mixing a core British cohort with a diverse group of members from around the world. The focus groups involved in this research drew on members of the Advanced Staff Course, a program attended primarily by those holding the rank of major (in the army, or equivalent). The RCDS embraces an international mix of defence practitioners, primarily at 'one star' (Brigadier/Brigadier General) level, with some international members at full Colonel, or equivalent levels. Those who took part in the research came from all continents and cultures, with participants not only from all continents, but also roughly all parts of all continents. Along the way, the research involved people from Middle Eastern countries, from all points of the African compass, from different Asian and Australasian countries, and from the Americas. There was a surprising degree of consistency. It is necessary to be careful about describing or referring to the group, because of the confidentiality involved, especially because some of them come from countries where, if they could be identified, it was considered that they might well find themselves in trouble. Agreement to carry out the research with the RCDS involved sophisticated discussions with the Senior Directing Staff there to ensure that all sensitivities in conducting such research were addressed.

The research suggests that there is surprisingly little difference between the nationalities that comprised the research groups. There were small differences, however. Those who had been closer to unpleasant situations tended to have stronger views about politicians' responsibility, for example. In some cases they tended to have stronger views about what it is necessary to do when troops are engaged in certain kinds of conflict. On the whole, though, there was very little difference, in terms of nationality. It is possible that this relative coherence in views represented the success of British defence diplomacy and defence education in bringing the international members to the RCDS in London and acculturating them. It might be the case that, if personnel are in London, in a common environment, they might think in convergent, rather than divergent, ways. It is, therefore, possible that, if they were in the field, these same military personnel might think in a divergent way. However, while recognising this question, it should be noted that it remains equally possible that, if the same members were in the field, their ethical judgements and sense of the issues might still coincide.

The focus group research that informs this book has two particular strengths. It allows the generation of empirical data, simply through the discussion that takes place, with participants offering knowledge and information drawn from experience, as well as giving expression to beliefs, values and attitudes. This provides the data with which to inform analysis. Secondly, in contrast to individual research interviews, the group process (especially when it involves the presentation of specific propositions or material—part of the research used in this volume draws on instances in which participants were shown visual material) allowed discussion and interaction between participants. As discourse developed, salient beliefs, values and attitudes were identified, as well as issues about which participants strongly agreed or diverged. Focus groups were facilitated by one individual—often, but not always, me—with other members of the research team observing and taking close notes, which formed the basis for focus group reports that presented the data generated by each session (in some parts of the research, where there was agreement to do this, back-up audio-recordings were made to allow checking and re-enforcement).[65] Material drawn from this programme of research is presented in Chapters 4 and 5, in particular, which form the core of the book's argument.[66]

The preceding sections establish the context for this original empirical work. Chapter 2 explores the need to comprehend contemporary warfare, in which the famous secondary trinity of Carl von Clausewitz—government, armed forces and population—has been transformed into a multidimensional formation, described here as the Multidimensional Trinity Cubed (Plus), or *Trinity³(+)*. Understanding the multidimensional trinity and the way in which war crimes issues play among its elements is essential to comprehending legitimacy and success in contemporary warfare. Chapter 3 considers the evolution of the laws of war and increased emphasis on the prosecution of war crimes at the end of the twentieth century, as well as the pressures for new law in the twenty-first century to meet the demands of contemporary war. Chapter 4 investigates how defence professionals judge the impact of war crimes issues on strategy, civil-military relations and their ability to do their jobs. Chapter 5 investigates the need for an understanding of strategy and military affairs in consideration of war crimes situations, and it introduces military voices to explore war crimes scenarios, including standoff bombardment, prisoners of war, and the use of cluster munitions. The final chapter concludes that, even more than ever, strategy embraces justice and law, with lawfulness and justness essential to success in military operations—but that these issues should never be considered without reference to the views of professionals as one part of evaluating them. In a context where legitimacy defines success in warfare, but legitimacy is fragile, as the relationship between war and war crimes evolves, no group has a greater interest in responding to these pressures and changes positively than the military. It is they who have the greatest need and desire to foster legitimacy in war, by getting the politics-law-strategy nexus right, through developing a clear understanding of the mutually defining relationship between war and war crimes, and in calibrating where war becomes a war crime in a multidimensional trinitarian warfare context.

2

STRATEGY AND THE
MULTIDIMENSIONAL TRINITY

The harmonisation of the nexus of strategy, law and war defines success in twenty-first century armed operations. Increasingly, pressures arise in relation to the proper reasons for conducting those operations, and in relation to their proper conduct. It is evident that this generates pressures on military personnel, as noted in Chapter 1, meaning that there is a need to understand better how these issues shape success. The key to this, as this chapter argues, is to understand how legitimacy operates in terms of strategy (the term itself is discussed below). Thus, this chapter investigates strategy in relation to the changed character of warfare, and the relationship of legitimacy to issues of justice as a measure of success. In doing so, it introduces the concept of the Multidimensional Trinity Cubed (Plus), expressed as an emblem, the *Trinity³(+)*, or *T³(+)*.[1] This concept is developed from the famous secondary trinity of Carl von Clausewitz—political leaders, armed forces and people. The *Trinity³(+)* is the context in which war crimes issues operate and affect success, and also that which has centralised them as they have taken on a new significance in contemporary wars.

After introducing contemporary warfare, this chapter develops the notion of strategy, before considering this strategy and its effect in the context of contemporary warfare. Having established the interim conclusion that the purpose of contemporary strategy is broadly to generate a quality or a condition—the measure of success—the next section explores success in relation to the quality of legitimacy, building on previous work in arguing that critical legitimacy is the key to success in the contemporary era. The final part of the chapter then explores the concept of the *Trinity³(+)* as a framework for understanding critical legitimacy and success in an era of multiple partnerships, audiences and communications channels. The *Trinity³(+)* forms the context in which the testing questions surrounding war and war crimes in the contemporary period play out.

Contemporary Warfare

The essence of war does not change. But its particular manifestations do. The character of warfare changes from period to period, or context to context, yet its fundamental nature is necessary and eternal. Who practises the arts, science and crafts of warfare, and how they do so, is contingent. War is always and only for political purpose—it is that political purpose which gives it a special condition in human affairs and legitimacy as the means of settling political matters when other means do not apply. It always involves dedicated social groups; armed forces that are trained (even if that training is rudimentary and very limited, far from the sophistication of the most advanced armed forces) and disciplined in the management and application of restrained coercive violence. Restraint is a vital element of this. It is a reflection of skill and discipline, and it is also a measure of the degree to which the use of these unusual means is still subject to prevailing rules and conventions. While the details and form of these rules and conventions might change, they are nevertheless present and mark the boundaries between acts that are only permissible in the case of war, and those that are not acceptable under any circumstances, even war.

From the late twentieth century into the twenty-first, a major shift in the character of warfare—that is, in its main features and dominant forms—occurred, as discussed in this section and in the following one on strategy. This was due to a range of factors. One important feature was the changing international order,[2] itself a reflection of and a driver of changes in statehood,[3] both of which determine the character of warfare. The type of warfare that became conventional in the twentieth century, involving the regular armed forces of states, gave way to a form of armed conflict dominated less by the application of major armed force, aimed at an opponent's centre of gravity, and more by a form of armed conflict dominated by other factors. Contemporary armed conflict differs from traditional, conventional warfare in its character and qualities. In his work on the changing qualities of armed conflict, Rupert Smith offers key characteristics of contemporary warfare that set it apart from the previous era of what he calls 'industrial' warfare: contemporary warfare is fought not for victory but to create political or strategic conditions, non-state actors are central, and the key to war is the struggle for the will of 'the people', because war is fought amongst the people.[4]

Large groups of armed forces engaging in epic set-piece battles have little relevance in the twenty-first century. They were once vital, and may well return to importance in the future, though this will likely be in a new guise, if they do. However, this change does not make regular and professional armed forces irrelevant. Indeed, the skills of well-trained professionals may be in even greater demand than before because of the new subtleties and challenges of using what is, in truth, the very blunt instrument of coercive force in the context of the twenty-first century. The type of application of armed force that characterised the World Wars of the twentieth century, for example, will not work in the socio-political conditions of the early twenty-first century, but armed force will inevitably remain a clumsy instrument. Therefore skill in its necessary application will be at a premium because the chances of something going wrong with significant consequences are so much greater. The application of kinetic force—that is physical force that generates blast and fragmentation—to destroy life or property, requires unprecedented guile to be effective in its use. The creation and application of the means and methods of armed force for 'total war' developed between the Napoleonic era and the Cold War. In this type of warfare, overcoming the enemy by finding their power centre, and then applying mass force to destroy it, was the objective. By the early twenty-first century, that had changed. Instead of seeking to destroy the enemy by applying greater amounts of destructive force, the purpose became the achievement of a quality, rather than an objective, physical demand. William S. Lind, and then Thomas G. Hammes, labelled this shift as 'Fourth Generation Warfare'.[5] Others have characterised it as '3-block warfare',[6] or a shift to 'hybrid wars'.[7] The common features of all these are relative complexity; the salience of politics and the will of population groups and the recognition that brute force alone will not win the war, and often might make it harder to win, so that any use of force should be judiciously calibrated to the political and social contexts of the operation. Lawrence Freedman described this as the *Transformation of Strategic Affairs*, where narrative replaced sheer brute force as the decisive element in warfare.[8] Following Freedman's logic, Joseph P. Nye encapsulates this:[9] 'It is not whose army wins, but whose story wins'.[10] Theories of contemporary warfare (from a mainly American perspective) have focused on how the most advanced technical developments, linked to the cultural aspects of warfare, in a diverse and network-oriented environment produce an accumulation of effects that cause the collapse of the enemy, where once the use of decisive major combat was the instrument for achieving victory.[11] This produced effects-based warfare, in which the message became as important as the missile; only if the missile sent the right signal did it serve its purpose.

The problems of legitimacy surrounding Iraq, or the Global War on Terror, were manifestations of this changing character of war, and the changing relevance (if not character) of war crimes and emerging legal issues at the heart of any conceptualisation of war. This shift in the character of warfare—and its relation to the eternal essence of warfare—can be explained by reference to the famous Clausewitzian 'trinities'.[12] Carl von Clausewitz's primary trinity emerged from the theory that war, as a political phenomenon using armed force, was governed by the interactions of reason, chance (or the interplay of probabilities) and passion. This captures the very nature of war along with its political purpose, the involvement of armed forces (whether or however force itself is employed) and conventions. Clausewitz's secondary trinity comprised the government, the armed forces and the people, which is also relevant to contemporary conceptions of war.[13] Indeed, it offers a clear way in which to view the altered character of warfare while retaining a hold on the essence of war.

Thus, those such as Mary Kaldor and Martin van Creveld, who have declared the erroneous notion of 'post-Clausewitzian' warfare by arguing that Clausewitz is no longer pertinent, are mistaken.[14] Creveld posited that Clausewitzian-type warfare was obsolete, and that the trinity no longer applied—'the Clausewitzian universe', he wrote, was 'out of date'.[15] He was right to identify that the application of mass force directly by one state against another, which was the mainstay of nineteenth- and twentieth-century thinking, was unlikely to occur again, but his inference that this meant that Clausewitz's principles no longer held force was flawed. His assertion that the trinity had become irrelevant was fundamentally wrong. Clausewitz maintained that warfare was the outcome of a trial of physical strength and a tussle of will: both were always present. From the Napoleonic era to the Cold War a conventional type of warfare dominated, in which victory in a trial of strength, and the power this gained the victor, determined judgements of military success or failure. In the course of the Cold War, while the character of warfare was undergoing a crucial transition, the balance shifted to the other end of the scale. By the end of the twentieth century, the struggle for power and influence took precedence in war. Indeed, winning the battle of wills had largely become the route to success in any trial of strength between states. The balance between these elements had reversed, but that balance still applied to both trinities: to reason, chance and passion, and to political leaders, armed forces and peoples. The secondary trinity still operated in every single conflict situation: political leaders, an armed element, and communities remained the relevant variables in any armed conflict. In this context of a shift towards winning the struggle of wills in order to win the trial of strength, the outcome of any war, in large part, was defined by the need to 'win' through success at the level of 'hearts and minds'. As Smith asserts, the battle for 'hearts and minds' has gone from being a support activity in military operations, to being their central purpose.[16]

In contemporary warfare, as noted, large set-piece battles between armed forces rarely occur. Where they do occur, they generally have little salience—although this does not make them irrelevant. However, the application of kinetic force to destroy through blast and fragmentation, ideally damaging the opponent's centre of gravity,[17] which characterised warfare from Napoleon's campaigns through to the Cold War and the advent of nuclear weapons,[18] has been largely replaced by a demand for the adept use of force to achieve a particular effect, or condition, that is not necessarily about destruction and physical control. This reflects a world where the convention in conflict has shifted away from the massive application of force to overwhelm the opponent toward a greater emphasis on coercive control (or something along those lines). This was proven by the US expedition in Iraq, beginning in 2003. The traditional combat phase of 'industrial' warfare was quickly achieved, leading to the famous photo-opportunity for US President George W. Bush on the USS Abraham Lincoln, beneath the banner 'mission accomplished'.[19] Subsequent events demonstrated, though, with great effect, that this phase was barely a prelude to the years of armed conflict that followed—the real warfare of the twenty-first century.

In contemporary warfare, rather than seeking to destroy the enemy through the application of greater amounts of destructive violence, the aim is to establish what, as noted above, Smith correctly identifies as a set of conditions. Contemporary strategy aims to achieve a quality, not to obtain a concrete physical objective, even if the latter may sometimes be a contingent requirement. The remainder of this chapter turns to strategy in the context of contemporary warfare to explore precisely what this means, how to understand the character of contemporary armed conflict, and the difficulties of using armed force in this environment.

Strategy and Strategic Effect in Contemporary Operations

Just as the term 'war' is used as a metaphor for any matter involving, or wishing to give the impression of, a major engagement in social struggle, so the term 'strategy' has taken on myriad applications. In business and management studies, as well as in the statements of government ministers or their panjandrums, for example, the term has wide currency. So, MBA students might encounter the notion of 'business strategy' in their curriculum—or even 'Clausewitz for managers!' Furthermore, on almost any day, of any week, at least in a Western liberal democracy, it seems inevitable that a politician or a functionary will announce, or comment on, some 'strategy' or other for dealing with a difficult issue on the multifaceted government agenda. Sometimes, statements of this kind might mean little more than saying that the government, or some entrepreneur, has a notion, or even a label, to apply to an issue. It might mean that they have an overall approach, or that they have a conceptual understanding of whatever the issue is and how to go about addressing it. It might even mean that they have a cunningly structured plan. This is the kind of approach reflected in the following definition, drawn from the world of public relations, marketing and communications: 'Strategy is probably best defined, for argument's sake, as planning, with added ingredients of creative flair and business insight'.[20] While accepting the qualification that this definition is only 'for argument's sake', for the student of war a definition of this kind is perhaps where the argument begins.

For such a student, strategy is about considerably more than planning, even if, as in any walk of life, there is scope for occasional touches of flair and insight in planning. Strategy is not about planning. Planning may be expected to follow from strategy and to be encompassed within it, but planning is only concrete and empirical. There should be concrete and empirical manifestations of strategy, including planning and the outcomes of planning, but strategy is an intellectual exercise and a practical process.

It concerns the conceptualisation of problems and their solutions. There are many contemporary reallocations of the term—economic strategy, business strategy, political strategy, marketing strategy. Each of these exploits one aspect of the original usage; the relationship between means and ends. Each is concerned with the way in which means to achieve designated ends can be provided, or the way in which available means can be applied to obtain specific aims, or the interactive process by which means and ends are calibrated to each other. With reference to the business of generals, broadly defined, strategy is about relating the means of war and the ends of war to each other. And, however it has been adopted and adapted in other spheres of activity, strategy remains originally and primarily a term associated with war.[21]

Strategy is the brain in the body of war. While law might define war, and legitimacy might determine success, it is strategy that provides the guiding intelligence. It is, in its narrowest terms (derived from its etymology) the business of generals (*strategos* in Greek means general). However, while it is business that involves generals, it does not relate to the military alone. As Clausewitz reminded us, the purpose of war is political and, while the operation of warfare is a matter for the military, there must be constant interaction between the military and the political. Strategy is about translating political aims into military objectives, which will contribute to a successful political outcome. It is, therefore, about the relationship between ends and means.[22]

The ends involved are both political and military—the latter should contribute to achievement of the former. As Clausewitz advised, this is where the big questions of morality and morale, as well as how much and how little force, overall, are to be found; where 'Strategy borders on political science, or rather where the two become one'.[23] The means are various, but focus on force, specifically the creation and application of armed force (though, in a globalising world, the instruments available through dual-use capabilities of all kinds increasingly extend beyond conventional weaponry).[24] The creation of force has two aspects. The first is destructive kinetic force—the use of physical mass to disrupt or force to move some other physical object. The second is the creation of the body that will employ that kinetic force—the military. Application—how those means are put to use to meet the needs of a particular situation—is therefore the hub of strategy.[25]

Although strategy is ultimately about 'doing' something, its essence lies in 'thinking'; from an elementary starting point—the creation of force and its application—a vast, often subtle, and possibly infinite, array of conceptual and practical issues extends. These are the battles and separate campaigns that add up to the overall strategy and war. Strategy 'links together the series of acts' that drive the effort to win the war. While policy sets the political objectives to be achieved through war, strategy is the translation of those objectives into an aim 'for the whole military action'.[26] In a war, each battle is one part of a whole, in which, ideally, successful strategy connects all the different actions and weaves them into a whole that is enough to overcome the opponent, but that avoids any unnecessary expenditure of resources.[27] Despite its obvious practical connotations—strategy begets plans and practical operations—strategy in its essence is a conceptual and philosophical enterprise.[28] It is about embracing the totality of a situation and reducing it to an ideational structure in which the available means, the desired ends and the various limitations on each are all balanced—including the necessary considerations of prudence and ethics, destructive capacity, manoeuvre and other factors. It is by no means a simple business. At times, the attempt to reconcile all of the relevant factors into one usable approach can be excruciatingly difficult—as history testifies.[29] That difficulty is amplified in the contemporary era because of the new complexities of armed conflict; the actors are often more numerous and less well defined, the means often ambiguous, and the ends less concrete than in the past.[30] The difficulty of rendering strategy is even greater in environments of open discussion—such as those found in liberal democracies, where batteries of critics, equipped with no better than incomplete understanding of a situation and of all the information to be taken into account, increase the complexity of rendering greater elegance to the strategic equation by constantly 'knowing better'.[31]

Strategy is not therefore about the conduct of operations, but about the thought that goes into them and the conceptualisation and imagination that enable the means available and the ends desired to be reconciled. Equally, therefore, strategy is not about plans—although plans will inevitably follow as conceptualisation is translated into operation. Plans are inadequate, in themselves. Strategy requires conceptualisation and imagination such that, when the initial plan is met by the adversary's counter, flexibility is available and adaptation possible. Thus, intelligence, broadly drawn and defined, and adaptation are essential aspects of strategy.

Strategy requires intelligence. It requires it on three discrete but interrelated levels. The first, which perhaps springs most readily to mind, concerns specific and often secret information about the opponent (and measures to ensure that the opponent cannot gain such information about one's own forces and intentions). This is the meaning of 'intelligence' that many will leap to on hearing the word in the context of strategic and military affairs. However, this is just one aspect of intelligence, understood more broadly as 'knowing your enemy' and defined in the ancient classic *The Art of War* by Sun Tzu, which is perhaps more an aphorism-based treatise on intelligence (in all senses discussed here) at the heart of strategy than on the 'art' of war in terms of actual conduct.[32]

This broader realm of intelligence involves not only specific information about an opponent's specific force disposition and intentions, but also understanding about the character of the individuals involved and of the wider political, social and cultural environments that surround the opponent's armed forces.[33] In essence, this means being able to benefit not only from the detail and impression gathered by secret means (whether human or technical), and evaluated and assessed by experts on process and product, but also from a wider body of knowledge and understanding available from various sources in society—especially expertise subsumed under the broad catch-all heading of 'area studies', which mixes linguistic ability and broad country or regional familiarity with knowledge and understanding of different aspects of life (such as culture, politics, society, economy, history and so on). Without this type of in-depth intelligence, the chances—always significant, in any case—of misjudging the opponent will be amplified.[34]

The third level at which intelligence is essential to strategy concerns the capacity to absorb, process and reflect on information—including the imagination to put oneself in the opponent's boots. A political leader or military commander requires the qualities not only to inspire and lead, but also to extract and interpret whatever is most salient from the available information on their own forces' capacities and character, and those of their opponent. As situations shift, demanding development of their interpretation, good leaders reflexively have to adapt in the interests of success. This is because it is almost impossible to conceive of a war where the initial scheme adopted by one side is not required to change as victory, or success, is pursued.[35] Opponents, generally, in their own pursuit of success, if they are wise, do not conform to their enemy's scheme. Thus, although strategy is about conceptualisation, it is steadfastly empirical at the same time, always dealing with the realities of an intelligent opponent who is not merely an object to be removed by kinetic force in a purely physical sense, but who will react, adapt and show innovation, wherever possible, so as to out-manoeuvre the strategy in place.

At times, identifying a centre of gravity and crushing it through massive use of destructive force might be the appropriate means to achieve success—as in Napoleonic warfare, familiar from Jomini's description and Clausewitz's reflection.[36] At other times, the emphasis is far more on the intellectual and spiritual faculties of avoiding a trial of strength by seeking to win by wit,[37] as in Liddell Hart's 'indirect approach',[38] or the 'deterrence' theory of nuclear strategists.[39] Knowing the enemy is essential. Until an opponent—actual or presumed—is present, there can be no complete or clear strategy. Even though strategy is a matter of intellect and concept, it can make little sense as a purely abstract or arbitrary discipline. Strategy only makes sense in terms of an opponent, and part of recognising an opponent is acknowledging that the enemy is neither fixed, nor inanimate. In this context, it is critical to understand that no particular means—especially those offering technical superiority—can determine an outcome in itself. The key lies in how technical means are used, how they are used to achieve the desired end and how they are used in relation to the opponent. All of these points must be synchronised for success.

Thus, strategy is predicated on posing the right questions and answering them correctly. At the broadest level, these include the following sets of questions: 'what do we want to achieve?'; 'what do we know about the opponent, in terms of their capacities, intentions and will?'; 'what do we know about ourselves in terms of these same factors?'; and 'how best can we translate what we know into a scheme to secure a successful outcome?' Beyond these issues, there are numerous other questions that might be posed and answered—too many to set out here.[40] However, among them, at some point, must be consideration of how force is to be used at appropriate levels and in appropriate ways.[41] The posing and answering of such questions forms a basic, but comprehensive, guide for thinking problems through strategically. The key to them is that they start at the far end—the desired outcome—and then work backwards, through sets of questions. These questions first address conceptual and practical issues at the strategic level, and then, once that level is established, transpose them to the operational level in order to translate concepts into practice. Coherence, both in addressing all the questions and reconciling the different levels, will provide the basis for success, and for dealing with the challenges thrown up along the way, when the opponent's actions compel adaptation.

Legitimacy and Strategic Success in Contemporary Warfare

The importance of strategic coherence cannot be ignored. Once the strategic initiative has been taken, to whatever degree, success at the strategic operational level will be a function of such coherence. That might mean using force in some cases while avoiding it in others. It probably means an attempt to maximise the degree of consent so as to oil the wheels of the operation and ensure that the desired strategic condition is not undermined by any action that could adversely affect the will of whichever people, or peoples, might be relevant. The employment of force and restraint has to be integrated into the framework of the intended end-goal of the mission. In this sense, the use of force is one particular instance of the salient phenomena, which can provide the focus for support: the use of force, or a failure to use force, among other actions, provides the issue around which belief and discourse—positive, or negative—revolve.

This issue can be understood by references to change in military peacekeeping, where a shift also occurred in the 1990s from traditional peacekeeping to new strands, including what can be termed 'strategic peacekeeping'.[42] Thus, in contrast to the strategically static nature of traditional peacekeeping, where the initiative lies with parties to the conflict, the type of situation relevant to the present discussion is strategically dynamic. It is one in which consent may well be challenged, although maximal consent is still the ideal. Even where there is some consensual basis for the deployment, as was the case in Bosnia and Herzegovina, there are still some parts of the mandate which go beyond that, and which are subject, for example, to Chapter VII enforcement measures authorised by the UN Security Council. So, there is a complex: the mission is based on the need to maximise consent, as far as possible, while recognising that there is a situation in which consent is not likely to be easily forthcoming—therefore, the Security Council has authorised those enforcement measures as part of the mandate (it should be stressed, only as one part of the mandate) to enable certain things to be permissible. The strategic initiative lies with the external actors. By contrast, in a conventional peacekeeping operation, the strategic initiative lies with the parties to the conflict who, having made it clear that whatever strategic objectives they may have had they feel unable to keep pursuing them, ask for help, meaning that the forces are deployed at the initiative of the parties. The external response confirms a largely static situation. In the strategic peacekeeping context, there is a difference in that, at the strategic level, a response is being made to a continuing, dynamic armed conflict.

Whether or not strategic peacekeeping is the right term is open to discussion. Although it is a useful term for carrying the discussion forward, it might not be definitive. Furthermore, it is a problematic term, given that traditionally peacekeeping could be seen as an entirely passive activity in which there is no strategic initiative taken by the force involved, or its international sponsors. Similarly, terms such as 'peace enforcement', or the more generic 'peace support operations', are used in different ways, depending on the authors and conflict involved. The virtue of the 'strategic peacekeeping' label for this activity is that it does at least focus on the strategic level. That strategic level focus makes legitimacy of overriding importance.

Legitimacy is a compound concept.[43] It is a quality, or phenomenon. It is the result of processes of legitimation, or legitimisation. The three elements of this compound are: bases, performance and support. The bases comprise rules, norms, laws, or statements. They can be explicit and stated, or they can be implicit and un-stated, and they can be self-ascribed, or ascribed by others. The bases of legitimacy are not only an actor's own beliefs, but those of others—what they believe that actor is doing, or should be doing. Among other elements, bases for legitimacy might include: relevant Security Council resolutions; exercise of the right to self-defence; humanitarian assistance; perceptions of interest; why troops or people believe a force is deployed; and, *de facto*, what that force is actually doing, irrespective of formal authorisation or mission. However, whatever the bases for using armed force, legality or perceptions of lawfulness will almost always be relevant.

Legitimacy is also about performance. This refers to how a force achieves its aims, and how well it does this. Often, weak, obscure or even doubted claims to legitimacy, could be successfully addressed through good performance, just as good bases—and the corresponding belief that something is being done for the right reason—can mitigate poor performance. Crucially, this relates to military culture and whether or not the soldiers are performing well, or feel that they are, and whether or not they have the respect of their own national communities, as well as that of the host community and other external actors.

The final layer of legitimacy is support. This can mean support either for the performance of the force, or for the reason that the force has been deployed (which may include the formal mandate, or not). However, neither accepted bases, nor good performance, can necessarily sustain legitimacy forever, in the absence of the other. This is especially so if either one is too severely compromised for the other to be able to mitigate, or compensate. This is because each of them relates to support. However, support, while generally recognisable as an idea and central to the overall concept of legitimacy, is hard to isolate. In the context of a globalised, internationalised, transnationalised environment, isolating support becomes that much harder: there is not only a single community that requires support, but an array of them, if operations are to be sustained and successful in the long term. Each military contingent is locked into an overall framework in which legitimacy stems not only from their own sense of purpose and performance, and the support of their home society and government, but also the support of other contingents with whom they might be operating, the societies and governments of those forces, elements within the country where a force is operating and, then, an international community of critics and potential supporters around the world, connected by twenty-first century communications.

The key to using force successfully is an appreciation of different levels of warfare, and the relationship between capabilities at one level and another. However, in the contemporary context, the traditional hierarchy of levels—political, strategic, operational and tactical (all always defined in relation to each other)—is still present, but, in practice, the hierarchy does not clearly operate as expected; one level does not determine the next in a straightforward manner.

While building on his characterisation of the new idiom of warfare, Rupert Smith indicates that commanders need to think carefully about the level at which kinetic force is applied, and the degree to which it is applied to avoid undermining the overall aim of a mission. Any use of force needs to serve the purpose of creating a political or strategic condition, in a context where non-state actors are prevalent (including at the level of multi-state international organisations, coalitions, partnerships and so on, whose particular concerns may not impact directly on the use of force, but which still need to be satisfied, and the friction between which must be minimised). Success is about avoiding defeat and achieving aims that are focused, above all, on the key factor: the struggle for the will of 'the people' because war is fought amongst the people. However, as Smith notes, the 'people' include, in some sense, the 'global theatre' of third parties who watch wars, express views on them, and even influence their aims.[44] It is this multidimensional arena that distinguishes contemporary war so clearly from previous forms. This is discussed in the final section of this chapter.

The Multidimensional Trinity Cubed-Plus (Multidimensional Trinity³(+))

In the contemporary context, more than ever, legitimacy is the key to success, although it can be argued that legitimacy has always been vital to success in warfare, in one sense or another. Philip Bobbitt, for example, has argued that law, or legitimacy, and strategy have always been two sides of the victory coin—law has historically been invoked to confirm military success, while armed force is needed to enforce legal claims.[45] It is undoubtedly the condition required for success in contemporary war. However, while legitimacy is perhaps more important than ever in the era of contemporary warfare,[46] it is also harder than ever to establish and maintain, because it is affected by the problem of multiple constituencies.

This problem is a reflection of the globalised, internationalised and transnationalised world in which armed conflicts are less state-centric than in the past. Although the state remains the key point of reference, the realities of armed conflict mean that the involvement of non-state actors, whether of sub-state groups within a country or a transnational network, such as al-Qa'ida, or of multinational coalitions, alliances or partnerships, prevent the individual state and its armed forces from acting freely, if at all, on its own. All of this means, rather than two sides straightforwardly engaging in conflict with each other, warfare tends to involve multiple constituencies. This is the outstanding feature of 'post-modern' war in general.

So far, strategy has been implicitly discussed in an assumed binary form in this chapter—the opponent and ourselves. In practice, warfare was, and is, rarely like that. Throughout history, warfare has involved alliances and coalitions, or supporters and backers, on at least one side in an armed conflict, even if there has been a clear leader of those formations. In this binary form, the notions of legitimacy and success as victory can be related to the famous Clausewitzian secondary 'trinity' of government, armed forces and the people at home, noted above.[47] This was a simple trinity, reflecting key aspects of nineteenth-century statehood. With only slight modification, the essential character of the 'trinity' is linked to the importance of legitimacy and of 'hearts and minds' as applied to contemporary warfare. Understanding of the trinity in the contemporary context is vital to legitimacy. The trinity still operates in every single situation; furthermore, the relationships between political leaders, their armed instruments and the communities on whom they depend, or whose support they seek, become increasingly relevant.

That increased significance is due to the factorial expansion of the trinity. In this era, in the twenty-first century, a more complex, multidimensional trinity operates. The contemporary strategist has to take account not only of the traditional mirror trinities, of which Clausewitz wrote, but also the strategist's own, and that of the opponent. In the internationalised environment of twenty-first century warfare, there are multiple trinities; the home trinity and that of the opponent, in conventional terms, become multidimensional. When no state acts alone, then every engagement with allies, or partners, involves a honeycomb of trinities.

As mentioned at the beginning of this chapter, the expansion of the trinity in the twenty-first century can best be characterised as the Multidimensional Trinity Cubed (Plus)—which can be expressed by the emblem *Trinity³(+)*, or *T³(+)*. First, there is the home front, in each case, comprising political leaders, armed forces and people. Secondly, each aspect of the opponent's triangle of political leaders, armed forces and people needs to be influenced, as well as all of them at the same time. Thirdly, there are multiple global audiences, all being subject to the same information, and the same images, all affecting the environment in which any strategic campaign is conducted.

Each contingent has a Trinitarian relationship not only with its own political leaders and the political community, but also with those of the other members of the collective operation. The tactical-level action of each contingent needs to be coordinated, not only within its own country's context, but also with those of its allies, or partners. This means that the tactical-level action of any contingent affects the legitimacy of other contingents, and of the operation as a whole. In situations of complexity and ambiguity, the same set of relationships applies on all sides. Thus, in a conflict, there are two sets of multiply constituted trinities. In addition to this, there is a third category of trinities, which might be regarded as one, or as a set involving an indefinite, or even infinite, variety of others, that are not directly engaged in a conflict, but which form an international public, comprising multiple trinities—Smith's audience, or audiences, in the 'global theatre'. Thus, This set of audience trinities cubes the already multidimensional character of each state, or non-state, actor. The strategist's task is to devise strategy and operate, while maintaining a favourable equilibrium among these relationships. The condition of success is legitimacy—achieving the aim, whatever it might be, while avoiding, or at least successfully dealing with, critical challenges to the legitimacy of a mission. A key challenge in contemporary war is to be able to manage multiple constituencies of legitimacy—to understand, and operate, with the *Trinity³(+)*.

Issues of alliance, coalition, partnership, support and backing are more complex than ever in the conditions of contemporary warfare. It is these conditions that the *Trinity³(+)* encapsulates. The character of contemporary warfare means that conventional conflict between the regular armed forces of states has changed. The *Trinity³(+)* signals multiple audiences for, or potential reservoirs of, support (or challenge). Crucially, there is a need to be aware of transnational communities—something that is relatively important and a relatively recent factor, cutting across the boundaries of conventional states, and leading to a whole range of other problems. These communities constitute a key to legitimacy, if there is concern to avoid legitimacy crises. While legitimacy is a positive quality, it is not something that is easy to gauge positively. Where legitimacy can really be identified is in the face of critical challenges.

To understand the significance of legitimacy and the $T^3(+)$ is to recognise that there is strategic-tactical compression. This makes all tactical and operational actions potentially significant at the strategic level. In many cases, events at the tactical level have strategic impact. This has been an operational reality for some armed forces for some time, though not recognised in the dominant discussion in the US. In the US context, the phenomenon was symbolised by the label 'the strategic corporal', coined by US Marine General Charles Krulak in the 1990s,[48] although that Marine Corps understanding did not then penetrate other parts of the US military, leaving major lessons to be learned painfully during the Iraq and Afghanistan campaigns of the twenty-first century.[49] It is vital to understand the conceptual differences between one level and another. Greater challenges exist than in previous eras. To meet these, it is essential to take appropriate action at any particular level of the conflict to achieve the desired effect at the overall strategic level. In contemporary warfare, '[T]he severity of the challenges to strategy posed by ... highly asymmetrical small wars does not show strategy the door, but rather commands the strategist to work harder'.[50] This means recognising where a brigade-level formation is needed to overcome a battalion-based force structure and thereby ensure tactical and operational superiority.[51] Such superiority can then adeptly be transformed into strategic effect. Understanding how circumstances come to be defined—that is, at what level force can be used in a given situation—is essential to success. Any attempt to employ force at the wrong level is likely only to produce frustration and failure.

Operations always involve, and affect, strategic initiative on the part of those who decide to employ force. Once deployed, the force must ensure its legitimacy. Force commanders have to establish and maintain legitimacy, a process involving their reconciling diverse elements exterior to the force involved in conflict, as well as the sets of relationships within it. Critically, in the context of the *Trinity³(+)*, two operational factors become increasingly significant: the military culture of the forces deployed; and the degree to which the managers of the force can seize the strategic initiative.[52] As the complement to the extensive discussion of legitimacy above, grasping the initiative is a key aspect of strategic coherence. Leaders have to look at how to frame a strategic programme, either through design or opportunism, or, most likely, an admixture of the two. This maintains the momentum of the diplomatic, political and strategic processes, which the military operation supports. It is also crucial to what may be called 'defining moments'.

A defining moment is one in which opportunities are either opened up, or closed off (depending on approach and outcome), setting, or contributing to, the tone of the mission for the following period, and providing the focal point around which discourse and support for the mission accumulates, or dissipates. There are two possibilities for the salience of a defining moment. First, defining moments give momentum, in terms of performance, and, by giving momentum, they become *foci* of identity. Defining moments are a component part of the basis upon which an operation is carried out. The alternative is that the response in a defining moment is inappropriate and the mission is compromised and subject to dissipating energy, or inertia. These alternatives will affect legitimacy—the key to success—in a positive or negative manner, respectively. One of the big problems that the international force in Bosnia faced, for example, before 1995, as did others elsewhere, was that they could regularly do good work and achieve things in positive ways, but this was not noticed.[53] Rather, the general outcome and the broad perception of the force's performance were defined by notable, negatively salient moments, such as the halting attempts to use force to protect the Goražde, Sarajevo and Srebrenica 'safe areas', in 1994 and 1995, where incoherence was marked by the gap between force commanders' being ready to exert armed force and civilian political and diplomatic leadership being ineffectual. In contrast to the experiences in Bosnia, prior to 1995, a positive impact on legitimacy requires 'defining moments' to be recognised and determined as essential points to be exploited, as part of a coherent strategic approach. Flexible and adaptable engagement of this kind is vital to success in contemporary warfare, where effect is critical.

The successful exploitation of defining moments gives the clarity necessary for the effective use of an operational capability within a given, complex strategic environment in contemporary warfare. This coherence is crucial to strategic operations. However, strategic operations are not like an equation: there is no way to say, at any stage, that two plus two will equal four. Rather, strategy is more akin to sailing, or producing and rearing children—there are aims, and there is an understanding of the means available to carry out the mission, but any action occurs in a changing environment, where the character of the sea, or child, determines how effective a particular action is. This is why when trying to understand the way an armed force can attempt to maintain momentum and coherence at the strategic level, while using force judiciously, one of the most important dimensions to recognise is the exploitation of these defining moments or, defensively, the capacity to counter their exploitation by the opponent.

The obverse of this is perhaps even more important to grasp: those same moments become all the more salient if they focus on something that goes wrong. While it is important for those conducting operations to understand the need to exploit these chances with judicious action, it is even more important to realise that injudicious action can have disastrous effect. Whatever the particular circumstances, the perception of wrongdoing can fatally undermine a mission and result in failure—all the more so, if there is a substantive basis for such negative perceptions.

Perceptions in this context are shaped by images, more than anything else, as I have argued in earlier work.[54] These perceptions affect legitimacy and so also, in the terms outlined above, the prospect of success. In the last decade of the twentieth century and the first of the twenty-first, pictures affected and indeed changed the world of crisis diplomacy and the way in which crises were handled. Observers could instantly recognise and understand the significance of images, such as that of Fikret Alić at the barbed-wire fence of the Trnopolje concentration camp in northern Bosnia, which flashed around the globe and shocked it into action in 1992. Similarly, the images of ethnic cleansing, whether bodies cut in half in doorways or columns of refugees fleeing a similar fate, became too familiar and shaped international engagement with the criminal strategy at work there. For example, the aerial and satellite images of major earthworks, suggested mass grave sites around Srebrenica in July 1995, the markers of mass murder, and a film from the ground showed men and boys being separated from females, each group placed on buses, with the males being transported to their deaths at mass murder sites, and the women and girls being deported.

These images from Bosnia led the way, but each conflict over a twenty-year period was marked by the images emerging from it—or occasionally their complete absence (for example, the victims, legitimate or otherwise, of 'hidden' drone attacks by the US—of course, as occasional video releases confirmed, there were usually images captured by these devices). As a result, those problems were treated differently in a world where it had become almost 'no picture, no conflict' and there were competitions, in effect, for the most awful images and interpretations of them. Perhaps no other image had such devastating impact as that of the Twin Towers of the World Trade Center in New York City, explosively sliced open on the higher floors by commercial passenger aircraft used as missiles, and then crumbling to the ground in clouds of computer screens and concrete. Perhaps no images were as damaging as those emerging from the US abuse of prisoners at Abu Ghraib in Iraq, which virally replicated themselves around the world—pictures captured and disseminated using the same kinds of digital image device that had transformed the world in general, and that of crisis and conflict management in particular. Images decisively affected and shaped events dominating the international agenda. They were the impetus for engagement and action. They constituted evidence surrounding atrocities and contentious events. And in many ways they have come to be the decisive elements in engagements surrounding the use of force, defining the outcome, as argued elsewhere.[55]

As noted earlier, this is no longer a world where a decisive battle at a centre of gravity will shape an outcome. It is actually the images that define the outcome. For example, it is reasonable to suggest that, if the US-led adventure in Iraq was not already lost by the time the images of Abu Ghraib emerged, it was never going to be winnable from that point onwards. The phenomenon of images, therefore, has shaped the world in ways that were unimaginable two decades previously. This is because of the growth in global communications and the way that the digitisation of imagery, and other forms of communication, have re-shaped the world and changed the pressures on international security. It is a sad reflection, however, that the images that mostly 'work' and are salient are those that focus on war crimes. At a minimum, images generating accusations of war crimes make it even harder for those involved to succeed—all the more so, when, as at Abu Ghraib or Srebrenica (as different as those cases are), those images tell the truth of abuse and criminal activity. It is such images of abuse, inhumanity and war crimes that will penetrate the picture-rich contemporary environment.

The multidimensional character of the type of operation under discussion means that it is important to consider the ways in which an appropriate force might be put together and, in the process of putting it together, how it could be made successful. The key to understanding questions of success is the concept of legitimacy. However, understanding the relevance of legitimacy to all such operations depends on recognising that they are carried out at the strategic level. The legitimacy of operations, as discussed above, depends particularly on their defining moments. Among the most defining and salient of all moments are those that affect perceptions of 'wrong' and 'right' in warfare—especially when borne by images appearing to confirm them. It is the suggestions and images of 'wrongdoing', above all, that determine the legitimacy of actions involving the use of armed force.

In contemporary strategy, the interpretation of action became more important than the action itself. Combined with a number of other elements, this gives warfare a new character. The competition for legitimacy is a competition for a dominant narrative, albeit based around military operations, *inter alia*. In this context of contested legitimacy, legitimacy is almost always fragile, in keeping with the changed character of relations in the $T^3(+)$ environment.

This is where accusations of war crimes and misconduct become highly important. Along with powerful images, it is issues of lawfulness and ethics—right and wrong—that shape narratives of legitimacy. This is the context in which the military increasingly has to operate in countries such as the UK. Increasingly complex operations involve ever more finely judged decisions on using the blunt capability of armed force. Greater decision-making scope, and also understanding by the multiple audiences in the *Trinity³(+)*, is desirable for commanders in action. However, the opposite tends to be the case. At times, it seems that almost any operation in which a civilian dies, is met with charges of misconduct and alleged criminality from one quarter, or another.

STRATEGY AND THE MULTIDIMENSIONAL TRINITY

The *Trinity*[3](+) is the context in which such accusations, with their multiple reverberations through multiple audiences, affect the success or failure of a strategy. It is vital to understand this context in order to understand the questions and pressures affecting the use of armed force in the early twenty-first century. As war crimes accusations—and, indeed, prosecutions—have increasingly come to address the normal conduct of military affairs, rather than the exceptional and clearly illegal, the need to understand how defence personnel should think, and the kinds of judgements that might be relevant, is imperative. Understanding the calculus of armed force, as well as the views, values and beliefs of practitioners, should be a vital factor in any attempt to investigate war crimes issues. Against this background understanding of strategy and the kinds of considerations that have to be made in the conduct of warfare, amplified in the age of multidimensional warfare, the following chapter charts the evolution in the prosecution of war crimes in the late twentieth century and the rapidly changing legal and judicial environments that contributed to the salience of war crimes accusations and issues of wrong and right in the conduct of contemporary military operations.

3

PROSECUTING WAR CRIMES

Right and wrong are central in war. The use of armed forces to achieve political purposes is intimately linked to justice, both in the reasons for using armed force and in the manner in which armed force is used—the twin elements of Just War theory (see Chapter 1). The developed ethics that surround the use of armed force offer one set of boundaries, delimiting what is and is not acceptable, when there is resort to destructive political violence. Wrong and right in warfare are often hard to determine; the processes that negotiate the sense of wrong and right are challenging to manage. This is because large-scale multiple actions involving death and destruction are present. The translation of 'right' and 'wrong' codes into law, though, makes the definition of right and wrong easier, as 'right' and 'wrong' demarcate the boundary between lawful and criminal action. In other ways it makes no difference, while in yet others it makes the distinction harder. In practice, the apparent clarity of legal definition becomes an often-murky business. This is because the boundaries of legality and criminality depend on assessments of necessity and proportionality, as in the consideration of what constitutes a Just War. Yet, in criminal proceedings, evidence is introduced in the attempt to prove charges beyond reasonable doubt. This means that wrongdoers could be extended the benefit of the doubt, as either necessity and proportionality, or empirical evidence of direct responsibility, are often elusive.

These issues, which emerged more strongly at the end of the twentieth century and the start of the twenty-first, came to prominence because of rapid developments in the prosecution of war crimes, especially when the issues involved were less clear-cut than cases involving the massacre of civilians. The era of international prosecution was also one of change, involving both the strategic context and the legal environment. Increased attention to enforcement was a culminating point for a major phase in the evolution of the laws of armed conflict. The post-Second World War military tribunals began a phase of both customary and legal innovation. This continued through the formation of the International Criminal Tribunals, first, for the former Yugoslavia and then for Rwanda, followed by the Special Court for Sierra Leone and the emergence of the International Criminal Court. The evolution in the law continued through each new framework for prosecution. This chapter explores the evolving context of crime and prosecution, in relation to warfare, and the pressures this creates, paving the way for later examination of military attitudes to these changes. The first section in this chapter describes the evolution of the laws of war in the twentieth century; the second summarises the history and development of war crimes prosecutions; and the third reviews the development of international criminal law in the late 1990s, in connection with international prosecution. The final section, focusing on issues concerning the Global War on Terror, argues that the newly evolving strategic environment means a continuing demand for legal developments, which will put greater pressure on those conducting armed operations.

The Evolution of the Laws of War

The laws of war always existed. But those laws always developed to fit their historical and cultural context. Evolution occurred from one period to another, over time. The first recorded laws of war, as far as I have been able to establish, were elaborated in the Old Testament of The Bible, in Deuteronomy.[1] And they were not necessarily what we would expect now. These rules were basic and had what an early twenty-first century Western audience might judge to be an unexpected character. There were three elements, or levels. The first was the distinction between cities that surrendered and those that did not; this was the most humanitarian action available, involving enslavement of the inhabitants of the capitulating city. The second and third elements involved a distinction between 'near' and 'far' cities. The intermediate level applied to far—away cities, where only the males were slaughtered, while the women, children and cattle were spared and taken as the victor's spoils. The third level was to massacre everyone in nearby cities. Perhaps the most striking feature of these rules was the imperative nature of the law: it dictated how the ruler should behave. This was not law that permitted or limited action; it determined what should be done. While there have been some in recent times who might welcome rules of this kind, by the 1990s, the world could not condone such action. The world in general, and the West in particular, has found it increasingly difficult to tolerate such an approach, however hard it was in reality to respond successfully over twenty years.

By the end of the twentieth century, the understanding of the laws of war had changed significantly. 1863 saw the invention of the US Lieber Code[2] and the founding of the International Committee of the Red Cross, which would become the custodian of international humanitarian law and also provided the forum for the formation of the Geneva Conventions in 1864; the combination of these innovations spurred the development of international law.[3] The first Geneva Conventions, succeeded by the Hague Conventions of 1899 and 1907, emerged at the start of a century that saw the creation of an international code on the conduct of armed conflict and the protection of human rights through the elaboration of an existing web of conventions, declarations and treaties.[4] Nazi mass murder during the Second World War provided the most important catalyst for this change, as the century developed.

The Nuremberg International Military Tribunal, established to prosecute senior figures from Hitler's regime, amplified existing international humanitarian law.[5] Nuremberg was vital because instead of seeking revenge and summary execution without trial, it instead sought justice. It also marked a new period of the development of international humanitarian law. The period between the end of the Second World War and the last decade of the twentieth century saw various innovations, which marked new high ground, such as the adoption of the Genocide Convention in 1948 and the Geneva Conventions of 1949. Universal observation could not be guaranteed, but there was certainly acknowledgement in the global context of the United Nations that these were standards applicable to all conflicts covered by the laws thereafter. There was also a seemingly unstoppable trend, confirmed in the press and public discussion of every contemporary conflict in the world, that these laws should apply to all armed conflicts. Thus, the laws developed for international armed conflicts were seen as applicable to non-international armed conflicts.* This is understandable given the degree to which Iraq's invasion of Kuwait in 1990 proved that purely international armed conflict, one state against another, was an exception that served to prove the rule that one of the key characteristics of contemporary armed conflicts is their non-international character, even if they might often be mixed with international elements.[6]

The principles that underlay notions of *jus ad bellum* and *jus in bello* began to be codified as aspects of international humanitarian law from the late nineteenth century onwards.[7] The difficult boundaries of what constitutes right and wrong in the ethical sphere gained a black and white legal character. However, the emphasis, over time, has been far greater on standards in the conduct of war than on the reasons for going to war: whatever has been restricted and outlawed, it has not been the actual act of going to war (although the idea of waging 'aggressive war' has become unacceptable in the UN era, as the UN Charter, and increasingly state practice, allowed the legal use of force only as an act of self-defence, under Article 51 of the Charter, or as a Chapter VII enforcement measure authorised by the UN Security Council). In the course of the twentieth century the foundations laid in 1899 in The Hague Conventions were developed extensively.[8] The terms of the Geneva Convention of 1929 and their considerably more robust descendants, the 1949 Geneva Conventions, amplified by the protocols of 1977, are now central to conceptions of the laws of war. The

---

* For the most part, the laws of armed conflict rest on treaty agreements between states on how states will, or should, behave in the conduct of war. The Hague Conventions of 1899 and 1907, and the Geneva Conventions of 1864, 1906, 1929 and 1949 were agreements between states that gave states responsibilities. As the protecting parties in these legal agreements, states agreed to ensure that their armed forces would conduct themselves in accordance with these rules of war and, if individuals within the armed forces did not meet those standards, then the states would take action to punish them. Thus, individuals were always subject to the authority of the state as a protecting power embracing international agreement domestically, not to 'international law', as such. States, notionally, were responsible to other states for their adherence to the terms of the law. The implication of this is that the laws of armed conflict do not apply in non-international armed conflict—that is, internal armed conflict, or other armed conflicts not fought between states party to the relevant treaties, or subject to other laws and customs of war as sovereign states in an international society of sovereign states. The formal exceptions to this are Article 3, common to each of the four Geneva Conventions of 1949, which gives broad and limited reference to basic protections in the case of non-international armed conflict, and its reinforcement in Additional Protocol II of the Geneva Conventions, from 1977 (see below).

Geneva Conventions are now treaty law, signed between states. In the manner of traditional state relations, they are deeply protective of the state and its interests. They do not apply where there is an internal conflict—an issue discussed below. The one exception to this, under the terms of the 1977 Additional Protocol II, is that Common Article 3 is accepted by those who signed and ratified the Protocol as applying to internal conflict[9]—that is, Article 3 of each of the four Geneva Conventions has the same wording, and this common thread applies to all forms of armed conduct, external or internal, or, more precisely, international or non-international.

The adoption of Protocol II by a large number of states has contributed to an understanding in which the terms of Common Article 3 are argued to have entered the canon of customary international law.[10] That is, in distinction from treaty law signed between states—which only applies to states that are party to treaties—there is a separate category of law, which evolves over time and is derived from factors such as major international agreements. These might be treaty agreements so widely accepted that their terms are said to extend more generally, even to non-parties. Alternatively, they might be normative expressions, for which there is considerable support among states, or products of state practice and international precedent. The customary approach also embraces elements of law considered so essential and immutable that they endure through time and space. Such law, in theory, according to the notion of *jus cogens*, cannot be overridden by another legal agreement.[11] Thus, while the Geneva Conventions constitute a clear, treaty-based set of rules for the conduct of war, they also contribute to a wider body of laws on armed conflict, which even take precedence over treaties.

Within the scope of customary law, the notion of Crimes Against Humanity emerged after the Second World War. Although there was no clear basis for what was essentially an invention in the London Charter of the International Military Tribunal at Nuremberg, there was a strong and understandable argument that the behaviour of the Nazis had been so extraordinary that it required an exceptional measure—the *ex post facto* invention and application of law—to do justice for the exceptional offences they perpetrated. While Crimes Against Humanity, as a category, became embedded in international humanitarian law, one of the key aspects it had been invented to cover was distilled in the Genocide Convention of 1948: the attempt with intent to destroy, in whole, or in part, a national, ethnic, racial, or religious group.[12] The evolving catalogue of potential crimes produced over this period reached a crucial point with the adoption of the definition of a crime of 'aggression' holding individual responsibility at the Kampala Review Conference on the Rome Statute of the International Criminal Court in 2010.[13] While it would be some years before that crime would be in a position to be charged, it had the potential to constrain war—the chief objective of international humanitarian and international criminal law and their proponents from the mid-nineteenth century onwards.

The History and Development of War Crimes Prosecutions

The register of laws and potential crimes developed during the nineteenth and twentieth centuries provided keystones for the development of a new field of law in the twenty-first century: 'international criminal law'.[14] This new field related the ethical and normative aspects of contemporary contributions to customary law. However, before the notion of international criminal law came to be developed and labelled as such—indeed, as part of its development—there was increasing attention to individual responsibility in the second half of the twentieth century and the early years of the twenty-first century. This led to the evolution of war crimes prosecutions against individuals through various means: *ad hoc* judicial arrangements; purely municipal (or national) prosecutions of nationals; municipal action under the doctrine of universal jurisdiction where a jurisdiction adopts the right to prosecute certain international crimes, disregarding the geographical location of the crimes or the nationality of the accused; and the normative standard setting of the permanent International Criminal Court.

The first international war crimes trial is generally recorded as that of Peter von Hagenbach, at Breisach, in 1474,[15] when a panel of judges from the Holy Roman Empire convicted him of breaching the 'laws of God and man' through his troops' conduct (rape, murder and pillage), and sentenced him to death. However, an earlier case is arguably that of William Wallace, popularised as Braveheart, the Scots leader who was tried by the English Crown of Edward I, following what, it must be recalled, passed for an international armed conflict, in the era of personal incarnation of sovereignty.[16] Analyses of the trial of Wallace usually emphasise the 'show' character of the proceedings and the treason charges against him, often noting that these were questionable; the Scotsman had laid claim to the Scottish Crown, he had never sworn loyalty to the English Crown and its sovereign King Edward I. Treason was one of the crimes for which Wallace was hanged, drawn and quartered, reflecting English victory and control over the Scots. But, the charges against Wallace also included an allegation of war crimes, including murder and rape—which were, by the law of the time, acceptable if conducted by the forces of the liege, on his behalf, but not by an individual in this way. This meant that Edward, as victor, was entitled to do whatever he liked, and did so in his cruel rout of the Scots,[17] while the same acts committed by, and on behalf of, his defeated opponent were unlawful. Thus, the second element in the indictment was probably the first recorded (and quite possibly the first, in any case) war crimes case. The indictment accused Wallace of something akin to 'Crimes Against Humanity' and breaches of the laws and customs of war in the campaigns he led in northern England: '... he invaded the Kingdom of England and especially the counties of Northumberland, Cumberland and Westmorland, and all whom he found there loyal to the King of England he feloniously slew in different ways...'[18] This was a clear and recognised distinction, which constituted 'victor's justice', long before that phrase was applied to the Nuremberg trial at the end of the Second World War, the first truly international war crimes prosecution.

Two International Military Tribunals (IMTs) for the prosecution of major war criminals, in Nazi Germany and the Far East, respectively, were established following the close of the Second World War.[19] The latter, established in Tokyo, emerged on the coattails of the former, which was based at Nuremberg, in southern Germany, where the great Nazi rallies had been held in the 1930s. The International Military Tribunal at Nuremberg was the first of these. Its creation was partly a contingency of the weak Leipzig process after the First World War,[20] where the Allies had permitted Germany to try its own war crimes suspects, but the process and outcome had not been satisfactory. In larger part, however, Nuremberg was created as a response to the unimagined scale and character of the Nazi campaigns—though historical perspective on the Holocaust should never occlude the reality that Nuremberg was impelled by the will to punish 'waging aggressive warfare' and that other matters, such as Crimes Against Humanity, were derivatives that could only be charged as examples of the horrific way in which Nazi Germany waged aggressive war.[21]

The charter, which underpinned the IMT at Nuremberg, was agreed at the London Conference between the four allied victors in Europe: the United States, the Soviet Union, the United Kingdom and France.[22] These states brought elements of their diverse legal backgrounds and views together in the invention of a court and, to a large extent, the invention of the law to go with it. The IMT at Nuremberg began a blurring of boundaries that has continued to mark the realm of international criminal law. This was done with the adaptation of treaty agreement terms between states to allow for charges to be brought for individual responsibility in some cases (Count 2, 'Crimes Against the Peace'), while new law was wholly invented to meet these new circumstances (Count 4, 'Crimes Against Humanity'). The improvisation and legal innovation involved in the Nuremberg Charter and its Tokyo derivative raised questions about the appropriateness of measures, as key legal principles were breached, such as *nullum crimen sine lege* (no crime without law), meaning that there could not be a crime where the law had not already prescribed one (with *ex post facto* legislation, of any kind, and retrospective application also questionable in liberal legal doctrine).[23] Thus, three counts, incorporating four crimes, could be charged at Nuremberg. The first count included the possibility of a second crime in connection with the first: the charge of crimes against the peace could be joined by conspiracy to commit crimes against the peace. This was, in part, because the French and Soviet participants did not have a concept of conspiracy (in some senses, the practice called 'conspiracy' was how business could get done, in those places) and so could not accept a separate count. Still, Franco-Soviet unfamiliarity over 'conspiracy' was a small affair, compared to the way in which the framers of the Charter effectively created new law through expansion and invention of existing agreements. Crimes against the peace was a Nuremberg invention, derived from the 1928 Kellogg-Briand Pact against waging aggressive war, a treaty agreement to which Germany was a party.[24] However, as far as that pact created responsibility for any violation (and it was a relatively flimsy basis for generating 'crimes against the peace'), this was not individual criminal responsibility, but state responsibility. The second count was war crimes, in relation to the Hague Conventions, the best-established element of law applied at Nuremberg. Hague law, though, while far more substantial and established as an instrument of law than the Kellogg-Briand Pact, still applied to states and was not created as a matter of individual criminal responsibility, at the international level, at least. In this way, two of the counts concerned the translation of international law regarding state responsibilities into crimes for which individuals were suddenly to be held accountable. However, if the first two counts could claim some basis in existing law, even if the claim was questionable and the law involved did not apply to individuals, the final count was a complete invention—Crimes Against Humanity. This new legal category was invented *ex post facto* and applied retrospectively, once more, contradicting defence arguments, conventional wisdom and Western legal philosophy, but making sense in the circumstances.

This count breached a basic principle of the Western liberal legal tradition: *nullum crimen sine lege*—if the law did not exist, there was no crime.[25] As one of the defendants, Reich Marshall Hermann Goering, complained to the court, nobody had previously said that these were crimes. Defence lawyers filed a motion on this issue, which the judges addressed with subtlety in their verdict:

The maxim *nullum crimen sine lege* is not a limitation of sovereignty, but it is in general a principle of justice. To assert that it is unjust to punish those who in defiance of treaties and assurances have attacked neighbouring States without warning is obviously untrue, for in such circumstances the attacker must know that he is doing wrong, and so far from it being unjust to punish him, it would be unjust if his wrong was allowed to go unpunished.[26]

There were also questions about the application of the law only to one party to the conflict—Germany. Defendants were denied the chance to argue a *tu quoque* defence that the Allies had done the same things. Yet, while the *tu quoque* defence was not allowed, charges were not pressed against Admirals Karl Doenitz and Erich Raeder, relating to submarine warfare, as the allies had also broken the 1936 London Submarine Protocol—or, as Doenitz's lawyer argued, acted lawfully according to the same interpretation as used, in effect, by the US and others.[27]

The circumstances of the Second World War, most notably the programme of industrial mass murder of Jews and others in extermination camps, were taken as ample justification. These were extraordinary circumstances that required extraordinary measures. However, while the questionable steps taken were undoubtedly justified, on balance, they were more than ample evidence that Nuremberg was a matter of 'victor's justice'.[28] The crucial thing was that it was, indeed, justice, rather than straightforward revenge. It was due process rather than summary execution. It thereby established clear lines of future responsibility, even if the due process used was also deeply flawed regarding many matters. The flaws related to issues such as: the admission and availability of evidence; the scope for defence; the limited (effectively non-existent) right to appeal; and the unequal application of the law—only major figures on the losing side were prosecuted, with no question whatsoever of admitting the possibility of cases against the

Allies (this last aspect was compounded by the rejection of any *tu quoque* defence). Not only did the exceptional situation created by Nazi Germany justify the establishment of the IMT, despite its weaknesses, but, in retrospect, so too did the legacies it created, both in terms of international judicial precedent and the rehabilitating impact on West Germany.

Although Nuremberg and Tokyo are often assumed to be synonymous, the latter had even greater question marks against it. All the same issues could be raised and amplified. In addition to this, rather than being created by treaty agreement between Allies, following the creation of the IMT at Nuremberg, the Tokyo IMT was effectively created by fiat of General Douglas MacArthur, the US officer commanding in the theatre, with a petition to him as the only slender route for something akin to appeal.[29] There was significant dissent on verdicts from three judges (all among the non-Americans appointed to the Tribunal to represent Japan's main victim countries),[30] further bringing the outcome into question. And the impact on post-1945 Japanese society was not comparable with the effect of Nuremberg in helping to transform German society.[31]

Developing International Criminal Law in the 1990s

After a hiatus of more than forty years, attention to war crimes issues began to emerge more strongly. In the decade and half after the Cold War closed, there was increased attention to issues of lawfulness in the conduct of military operations. In part, this involved the emergence of international tribunals for particular cases and the International Criminal Court (ICC), which simply raised awareness of the Laws of Armed Conflict and international crimes at a broad level. However, awareness of the importance of legal issues and the prospect of war crimes prosecutions did not necessarily equal developed understanding. For example, it is striking that senior UK officers still did not understand how the ICC was intended to work, with the UK's having entirely embraced the ICC Statute in UK law.[32] Chief of the Defence Staff, Admiral Sir Michael Boyce, sought assurances that UK military engagement in Iraq would be lawful and not result in prosecutions there.[33] Boyce's fears were misplaced, on two levels. On one of these, any concerns about involvement in potentially unlawful action *per se* were irrelevant, as the ICC had no jurisdiction at that point for handling questions of aggression.[34] On the other level, the principle of complementary jurisdiction meant that there was no realistic prospect of any UK soldier appearing before the ICC. Complementarity meant that the ICC could only have authority to deal with cases where the national courts of States Parties to the Statute had failed, whether through inability to deal with cases, inadequate investigation and process, or where the UN Security Council referred a matter to the ICC under Article 13 of the Rome Statute and Chapter VII of the UN Charter (it is unlikely that the UK, as a permanent member of the Security Council, would not exercise its right to veto, should the question of that body's referring a British case ever emerge). ICC jurisdiction could only apply if an individual accused of war crimes belonged to a State Party to the ICC Treaty or if the suspected crime were committed on the territory of a party to the Treaty, and if no action were taken at the domestic level. Boyce's crucial misapprehension in the case of the UK was that both British culture and the measures already adopted by the authorities made this an unthinkable prospect. The ICC statute was taken into UK law in almost its entirety (and with only small differences where the wording was not exactly the same) to ensure that all matters would always be handled in the UK, with no friction over terminology or crimes. This was intended to mean, and in practice meant, that there was no prospect of UK personnel finding themselves in the ICC dock,[35] although, ironically, adoption of the ICC statute did mean the first trial and conviction of a serving UK soldier for war crimes—that of Corporal Donald Payne, discussed in Chapter 1.

This was in sharp contrast to the jurisdiction of the *ad hoc* International Criminal Tribunals (ICTs) for the former Yugoslavia and for Rwanda. These were established under the authority given to the UN Security Council in Chapter VII of the UN Charter to deal with 'threats to international peace and security' by using enforcement measures, which have binding effect and override any other instrument of international law.[36] Thus, the mission of the *ad hoc* Tribunals was to restore and maintain international peace and security by criminal justice proceedings against individuals who were war crimes suspects, who had not faced the test of criminal law, and whose continued liberty as individuals constituted a threat to international peace and security. The ICTs had overriding authority, limited by a range of factors: geographic, temporal and personal. The geographic, temporal and personal limitations for the ICTY were that the court could only try cases involving individuals committing offences on the territories that made up the Socialist Federative Republic of Yugoslavia after 1 January 1991.[37] In the case of the ICTR, the limitations were that the relevant law applied to individuals on Rwandan territory, Rwandan citizens on neighbouring territory, and, in any case, for alleged crimes committed between 1 January and 31 December 1994.[38] These *ad hoc* bodies under the UN Security Council had complete primacy within their boundaries of temporal, geographical and personal jurisdiction, in theory, superseding any relevant aspect of municipal or international law, or claims founded in them. This primacy over national jurisdictions was not repeated in the ICC Statute.[39] Yet another model was developed for the UN Special Court for Sierra Leone (SCSL).[40] This was a joint enterprise between the authorities of Sierra Leone and the international community, established with Chapter VII authority—often regarded as a 'hybrid' body. It included elements of national law and included the participation of Sierra Leone in all respects. Yet, it also clearly reflected the influence of both the ICTs and the later ICC—and ultimately it was an international body.[41] This was evident both in the fact that Sierra Leone itself could not dissolve the court and also in the SCSL's case law. Versions of this hybrid model, sometimes international, sometimes embedded in municipal law, but with significant international involvement, making them, in effect, 'internationalised' courts, followed: the UN Special Tribunal for Lebanon, the Extraordinary Chambers in the Courts of Cambodia, the Iraqi High Tribunal, and the Bosnia War Crimes Court, for example, In addition to the advent of these international judicial bodies, the emergence at the end of the Cold War of jurisdiction to tackle international crimes under a doctrine of universal jurisdiction made a difference, resulting, for example, in the introduction of the War Crimes Act in the UK and its equivalent in Australia in the early 1990s (which fortuitously generated a small body of practitioners with relevant experience before the first *ad hoc* international tribunal (for Yugoslavia) was created.[42]

The laws of armed conflict, which evolved and developed significantly over a century and a half, were fundamental to developing the Statute of the International Criminal Tribunal for the former Yugoslavia (ICTY), devised by the UN and representatives of the Security Council states, and adopted by the UN Security Council in Resolution 827 of 25 May 1993. This extraordinary use of Security Council power and authority to establish international judicial intervention was seen by many as a fairly empty political gesture.[43] It focused attention on the atrocities being committed and it demonstrated international concern. This was the outcome of interactions involving the integrative subset of international politics and international law—that is, international peace and security—along with a raft of other factors: the evolution of the United Nations; the evolution of war and the laws of war; the outcome of the Yugoslav War; the assertion of human rights; and the calibration of the use of power. The key to establishing this international judicial body was the combination of politics and the related reinterpretation of 'threats to international peace and security' decided by the UN Security Council Summit of Heads of State and Government in 1992. This made possible an action that would previously have been unthinkable. The ICTY was created not as a purely judicial measure. It was part of a legal-political sandwich, where political authority (the Security Council) created a purely judicial body (the Tribunal) for political purposes (the restoration and maintenance of international peace and security in the region).

This development was largely linked to a new understanding of issues concerning peace and security. Radical changes occurred in the 1990s, including new interpretations concerning threats to international peace and security. These were confirmed by the UN Security Council. It was the Security Council's altered definition of international peace and security[44] which confirmed the shift in attitudes towards ending the absolute protection provided by state sovereignty, and pointed to the increased importance of human rights as a factor in peace and security. This was a process of codifying something that was already in effect—as noted elsewhere, the authority for the UN Security Council to take action contrary to conventional protections of sovereignty had been 'generally unnoticed for forty years',[45] even though the founders of the UN had allowed for this provision in Article 2 (7) of the UN Charter. While the provision for action had been included in the Charter, the Cold War compress that followed the foundation of the UN meant that there was little Security Council enforcement action under the provisions in Chapter VII. Only ten matters were handled under Chapter VII before 1990. Although they sowed seeds for the type of action that would come in the 1990s, including issues of sovereign rights and protections, none was as radical as that which occurred in the 1990s.[46] In line with this, the Security Council passed Chapter VII resolutions concerning a wide range of problems, all essential departures in terms of sovereignty in international relations and the management of international peace and security.[47]

This novel use of Chapter VII powers, turning on the nexus of international security and international law, represented a new step regarding the position of the state and its qualification of sovereignty. The increased importance of the individual and the emphasis on justice marked a new understanding, derived from Nuremberg and translated through the creation of international tribunals for the former Yugoslavia and Rwanda: there could only be peace if justice prevailed. Where there had been gross abuses of human rights, the traditional protection offered to the state by sovereignty had to be removed in the interest of justice and, through justice, peace. That meant that the protection and privileges of exercising sovereign rights also had to be suspended, if arrangements for governance were to be found that satisfied the need for peace.

The operation of the Yugoslavia Tribunal, as a judicial body, needed to ensure due process—including corrections to the legal failings of Nuremberg and Tokyo, as prescribed by key participants in those earlier processes.[48] However, in terms of its operation, this purely legal body was the filling between two slices of politics, as was the case with the other *ad hoc* international courts created in the wake of the ICTY, for Rwanda and Sierra Leone—the former following the Yugoslavia model, the latter operating as a joint venture between the UN and the local judicial system in Sierra Leone, with the purpose of both strengthening the domestic legal system and bringing the issue of justice within the relevant political community itself, given that it was possible to do so.[49] The political-legal dynamic was also pertinent to the ostensibly domestic, yet internationally influenced, Iraqi High Tribunal[50] (which, at one stage, might have been formed as an international body)[51] as well as the war crimes courts in Bosnia and Kosovo, which formally involved international judges and lawyers by treaty agreement, and the Extraordinary Chambers in the Courts of Cambodia. It too, therefore, can be seen as part of an evolving canon of international judicial intervention, notwithstanding that court's clearly non-international focus.

The creation of *ad hoc* tribunals for the former Yugoslavia and for Rwanda, based on decisions of the UN Security Council, constituted another stage in the application of international humanitarian law, and the application of constraints on war. In these instances, unlike at Nuremberg, all the laws in question were already agreed and in existence. Interpretation and application of such laws appeared to have found its time. Developing this, in 1998, a UN conference supported by 120 states agreed on the Draft Treaty for a permanent International Criminal Court.[52] As the twentieth century closed, there could be no doubt that, whatever the remaining differences over detail, there was broad consensus among states to seek ways in which to uphold and strengthen international humanitarian law and the protection of human rights. This was geared to the need for international peace and security. Thus the development of justice regarding international life and conflict had been transformed from restraining the conduct of war to being an instrument of post-conflict peace.

The Yugoslavia Tribunal took time to grind into action, under considerable pressure both from public and media criticism of apparent inaction (reflecting no understanding, or even will to understand, the practicalities involved), and from those in the international community who had been responsible for its creation—the key members of the UN Security Council. The latter did not offer comprehensive commitment to their remarkable innovation in the early years, and many of the problems the Tribunal faced were practical—beginning with finding personnel and premises.[53] The UN Security Council's authorising the creation of the ICTY was only the point at which the practical aspects of a working Tribunal started to be put in place. First of all, the UN General Assembly had been required to appoint judges in a beauty-parade selection process, where politics clearly counted far more than experience and competence. Then, it had been necessary to found a registry and judges' chambers. And lastly, there was a need to establish a prosecutor's office, incorporating investigators, legal analysts and trial attorneys. Alongside these offices and underneath them (literally, as it turned out) there was a UN bureaucratic-administrative office (unlike each of the others, there would be a strong case for arguing that this was wholly unnecessary in operational terms—only the 'UN way' required this cumbersome addition and diversion of resources).[54] Finding premises in The Hague, and moving into them, all took time. So did the recruitment of sufficient personnel (both by the UN and by secondment from governments, at this stage). The establishment of a rudimentary operation took over a year. The search for a Chief Prosecutor was drawn out, primarily because of UN politics.[55] In spite of these realities, the Tribunal was already coming under pressure to produce demonstrable results.

Other problems in establishing the Tribunal were more conceptual. Unlike the Nuremberg and Tokyo Tribunals, this *ad hoc* body would be an international civil court, not military, with vastly different authority, operational and ethical considerations. Unlike the post-Second World War military tribunals, the ICTY was created, in part, as a deterrent while the war continued, rather than as a purely post-conflict instrument of justice. Unlike Nuremberg and Tokyo, the Yugoslavia tribunal would be conducted by a mixture of third parties—outsiders—on behalf of the UN, rather than by the victors in the conflict. Lastly and, most strikingly, as a consequence of all the preceding factors, whereas the victorious Allies in the Second World War had twenty-two major figures in custody to try—even if some even more major figures escaped justice though death, or flight (or possibly their value to the Allies, especially the US, who protected them, as was the case with many who had been involved in scientific work under the Nazis and were absorbed into Western weapons programmes or security apparatus)—the Tribunal in The Hague had no suspects in custody and no obvious means of changing that situation, when it started work. Nonetheless, over the years, the Tribunal began to work effectively and to expand. This resulted in a remarkably successful position where, by mid-2011, of the 161 persons indicted by the Yugoslavia Tribunal, not one remained at large,[56] while the performance of the Rwanda and Sierra Leone courts, in this respect, was strong, especially once former Liberian leader Charles Taylor was, in March 2006, taken into the custody of the Special Court for Sierra Leone.[57]

Despite their being grouped together under the umbrella of post-Cold War peace and justice developments, the bodies to emerge have had not only different provenances and jurisdiction, but each has had a different set of crimes under its responsibility, reflecting evolution not only in the encompassing field of international humanitarian law, but also in the refining of criminal law, tailoring it to the needs of situations and taking account of previous developments. This can be seen through summary comparison of the crimes chargeable at the three purely international bodies, the *ad hoc* international tribunals for the former Yugoslavia and for Rwanda as well as the ICC,[58] and the effective evolution in international customary law that occurred.[59] The purpose of this comparison is certainly not to offer any definitive assessment of that evolution,[60] which resulted from a 'particular emphasis on developing international law'.[61] Nor is it to investigate the presumably complex reasons behind the choices of offence in the various statutes, or their ordering in the statutes, or the interrelationships between these different elements of international criminal law. These are matters of interest that would require sophisticated attention in their own right.[62] The more limited purpose in the present context is to indicate that change has occurred with considerable historical pace—and that it continues to do so, altering the environment in which soldiers operate and increasing the potential pressures they face as it does so.

In line with the developments in international humanitarian law outlined above, there were four crimes that those who faced the Yugoslavia

Tribunal could be charged with. These were encapsulated in Articles 2–5 of the Tribunal Statute. Under Article 2, the Statute provided for action over Grave Breaches of the Geneva Convention.[63] To apply this provision, the Prosecutor needed to establish that the alleged offences were committed in the context of an armed conflict, and that the armed conflict was international in character (rather than domestic), before the alleged victims could be regarded as protected persons under the law. However, reference to the Geneva Conventions was restricted to Common Article 3 of the conventions supplemented by Additional Protocol II (1977) and moved down the order to Article 4 (the last criminal category) in the statute of the International Criminal Tribunal for Rwanda (ICTR). In the Rome Statute of the ICC, Grave Breaches of the Geneva Conventions were subsumed as one sub-paragraph within a single macro-Article 8 dealing with war crimes as a broad category (with considerable additional detail included, making for an extensive list of acts covered by the crime category) and placed as the last category of existing crime. It is possible that this suggests, as would the changes between the Yugoslavia and Rwanda Statutes, that genocide and Crimes Against Humanity might be deemed to be more serious within a hierarchy of already very serious crimes, recognised as being out of the ordinary by their status in these documents. Of course, this is just conjecture, and it is likely that those responsible would argue that they intended nothing in line with this suggestion—it was merely how things turned out. The broad war-crimes category in the ICC Statute also includes an expanded version of the notion of laws and customs to that introduced under Article 3 of the ICTY Statute.[64] With reference to the ICTY Statute, it was necessary to prove that there was an armed conflict, as with the Grave Breaches provisions. However, it was not initially clear whether this also required international character—in the course of proceedings, the Tribunal's Appeals Chamber significantly clarified this, by placing Common Article 3 of the Geneva Conventions squarely in the domain of custom. Any haziness regarding the sweep of laws and customs under the Yugoslavia Statute was cleared in the ICC Statute, where different elements of law or acts are clearly laid out in paragraphs 2(c) and (e), which can be considered in the context of non-international armed conflict, whereas the items listed under 2(b) pertain only to cases of international armed conflict.

Genocide and Crimes Against Humanity appear in all three statutes. However, while the wording of the Genocide articles is exactly the same, lifted directly from the Genocide Convention, in both the Rwanda and

Rome statutes it is elevated to the first rank, whereas it appears behind both articles relating to war crimes in the Hague Statute. It seems evident that placing Genocide as the first crime in the Rwanda Statute was in recognition of the clear genocide that had occurred there and that genocide was the most important issue in that context. The retention of genocide at the head of the crimes listed in the Rome Statute reflects the evolution from the ICTY to the ICTR, as well as that which has emerged as an implicit hierarchy within the ranks of the most serious crimes, with genocide seen by some as the ultimate and most serious of these crimes. This status was also an implication of the Prosecutor's decision to add charges for genocide in Bosnia to the list of charges against former Serbian leader, Slobodan Milošević, after he was already in custody. Those charges would have been hard to prove though, had Milošević lived to face a verdict. This is because the tests to establish both subject-matter jurisdiction and individual responsibility for genocide are hard to satisfy. Indeed, jurisdiction and the elements of the crime are, in many respects, intrinsically linked. The only distinction might be where jurisdiction to hear Genocide charges existed solely on the basis of evidence showing systematic features, including planning and intent. However, it was not established at trial that the motivation of the individual in question was to destroy, in whole, or in part, a national, ethnic, racial, or religious group, as such.*

---

* Different Trial Chambers at the ICTY found that genocide had occurred, but did not necessarily find the accused guilty of direct involvement, or personal intent. In the case of General Radislav Krstić, he was acquitted of genocide, but convicted, in effect, of aiding and abetting genocide, providing the logistics for the mass murder at Srebrenica in Bosnia in July 1995. Thus, the judges found that although genocide had occurred, it could not be proven that Krstić had this intent, only that he facilitated others who had that intent, in effect. (*Prosecutor v. Radislav Krstic Judgement*, IT-98–33T, 2 August 2001 and *Prosecutor v. Radislav Krstic Judgement*, IT-98–33A). In the case of Goran Jelišić, a self-confessed 'Serbian Adolf', who admitted to multiple counts of murder under the charge of Crimes Against Humanity, but pleaded not guilty to charges of genocide, the initial Trial Chamber found that, although genocide had been committed, it was not proven beyond reasonable doubt that the intention of the accused was genocidal. The Appeals Chamber found that a reasonable court might have found the evidence sufficient for a conviction of genocide and that the initial Trial Chamber had erred procedurally, but decided not to order a retrial. (*Prosecutor v. Goran Jelisic, Judgement*, IT-95–10A, 5 July 2001). In June 2010, Vujadin Popović, the Chief of Security of the Drina

The differences regarding Crimes Against Humanity are more striking than anything else in the statutes. In terms of the ICTY Statute, first, a nexus with armed conflict was required. This was in line with the historical record from Nuremberg and provided a contrast to the emerging discussion of such crimes as having international character requiring no connection to an armed conflict.[65] That understanding applied to the later ICTR and Rome Statutes, both of which reverted to the prevalent interpretation in international humanitarian law and dropped the link with armed conflict.[66] However, Article 5 of the Yugoslavia Statute did require the Prosecutor to establish that the alleged crimes were part of a widespread, or systematic pattern.[67] It was not enough, therefore, simply to record, for example, that a murder had occurred. Rather, it had to be established as one of a number of relevant, widespread or systematic crimes. The widespread nature of such crimes might be established with evidence of similar incidents, of a particular, but not necessarily defined, frequency, in a suitably defined geographical area, or set of areas, by the same, or similar, actors. The leap to 'systematic' required evidence of common enterprise, planning, organisation and intent. Thus, one test is to show empirical frequency, the other is to identify clear and conscious design.

Secondly, while Crimes Against Humanity as a category was effectively elevated in both the Rwanda and Rome Statutes over its last ranking in the ICTY list, it also gained significant additional elements under the ICC Statute, starting with additional clarifications to items already listed under earlier statutes. 'Deportation' received the additional clarification 'or forcible transfer of population' and 'Improvement' gained 'or other severe deprivation of physical liberty' and so on. Rape, already subject to innovation in the jurisprudence of the *ad hoc* tribunals,[68] gained significant accompany-

---

Corps of the Bosnian Serb Army (VRS) and Ljubiša Beara, Chief of Security in the VRS Main staff, were found guilty of genocide (as well as extermination, murder and persecution) and sentenced to life imprisonment. (*Prosecutor v. Vujadin Popovic et al., Judgement*, IT-05–88-T). These were the first individuals to be convicted directly for genocide, rather than complicity in genocide or aiding and abetting genocide. However, given that convictions for complicity in genocide had been overturned on appeal in previous cases (*Prosecutor v. Radislav Krstic, Judgement*, IT-98–33A and *Prosecutor v. Vidoje Blagojevic, Judgement*, IT-02–60-A), the possibility remained that these convictions might be overturned on appeal.

ing details, incorporating 'sexual slavery, enforced prostitution, forced pregnancy, enforced sterilisation, or any other form of sexual violence of comparable gravity'. This extension of the rape clause reflected the great interest in, and attention to, sex and gender crimes not only by commentators, but also in the work of the tribunals, as well as, unfortunately, the prevalence of such atrocities in the context of contemporary warfare and the specific cases handled by the *ad hoc* frameworks. Persecution also gained significantly greater detail and specific successor elements, with the fresh categories of enforced disappearance and apartheid inserted in the list, before the concluding catchall clause of 'other inhumane acts'. All of this was supplemented by the definition and clarification of the terms used in these clauses.

In a context of rapidly evolving jurisprudence, where all parts of the law (except genocide—so far, at least)[69] saw significant adaptation, change and evolution, it was in the domain of Crimes Against Humanity that the greatest development occurred. Crimes Against Humanity as a category was placed among the most serious of all crimes, at the same time as it underwent the most radical and significant growth in definition and scope as an 'international' crime. This meant that it could be applied in national jurisdictions, if states chose to do so, against nationals from anywhere in the world, and for crimes of this character committed in any location in the world, not just by international bodies. Moreover, in many regards, Crimes Against Humanity formed the easiest part of the rulebook to apply to cases, given the tests required before the application of the other elements of war crimes-related law.

The importance of the Crimes Against Humanity category and the cognate development of other aspects of human rights and humanitarian law strongly informed another development in the context of pressure on militaries: the jurisprudence of the European Court of Human Rights (ECtHR). This began by dealing with cases relating to Russian conduct in Chechnya, in particular,[70] but spread its net to embrace the UK's armed forces,[71] *inter alia*,[72] even though these cases would have been handled by national courts already. In two key cases regarding Chechnya, the Court determined that the European Convention on Human Rights 'covers not only intentional killing but also the situations in which it is permitted to "use force" which may result, as an unintended outcome, in the deprivation of life'. In this context, the Court said that 'absolute necessity' was required for the military action and the use of force should be 'strictly proportionate to the achievement of the permitted aims'.[73] This perspective creates a situation in which the application of Article 2 of the Convention with its (seemingly) absolute protection of the right to life, might swiftly mean that almost every death in wartime could be characterised as a breach of the Convention. To mitigate this, the ECtHR has noted as follows:

Bearing in mind the difficulties in policing modern societies, the unpredictability of human conduct and the operational choices which must be made in terms of priorities and resources, the obligation to protect the right to life must be interpreted in a way which does not impose an impossible or disproportionate burden on the authorities.[74]

None the less, whatever the specifics of the cases and the relevant jurisprudence, the reality is that there is increased tension, as a result of this evolutionary legal step, resulting from the blurring—or coalescence—of international humanitarian law and human rights law. There is certainly a new context that requires a new 'framework', as Guglielmo Verdirame has rightly argued, suggesting that it is correct to regard the coming together of the two bodies of law as in need of 'coordination',[75] which adds to the pressure on those involved in the use of force.

This chapter has shown how the evolution of the law relating to warfare and the development of prosecutorial frameworks for enforcing that law have overlapped, interrelated and, generally, extended their impact and reach. In the late twentieth century and early twenty-first, the pace and pattern of change began to place ever greater pressure on those responsible for the exercise of restrained coercive violence for political purposes. Issues of wrong and right have always formed part of the definition and actuality of war, and continue to do so. But the significance of issues of right and wrong is greater than it has ever been. The importance of balancing political power, the military means to that power and ethics lies at the heart of the war problem, more than ever. War is not war but rather mob violence, or some other phenomenon, if the violence is without rules and conventions. But its deadly and destructive core means that its special status has to be underpinned by a strong sense of that which makes the use of force wrong or right—both empirically and theoretically.

The development of Just War notions to explore the boundary between war and non-war, both in terms of cause and conduct, gave rise in the nineteenth and twentieth centuries to formal and legal treatments, establishing that which was deemed acceptable, and distinguishing it from that which was not. With the advent of significant attention to war crimes prosecutions of individuals from the second half of the twentieth century onwards, and the development of international judicial bodies to handle cases, there was ever greater definition and refinement of the right-wrong boundary in war and corresponding changes in the strategic environment. The continuing interaction of ethics, law and war, generating the notion of 'war crimes', and the increasing attention to war crimes issues, particularly the developments in the prosecution of suspected breaches of the laws of war, have a major impact on international law, international politics and, eventually, strategy. Those changes, themselves, confirm the continuing relevance of the time-immemorial ethical negotiations of wrong and right in warfare.

Contemporary armed conflict occurs amid legal change. That change includes the energy channelled into enforcement of the laws of war through criminal prosecution, in both international and domestic contexts. The emergence of judicial bodies focused on prosecuting those who exceed the bounds of the acceptable in war is one factor creating an environment in which the conduct of military affairs has come increasingly under scrutiny. That growth in attention to prosecution in limited circumstances also prompted evolution in the interpretation of the law, bringing it more into line with prevailing conditions. All of this added to the pressures on defence professionals as they carried out their work. As the world has changed, so warfare has evolved, and, as warfare continues to change, the law will, of necessity, need to adapt. That change might involve new versions of, new interpretations of, or new Protocols to, the Geneva Conventions. It might entail new instruments of law altogether, or customary evolution as a consequence of continuing changes in practice and interpretation. However it happens, change is inevitable. Further change will mean greater pressures, multiplied by the context generated by the multidimensional trinity—the $Trinity^3(+)$. These greater pressures and their impact in the changing environment are the topics of the following two chapters, investigating the perspectives of defence practitioners themselves.

4

STRATEGY AND JUSTICE

While issues of wrong and right have always been at the heart of war, in the late twentieth century, attitudes toward these issues shifted, as seen in the previous chapter. The attitudinal context of war became more dynamic as warfare entered this new era, with new levels of complexity. In this multidimensional context, the business of soldiers was subject to greater scrutiny by communications media and lawyers. With these changes, pressures grew on members of the armed forces, as conventional military operations became ever more subject to allegations of war crimes by partisan activists, human rights campaigners and news media observers. This created conditions in which one author could ask: 'Is the military legally encircled?'[1] This was not just a matter of increasing war crimes allegations as service personnel were also growing more litigious: there were 5,665 new claims for compensation made in the UK during the 2005–6 period, of which 621 involved payouts totalling £28.3 million for employer liability claims.[2] Further, the indirect 'judicialisation' of war brought pressure from other sources too, such as coroner's courts (discussed in the final chapter).[3] However, without doubt it was the largely misunderstood, but still real, impact of the International Criminal Court and the notion of war crimes that generated most concern. When the UK ICC Act was debated in parliament, legislators were 'particularly concerned about the military, as we have had both formal and informal representations ... about the effect of this legislation on their ability ... to wage legitimate war ...'[4]

In a survey of experienced British personnel conducted at the Joint Services Command and Staff College, one study found that trials of service personnel had 'undermined the confidence of military commanders' and that, even though the 'perceptions' of these commanders were often 'misguided', they had the effect of 'diminishing the operational capability of the Armed Forces'.[5] This effect was considerably more pronounced among officers in the army than in the navy or the air force—perhaps because ground forces felt the effects of the legal context more than the other services at that stage. This is likely to be a result of the closer contact ground forces have with opponents, and sometimes civilians (an issue that emerged in research discussed in Chapter 5). A repeat survey could potentially find greater concern among flyers five years on, as allegations (albeit weakly founded) were made regarding air action over Libya.[6] Virtually half of the cohort (214 personnel) believed that the law had changed significantly since 2001, with 46 per cent 'confident' in their understanding of the law (though 35 per cent were not). 49 per cent were concerned that they would be accused of war crimes at some point because of their actions, or those of their subordinates.[7] Although there was almost certainly a lack of understanding among the cohort about the real questions that might arise, the atmosphere of anxiety was evident, as was the pressure that war crimes concerns were generating. Most strikingly of all, 43 per cent of all respondents (50 per cent within the army) believed that changes in the law damaged operational effectiveness, making it harder for the military to do its job when required.[8] Those expressing these views almost certainly really meant changes in the legal environment and growing attention to legal matters, rather than concrete changes to the law. The reflection here is generated by a sense that neither the law itself, where it had and had not changed, nor the broader contextual and attitudinal shifts regarding legal intercourse and pressures, can be believed to have been well understood.[9] What is clear is that change was perceived, and that it was felt to make life harder, prompting concerns about war crimes accusations that could affect decision-making. This marked a shift from the previous pattern of treating only the most extreme and unacceptable of actions in war as criminal.

Western forces, even—or especially—when on humanitarian missions,[10] are subject to charges of war crimes by segments of the multiple audiences in the multidimensional *Trinity³(+)* (discussed in Chapter 2). However, these accusations often lack the professional sense of the necessary and the proportional that the military and their lawyers would use in making judgements on the use of force. As the early twenty-first century has seen an increase in the complexity of the issues surrounding warfare, understanding the different aspects of these issues becomes yet more difficult. The ethical and legal considerations involved become more demanding—even as accusations are more easily made. While attention to war crimes has become closer and more intense, the point at which the lawful passes to the criminal might often be harder to locate, as previously 'normal' military operations become the focus of alleged crimes. As strategy, politics and law change simultaneously (rather than step by step, one after another, as in the past) so strategists, political leaders and lawyers have to contend with new and greater pressures. The issues of necessity and proportionality at the heart of Just War (and also lawful war, where laws apply) can be harder than ever to gauge.

The previous chapter explored the context of the evolving and ever-faster paced evolution of the law and the practice of prosecution, generating greater attention to the issues of wrong and right in warfare. The next chapter will consider military perspectives on what can be seen as wrong or right in relation to particular situations, in the view of military-political practitioners, by reference to specific hypothetical scenarios, which reflect elements of recent warfare. The analysis in this chapter draws on the same original empirical focus group research among defence professionals that informs the next chapter.* However, in light of the discussion introducing

* As explained in Chapter 1, this analysis is based on empirical research, including data from focus group research with senior defence practitioners. Some of the information relating to this, as set out in Chapter 1, is repeated here (and again in the following chapter) for purposes of clarity as the material that follows is considered. This is because readers of the manuscript, understandably, had forgotten this methodological exposition by the time they reached the empirical analysis itself—the intention is to make life easier for the reader, especially the academic reader dipping into one chapter in a volume (I recognise equally that this explanation can be irritating to non-academic readers, less interested in the scholarly underpinnings of research and distracted by footnotes). This was part of a wider programme of research, involving the War Crimes Research Group at King's College London, the Royal College of Defence Studies (RCDS) and the Joint Services Command and Staff College (JSCSC), in the UK, as well as the Humanitarian Law Center in Belgrade and the Center for Interdisciplinary Postgraduate Studies, University of Sarajevo. The bulk of the research used directly in this volume involved the RCDS, which embraces an international mix of defence practitioners, mostly at one star (Brigadier/Brigadier General) or equivalent levels.

this chapter and the evidence of perceived pressure among military personnel, it explores how war crimes issues do, indeed, impact on them and affect operational considerations. The focus is not on particular situations and the boundaries of judgement, but on how the military responds to the evident pressures that war crimes accusations produce, and the potential impact such accusations have on strategy and operations. The analysis proceeds in three stages. The first considers the degree to which senior military people sense increased attention to war crimes and legal issues, and the extent to which this affects their thinking, planning and conduct of operations, which all forms part of the changing character of both war and war crimes. The second section examines the importance of context, and the specifics of any armed conflict that must be taken into account when assessing issues of wrong and right broadly, as well as the application of the laws of armed conflict more specifically. The final section, extending analysis from appreciation of the importance of context, explores the salience of judgement within a given context. This includes questions about the relevant level of decision-making, and different degrees of exposure in different fields of

---

Those who took part in the research were an international mix from all continents and a variety of cultures. Participants were from all continents and roughly all parts of all continents. The research involved people from Middle Eastern countries, from all points of the African compass, from different Asian and Australasian countries, and from the Americas. There was a surprising degree of consistency. It is necessary to be careful when describing or referring to the group, because of the confidentiality involved, especially because some of them come from countries where if they could be identified, they might face censure, or punishment. All respondents volunteered freely, with no compulsion or obligation. The agreement to carry out the research with the RCDS involved sophisticated discussions with the Senior Directing Staff there. The type of research that was conducted has two particular strengths. First, it allows the generation of empirical data, simply through the discussion that takes place, with participants offering knowledge and information drawn from experience, as we well as giving expression to beliefs, values and attitudes. This provides the data for analysis. Secondly, in contrast to individual research interviews, the group process (especially when it involves the presentation of specific propositions or material—part of the research used in this volume draws on instances in which participants were shown visual material) allowed discussion and interaction between participants. As discourse developed, salient beliefs, values and attitudes were identified, as well as issues about which participants strongly agreed or diverged.

operations, as well as how any application of justice must be determined by reference to individual judgements in specific circumstances. The strong interest of the military to have war crimes allegations addressed emerges as a clear pattern, so long as the judgement of the professionals in the particular context is taken into account—even though any attention to war crimes puts pressure on them.

Strategy and Soldiers

The greater attention to legal issues and the rise in allegations of unlawful action that emerged in the final decade of the twentieth century and the first years of the twenty-first, can be linked both to the radically changed—and still changing—circumstances in which military missions occur, as well as the greater sensitivity associated with them. Situations emerged in the 1990s involving major international engagement in new places using new practices. This reflected a new and developing approach to the traditional protections provided by the sovereignty principle in international law. The greater the legal and political sensitivities associated with a decision to use armed action, particularly in the case of Western liberal democracies, the greater the pressures associated with the lawful conduct of those operations became; the more novel or fragile the *jus ad bellum*, the more likely it was that there would be accusations of wrongdoing regarding the *jus in bello*. One indication of this trend was that every NATO mission over Kosovo in 1999 was legally vetted with a view to protecting personnel against potential war crimes accusations (not that this would necessarily be an absolute protection) because the lawfulness of the operation itself was questionable.[11] That, in turn, could be said to have had an impact on operations, affecting some of the targeting choices made, and creating frustration in some military circles. A similar pattern emerged regarding action in Iraq that began in 2003. This is all part of a general and growing concern. The heart of these issues seems to lie in the relationship between interpretations of legality, accusations about legality, and discussions about legitimacy, morality, justice and so forth. There appears to be a correlation between the fragile legitimacy of operations and sensitivities surrounding them, with accusations regarding alleged commission of war crimes.

That there is increased pressure is clear. When asked whether or not there seemed to be increased attention to these issues and concomitant pressure, the initial response was the following:

War crimes and the law of armed conflict are more of an issue than in the past. More soldiers are facing potential prosecution. The balance has gone too far. This makes it more difficult to conduct operations. We now have 3-block war[12]—where are the boundaries? One thing is war fighting [*sic*], but you have to behave differently in PSOs [Peace Support Operations]. The issues are more complex. There is now a plethora of human rights interest and legislation.[13]

Another response echoed and augmented this:

There is a change in situations, in the nature of war. War is different. The values of the civilian population are different. The value of order is different. In my country, the value of not necessarily prosecuting officers/soldiers is that they fulfil orders, but there is strong social pressure questioning the morality of giving orders. I agree that things are more complex. The way we measure a war crime in a military operation today is changing. This is not the same as years ago. … This is good for human development. But it is difficult for commanders. We have not yet found the right equation.[14]

This agreement that there had been a change and that it had impacted on military actions was clear, although there were differences over whether this was necessarily a bad thing: 'The problem is not necessarily "3-block war", human rights etc., it is just that things are more complex'. In these more complex circumstances, the 'pace of political change is outstripping military change'. At the same time, the 'law reflects ethics, but it is one step behind'.[15] Developments such as debates over pre-emptive—or even more controversially, the notion of 'preventive'—self-defence are seen to have added to existing pressures. One respondent judged this to be 'criminality' (not reflecting any existing instrument of criminal law, it should be noted, however). Others expressed a varying degree of concern that change in the right to self-defence might be a cause for concern, even if a necessary step, because it raised questions about something regarded as a basic principle through which the armed forces could do their business.[16] Thus, the changing dynamics of politics and order at the global, international and transnational levels overlaps with changes in the law and in military capabilities and approaches. The relationship between legitimacy, legality and morality in the context of these operations was seen as central.

The nexus of political, legal, and military change, and the tensions and pressures arising, mean that the armed forces depend on a strong ethical framework, even more than they did in the past. Apart from one respondent who revealed that 'some of these details' were 'quite new' to him, participants in the research demonstrated a strong interest in, and a developed sense of, ethics. This applied even in cases where there was some degree of ignorance regarding particular details of the law. This strong sense of an ethical framework 'is critical for people who practise the profession of arms', because, 'unless you have a strong code of ethics, your day to day job is unbearable'. This view was generally held.[17] Certain principles might be obvious, such as: 'You don't butcher a guy who's dead. You don't shoot a guy again if he is down. The principle is you use one bullet'.[18] Others are not so straightforward. Whatever the issues, though, a clear recognition that necessity and proportionality act as the two key axes of analysis and action existed among interviewees. The former encompasses what is 'indispensable for securing the ends of war' and 'lawful according to modern laws and usages of law', while the latter dictates that 'Damage should be proportionate to the aim achieved'.[19]

Issues of legitimacy, legality and ethics matter, in the end, not only because of the professional ethos of defence professionals, but also because they are aware of their relationship with society in general. The concern is with the pressures that emerge in each military's social context. In a transnational, internationalised and globalised world, pressures are also often those of a wide international 'public'. This is because three parts of this puzzle—expectations in society, political demands and missions, and the law and military operations—may not neatly fit together in a period of immense, continuing change. As a result, expectations from society, while understandable, do generate frustration:

The societies who send people to war have no idea of what war is about. They want to apply their ethics. When you get the sort of criticism of the use of weapons in Iraq by people who don't understand them ....

This is because society has unrealistic expectations and the fact that 'What they are looking for is a precision that doesn't exist', was a widespread view. This captures the frustrations produced when trying to conduct military operations and maintain support, while major issues are matters of contention, and others result in questions, challenges and even accusations of criminality, without there being an accurate understanding of the nature of military affairs. This is particularly strongly felt to be the case regarding news media and politicians, with their false perceptions of what is required. In particular, 'Media generate a sense of familiarity and proximity, which is a false understanding'. This becomes a major problem where broadcast news media constitute a vital element in contemporary warfare.[20]

The changing means available to the military and the choices that these make possible also have to be thrown into the equation. The nature of a particular conflict, the nature of the engagements involved, and the missions that troops are largely committed to, present choices that were not necessarily available in the past. These choices are augmented by the availability of apparently precise guided munitions, at the same time as the environment is restricting the scope of choice, while there are increasing expectations of accurate, clinical and possibly death-free action. The rules of engagement, in this context, become ever more important. More attention has to be paid to them—if for no other reason than because people outside are trying to grasp what troops are and are not allowed to do in a particular situation (which is, of course, not the ideal reason to have clarity regarding rules of engagement). The nature of many contemporary engagements means that what troops are and are not allowed to do is often more constrained than it would have been at times in the past, or than it would have been in a full-blown, total action, such as the Second World War.

As rules of engagement (RoE) become ever more sensitive in an age of increasingly delicate expeditionary missions, governed by concerns of legality and legitimacy, they are possibly also a problem of military planning in coalition, or joint operations—which are the norm for most western and partner militaries in the twenty-first century. 'The RoE are important. We can distinguish through the RoE if a soldier acts in a wrong or right way'.[21] Although the research here focuses primarily on military attitudes to right and wrong, this aspect of the broad, changing war crimes environment also suggested that attention be paid to the practical and technical concerns transmitted to the operational and coalition levels. The fact that troops might operate under different rules of engagement is something absolutely recognised in the research findings. There are very significant differences among the rules of engagement, in particular situations. The issue is especially salient in terms of the way it feeds back into operations involving coalition forces, where the coalition countries may have differing ideas on the rules of engagement. How does the commander make judgements on what to do? There can come a point where someone will say 'sorry, I am not allowed to do that'. This 'question is all the more challenging when secondees are involved etc.',[22] making exchanges and jointness within coalition operations more complicated. This makes for difficult decisions:

Do you withdraw them? Do you allow them to operate under [a partner's] RoE? If you do, then you could be condemning an individual to be breaking [his own country's law]; what can you do? Ministerial decisions have to determine what happens. Should they go? What should they do? This places the issue of individual responsibility in a new context. How can this be handled?[23]

This confirms that, in some ways, responsibility goes back to the political level because it is the ministers at the political level who sign off on both the rules of engagement and on the terms of commitment.

Within this, there was a very broad perception that there were far fewer concerns with these issues among the United States personnel. In several cases, others (mostly, but not entirely, British personnel) cited examples, such as one from Iraq, stating that the 'US was not quite so judicious in its application of the law', that the 'whole of Iraq was a war zone' and in one case, an individual asserted that they had 'never found a US soldier who knew their RoE, nor was bothered'. Notwithstanding this, it was recognised that the most important thing in the situation 'was trying not to hurt non-combatants'.[24] In practice, the US rules of engagement in Iraq were probably much as those explained to one group of Marines on film by a sergeant. He seemed confused by the question (wondering why anyone would consider it), and eventually answered: '[I]t's combat! Just kill 'em!'[25] Whether that means they know wrong from right is a different question. There is quite probably a difference in terms of RoE, attitudes and behaviour. Differences may stem from experience in that particular operational environment, rather than the way the individuals respond (or would respond) to issues of wrong and right while investigating scenarios.

There is an understanding that the rules of engagement are 'a dialogue between the CO [Commanding Officer] and Higher Command'.[26] Despite this, however, circumstances change and the CO on the ground might well need to use lethal force beyond the rules of engagement. It is interesting that, in the research, in discussing these issues, the case of Srebrenica came up several times. That event clearly plays internationally across military minds (and not only because it continues to generate legal action, such as that involving Hasan Nuhanović, in the Netherlands—see Chapter 6). There was general assent to the hope that, if they had been there, each of the respondents would have behaved differently.[27] If the rules of engagement constrained them, they would have been justified in ignoring the rules of engagement—an approach that involves making a distinction between that which is lawful and that which is right and just. Soldiers participating in the research judged that rules of engagement were less important than a basic distinction between wrong and right. In this context, if an element of premeditation is available (rather than a spontaneous response to events), it was judged to be possible to seek a temporary change in the rules of engagement for 'next Thursday', as one respondent reported having done. But, this would not help 'where circumstances change rapidly, such as at Srebrenica'.[28] So, there is a tension; if someone makes a decision that goes beyond the formal RoE, because they deem it the right thing to do, are they going to be a hero for having taken the initiative to do the right thing, or are they going to be pilloried for having broken the rules? This is an example of the real dilemmas that can arise in these uncertain situations. It is fair to infer that military professionals, on the whole, would prefer ethically to err on the side of doing what is right rather than sticking to the rules—with the accompanying sense that their interpretations should be respected over rule-based technicalities.

In this context, although there are sometimes contradictory statements, the general—and generally correct—view is that 'the pace of change in law and doctrine needs to catch up with the pace of change in operations'. The legal framework and the preparation of doctrine are simply out-of-kilter with the kinds of things that soldiers now have to do.

Finally, in this section, the research found a sense that the pace of political change has been outstripping that of military change. This is all part of the broader changing environment. No one can show how the military can adjust to operate clearly in this changing political environment and atmosphere. This creates tension and frustration. The increasing scrutiny of the news media and the law accentuates the difficulties, in terms of successfully achieving real end-state objectives—complementing irritation with politicians who are believed not necessarily to understand what they are doing when they commit troops to operations. However, despite all the pressures and frustrations, when confronted with the proposition that these pressures for change and increasing legal scrutiny would undermine the qualities of the armed forces, military respondents replied with an absolute and unanimous 'No'.[29] In one case, having been shown an article from *The Daily Telegraph*,[30] in which retired Colonel Tim Collins had asserted, in response to the decision to charge eleven British soldiers with war crimes under the International Criminal Court Act,[31] that prosecutions of this kind would ruin the qualities that had made the British Army great, the consensus view was supplemented by one British voice, which said that Colonel Collins had clearly 'got his career choice right' in leaving the army.[32] This reflects an understanding that, despite the frustration and irritation that there is a greater propensity for prosecution of war crimes charges, '[T]his is good for us in the end, it's short-term pain for long-term gain'. So there is an awareness that the issues of accusations, allegations, investigations and prosecution have become an inevitable part of the contemporary military environment. But, this is leavened by the judgement that, if the armed forces retain the right qualities, increased scrutiny will not harm their achievements and, indeed, it will be in their interest.

Conflict and Context

It could have been predicted, perhaps, that issues of context and the specifics of any armed conflict would be relevant to an investigation of how war crimes issues impact on the conduct of military business and, especially, of how allegations of war crimes are to be interpreted. The same applies more broadly to issues of wrong and right. It is only possible to discern these adequately in light of particular circumstances. 'All decisions that commanders make in battle are', as Rupert Smith noted, 'therefore, those of the circumstances of that day'.[33] That which is alleged, or sought, to be justified has to be measured against the situation in which it has occurred. As I shall detail in the following paragraphs, the research undertaken indicates that no issue of right or wrong, or of alleged war crimes, can be addressed without a strong and accurate sense of context. However, several differences of context were identified, which could have salience on issues of wrong or right.

First, there was a clear sense among the research subjects of a difference between what they termed 'wars of survival' and 'wars of choice'—although, given that governments are reluctant ever to do anything that they are not obliged to do through necessity, it is better to understand this as referring to them as expeditionary (or contingent) missions. This difference could go either way on the scale of acceptability. The difference might make things more or less acceptable to some respondents, depending on the perceived nature of the engagement. 'There is a difference between "wars of choice" and "wars of survival." The public perception of people where there is choice can be of a mistake. But wars for survival have heroes, who are accused of committing war crimes'.[34] This distinction affects the way the troops' society, and other societies, perceive the nature of the context and, therefore, the degree to which more extreme actions might be seen as justifiable.[35] It also influences how soldiers themselves understand their role and context. As one respondent explained, the 'choice/survival distinction makes a difference'. This could be seen in the behaviour of particular forces, associated with strong accusations of war crimes in one context, but showing no propensity to such action in others: 'Many Balkan soldiers are in Iraq now, but they are not committing the same crimes [as they/their forces committed in their statehood war]'.[36] Similarly, many of the critical challenges that emerged regarding Iraq might have been different had the basis for the conflict been different:

If Iraq had declared war on us, it would have been different, in a war of survival. But, because it was an expeditionary campaign, as they all are these days, there is greater sensitivity. In PSOs, or peacekeeping, there is a higher threshold. It is a matter of expediency. How important is the law? How would the laws of armed conflict have an impact? They probably would.[37]

Thus, additional scrutiny and fragility accompany the limited character of contemporary warfare.

The second point is culture. There are, and always have been, differences in cultural context. Some strands of response suggested that, if there is a tradition of committing something that might be called 'war crimes', 'we cannot speak about a chain of command. For example, therefore, soldiers cannot be controlled completely'.

The rules of engagement, it was posited, could not be understood 'without reference' to that tradition.[38] This view might be questionable—for example, it ought to be possible to arrange training and education in such a way as to encourage change in that tradition. Yet, it is one that was expressed in the research sessions without dissent, reflecting the views of practitioners about the relevance of culture to context.

It is important to understand that cultural contexts differ.[39] Elements of thinking suggest that this is not just about warfare. 'Cultural contexts differ, even within countries', one respondent pointed out to general agreement, citing the example of morality and marriage, specifically the number of concubines a man might have as an issue within certain countries.[40] The real issue is what is acceptable to the armed forces and their society in a given context. The right and wrong distinction in armed conflict 'has to do with societies, what is acceptable to people'.[41] However, if we keep in mind the changing environment in a globalising world, this does not only encompass what is acceptable in a given community within a country, or to a country as a whole, but also what is acceptable in the world at large.

There is also a strong awareness that the same troops might behave differently in various contexts. Respondents asserted that German troops behaved differently in the Balkans and on the Eastern Front in the Second World War than they did in the West:

… in the Second World War, the Germans committed war crimes in the Balkans, not on the Western Front. The environment has a strong influence on the behaviour of soldiers of all ranks. If there is a culture of violence, then the other side feels free to use violence. They might behave another way at another time in another context.[42]

Ostensibly, the Germans' differential approach could be attributable to the Soviets' not having signed the Geneva Conventions.[43] However, although this might have been a pretext—whether implicit or explicit—for a different approach, 'cultural explanations, racism, were the genuine ones'. As one respondent said (drawing the agreement of others) 'it was a gut feeling, it was a cultural thing'.[44] The cultural dimension was felt to offer the real explanation. It was felt that a form of racism, rather than legal calculation, determined the nasty, brutal fight and the very different behaviour in the East from that which was seen on the western front.

Finally, there is a sense that differences of timing, enemy and operational context are relevant to differentiating that which is acceptable from that which is not. Bearing in mind that this was an international group of respondents, some of them were able to speak from their experience of armed conflicts, including some extremely unpleasant ones. This led to statements about the ethical tests and the boundaries of responsibility, in rapidly changing or extreme situations. One example came from a respondent with direct experience of conflict marked by atrocity: 'They abused women soldiers, but they brutalised us and that changed our ethics'. This prompted an observation by a respondent without such experience, but reflecting a general understanding of acceptability: 'There is a principle of belligerent reprisal. Under certain circumstances you can be unethical'.[45] Of course, there can be discussion in this regard about whether ethics changed, or not. What each person meant here was that when circumstances change, what was previously regarded as being unacceptable can become acceptable in the new circumstances. In other words, what was wrong becomes right. In this sense, it remains ethical. The act committed is right and justified. It is the product of a process of negotiating wrong and right, which makes it ethical, as such, so long as the outcome of that process is well-judged. It is recognition of the 'impact of time on your ethical framework' and the answer to the question, 'When does it suddenly become acceptable to do something?' The inevitability of change and how this affects acceptability could be seen in quite rapid changes in the law, induced by circumstances: 'In 1916, you can use gas. In 1919, you can't. And the use of land mines, Princess Diana has changed single-handedly'.[46] Thus, what is wrong and right cannot be regarded as absolute, or absolutely fixed. Different points in time, different cultural contexts and, certainly, different specific circumstances are significant for reconciling the ethical balance of wrong and right in warfare. In the words of two respondents:

A. I don't think the ethics change. But you make judgements about what to do. It is a question of operational necessity.

B. I agree with A. You don't alter the ethical framework. The underlying principles remain the same. You make a judgement in the circumstances.[47]

The point is the same, whether ethics changed or, perhaps more accurately, the ethics remained the same, but judgements changed within the ethical framework. These reflections are testimony to the kind of thinking that professionals in the management of violence have, at least at more senior levels. The enemy's behaviour is essential to a principle of belligerent reprisal—if that enemy begins to behave in a particularly gruesome way, then there might well be an entitlement to respond in kind. This is because responding in kind, among other things, might well be the only way to prevail. However, there was a concern that this might not be grasped by those outside the operational environment.

Overall, there is a sense among defence professionals that different situations, different contexts, and different types of conflict define that which is either acceptable or unacceptable. However, there is recognition that absolute restraints exist in limited areas—such as the legal prohibitions on using chemical shells and land mines, which were cited. Notwithstanding the few exceptions, the balance within those different situations, contexts and conflicts of that which is acceptable and that which is unacceptable might well change as circumstances change. Right and wrong will always be largely defined by context.

Justice and Judgement

If understanding the type and the context of a conflict are vital to understanding issues of judgement within it, how does that judgement relate to a sense of justness, in terms of Just War notions (as discussed in Chapter 1), and to a sense of justice, in terms of potential accusations, charges, or prosecutions concerning alleged wrongful action? If the specific circumstances are to be relevant and are to contribute to determinations of criminality, or otherwise, then it should be the assessment of peers that informs whether or not an action is justified, necessary or proportionate. Both decision-making and judicial processes need to be appropriately informed by the input of military practitioners. Justice depends on judgement in, and of, the circumstances. Only soldiers, in the end, can really assess these fully. This point is explored in the present section with reference to five areas identified in the research.

The first issue emerging from the respondents was a quite pronounced concern about exposure on these issues. There was a strong belief in the need to be judged by one's peers. It was generally felt that it would be 'wrong' to 'expose' soldiers to a court that 'doesn't understand' either the particular circumstances, or the business of the armed forces. What soldiers do, and what the issues were, in a given context need to be well understood: 'To be judged by one's peers is a fundamental principle. In a civilian court, this can't happen'.[48]

Secondly, there is a sense that the prerogatives of the commanding officer are changing. Previously, the Commanding Officer (CO) essentially had the right to say whether or not there was a charge to be heard—and in the field, under the court martial system (where present) the CO could arrange to be prosecutor, judge and jury. Now, responsibility has been taken out of their hands to a large extent. However, there was a sense among the respondents at brigade level and above, albeit subject to some dissent, that this was right, with one respondent saying: 'Should the CO be the final court? Six years ago, I would have said yes. Now, from Brigade level, I would say no. COs are too close to situations. It needs to come up, but not too far'.[49] On one level, this could be seen purely as an extension (or reduction) of the trial by peers point. But, it is really a concession, in principle, that others should judge allegations of criminal behaviour, not those closely associated with the accused, who might bring personal feelings—loyalty or spite—into the case.

The third aspect developed in the research involves the question of who it is that judges the case. This involves two levels of analysis—national-international and military-civilian. The first level concerns whether it is one's own society, or others, who should judge. There is a sense that, in general, criminal proceedings should occur in the country, or cultural idiom, of the accused, given the possibilities for different interpretations in different contexts:

There is an issue over whether you should be judged by your own society, or by others. The UK sees terrorism as a crime. But the US after 9/11 saw it as an act of war. There is gap between the European and US views.[50]

The differences on this issue—which, though not directly the same, have echoes in the Guantanamo context (as discussed in Chapter 6)—can be multiplied in line with the number of crimes or offences that might be charged. In this respect, it is curious to note that the UK decided to embed the International Criminal Court (ICC) Statute into English and Welsh, Northern Irish, and Scottish law,[51] so that there could never be any question of charges being raised that a British soldier could not face in a British court. However, given the request by UK Chief of the Defence Staff Admiral Sir Michael Boyce (later Lord Boyce) for clear legal advice from the Attorney General that action in Iraq would be lawful, meaning that no British soldier could be taken before the ICC, this seems not to be understood, even at the highest level.[52] It seems that the complementarity principle underpinning the ICC Statute, by which indictments can only be raised where national courts have not addressed a matter, has not registered. Nor does it seem to be understood that the UK had embraced the statute so as to ensure that there could be no grey area questions to be exploited for judicial or political purpose, either by the ICC itself, or by other countries. However, the UK model can only work where countries demonstrate responsibility in approaching war crimes issues. There are, and will be, other cases where the national courts are simply not available as an instrument of justice, either because of political corruption, or lack of competence. In such cases, the scope and necessity for international prosecutions remains.

Thus, there are situations in which international, or external, prosecution is pertinent. However, this leaves open possibilities of differential approaches, depending on the particular context of the perpetrators and victims. Context is, once again, relevant, in the extra sense that this differential approach might translate into the probability of facing criminal action in soldiers' own national contexts. The same action might get serious attention, or not, depending on the victim. Two cases from KFOR, the NATO-led deployment to Kosovo, were cited in this regard. On one occasion, a Serb civilian was shot dead. There was next to no criticism of this action. Although there was a brief formal and superficial inquiry, it dismissed the case. In another instance, two weeks later, two ethnic Albanians were shot dead. In contrast, this resulted in an eighteen-month inquiry, leading to court cases. In both examples, the troops were acting in self-defence and had already been fired upon. Therefore, there was ostensibly no difference between the two cases, in terms of the events themselves.[53]

The second level of analysis regarding 'who judges' concerns whether those judging are military or civilian. This chimes with the point, made earlier, about being tried by one's peers. The important thing is not so much that the court should be made up of one's peers, in a literal sense, but that the court should be adequately informed about the nature of the military profession, and what the issues are in a case (see below). Within the framework of the 'who judges?' question, there is an understanding that there are two discrete targets to be addressed: public opinion and justice. There were fears that it might not be possible to satisfy both targets at the same time. While it was felt that it ought to be possible to hit both targets, there was still a concern that, in some circumstances, it might not be feasible. So, soldiers might be brought before courts on charges that have political purpose, whichever type of court it is. There was a strong sense among respondents that the eleven British soldiers facing abuse charges in the Iraqi context fell into that category.[54] There was also the sense that, even if all eleven were to be acquitted, in terms of legal procedure and justice, then the outcome would be seen as a 'fix': 'If all eleven Iraq cases collapse, then there will be no credibility'. This complemented the analysis that the 'military justice system lacks credibility, so cases have to go more and more outside it' and that 'Justice has to be seen to be done'.[55] It was also noted that politicians were responsible for putting soldiers into court. For example:

... [T]he Attorney General is part of the government, political, and has to make decisions on whether to prosecute and there could be prosecutions for public opinion. The question of justice 'being seen to be done' is important.[56]

So—not unreasonably—there was an expectation that if the accused were acquitted the public would believe it was a result of a different kind of political fix—not because the acquittals were the right and just outcomes. The military personnel assisting the research believed that in this continually changing environment they were on a possible hiding-to-nothing. Nothing they could do would be right for everyone.

Following on from this, the fourth theme to emerge in the research is the importance of assisting courts, if they are going to be civilian. This requires explaining to the judge what was involved in military operations, starting with the basics. This is likely to be somewhat laborious and painstaking. One respondent had given assistance to a civilian court hearing cases against junior military personnel. While he was satisfied that, in the end, he and others were able to give the court assistance such as to ensure that the requisite understanding was available, this had not been achieved easily. Even then, it had only been achieved after a lengthy process, including the explanation of elementary matters: 'The judge asked really basic questions: I said the soldier had gone out on patrol; the judge asked "what does that mean?"'[57] While knowledge and understanding could be made available in a civilian court, there is clearly scope for weak attention in this regard. This makes trial by military peers appear a more just option. At a minimum, there was a 'need to agree that military operations are like fraud—at the extremes of what a reasonable person can understand and handle'.[58] Indeed, in the final analysis these are matters that 'only military personnel with experience and expertise can judge', and 'Judgement is about experience', which means that the only reliable judgement is the following: 'You have to put yourself in the place of the person making the decision'. Judicial process needs to be informed by military experience.

War is the most extreme activity. The question is what it is reasonable to expect. What is reasonable in the circumstances may seem unreasonable to those without experience.[59]

The inference is that it is likely that only those with cognate experience are equipped to judge.

The problems involved in making sure that courts are adequately informed make for a lengthy procedure—as could be seen in the international trials in The Hague and Arusha, where critics sometimes questioned why the process had taken so long. The extensive explanations of situations that had to be made in those courts illustrate this point. It is, therefore, important that courts should have the means available to understand military issues and circumstances. In this context—and recalling the principle of being judged by one's peers—there was a clear demonstration of the capacity for reflection among the senior military respondents in a philosophical reference to the ideas of Ludwig Wittgenstein.[60] One participant quoted his theory that 'we should only speak of that of which we have experience', so without experience no opinion may be expressed. This reinforces the sense that only soldiers can really know where issues of combat are concerned and, so, recognition of the need for the armed forces to work with the courts to inform them, to make sure that the situations in which alleged crimes occur are fully understood. Given the sense among the interviewees that attention to war crimes issues, and accusations of war crimes, are inevitable in the contemporary climate, this sort of awareness is necessary to ensure that justice is done. It is, therefore, in the military's interest to accept civilian criminal processes and engage with them, because the military justice system has become discredited and the public needs clearly to see justice done. For the armed forces to maintain the support and confidence of society broadly, they must ensure that things are done in this manner.

The need to maintain broad support in, and the general confidence of, society at large, explains why judgement concerning collateral damage is also important for the armed forces and should be assessed in context: 'The legitimacy of collateral damage changes with the context of the conflict', was a view expressed in focus group research that was met with emphatic and universal assent.[61] It is not possible to understand whether or not a case is significant, if the context is not understood. The starting point for this—reflecting the frustration and pressures already identified above—is the need to understand that people get killed and property gets destroyed in warfare. This is reflected in the following exchange between two participants:

A. If we make the law too prescriptive and unrealistic, we won't be able to fight.

B. The issue is working out what is in somebody's mind. It is the best intentions versus malign or careless intentions. The question turns on intentions, if you don't care about civilians and are hiding behind them, and you are addressing the balance of lesser evils.

A. War is a dirty business. There is no purity.

B. Trying to be too exact can be dangerous.

Warfare is clumsy, armed force is a blunt instrument and, despite the impressions suggested by precision guided munitions in certain respects, the realities of combat remain bound by that clumsiness and bluntness. There has to be acknowledgement of this in given circumstances. However, for that context to be properly understood, evidence of the issues involved and addressed needs to be available from sources as proximate to the event as possible; one suggestion was that 'operational logs and war diaries have to be kept'.[62] It is important that logs, reporting mechanisms, journals and so forth are kept, and that decisions are fully explained within them. Soldiers have to be able to 'say you can justify things, you can justify actions'.[63] In air operations, there are logs and decisions are taken largely beforehand. Army and Marine officers on the ground should write in their journals afterwards about what has happened and how they have made calculations and decided about what they have done.

The fifth and final part of this section concerns levels of responsibility. It makes a difference whether or not an individual infantry rifleman carries out an action. The starting point for analysis lies, for example, in the difference between two situations: of the infantryman using a rifle, having made eye contact, and the artilleryman, or airman, who cannot have clear and direct visual contact with the target. This means that, if there is a breach of the law, the 'crime is likely to be in the targeting process'. The issue is 'whether someone is negligently or wilfully committing a crime, or committing the lesser of two evils'. This is where the 'nuance of complexity is important. It is a question of demonstrating that, in the circumstances, you are pursuing the most humane options'.[64] The rifleman sees the target, and may see the potential collateral damage around—in a situation of crowd control, for example—and then gets the decision wrong. Psychologically, the rifleman's situation is different from that of a bombardier, say, pulling a lanyard, at a distance. Empirically, it is a different situation, because there is visual contact:

… it is a psychological question. The person can see and knows he has done wrong for sure with the rifle. The other doesn't.[65]

The position is quite different if we consider howitzers, or Multiple Launch Rocket Systems (MLRS), or naval or air action, where distance means that those who fire can never actually perceive the specific situation, and can never be sure what the impact is going to be. In the words of one respondent, this means that it is perhaps 'easier to commit crime at a distance',[66] because the lack of immediacy means that no direct engagement of conscience is necessary and the precise consequences are not knowable. Therefore, it is always possible for the perpetrator to think that something awful might not happen. In another respondent's words, 'I have never been behind an artillery battery, but, at 10 km away, you can't have the capacity to measure the impact on the ground'.[67] On the other side of this issue, the infantryman is likely to know exactly what the consequences of his action are at close quarters, reducing scope for reasonable contingent damage, or doubt.

The question is one of responsibility. In the infantry, the responsibility lies with the man who gave the order and the man who fires. Where the fire is indirect, the man who gives the order always carries the blame, but the gunner might not. Should the gunner be expected to ask for the plans etc. every time, before following an order?[68]

The chain of command is vital, therefore, in assessing questions of responsibility. It is important because of this dilemma, in terms of the rules of engagement, in making decisions when following orders. A somewhat simplistic notion of proportionality might involve a distinction between ten shells and eleven, with the former somehow acceptable, but the latter deemed to be excessive—a proposition I used as the investigator to prompt reflection. However, this approach, even less simplistically, was rejected: 'The number of shells can't be considered. The question is the nature of the weapons'.[69] A different version of proportionality—and one that emerged in an operational example mentioned in the research—might be that the RoE could permit the use of 120mm cannons, but prohibit using 155mm shells. And, yet, the commander's judgement might well be that the objective will be achieved faster, more safely and securely, and with less collateral damage by using 155mm artillery.[70] That is the level at which influence is being exercised, because of the nature of operations.

All of this leads to the point of decision making as being the most relevant to issues of responsibility and criminality, in particular, with respect to targeting decisions.

There are different levels of responsibility—this means the positions of those involved. Usually, crimes are committed by soldiers. But who is responsible is the question. Where does the buck stop? Is it at the political level? It is at the military level? If it is the military, which military level?[71]

Locating responsibility, therefore, is not necessarily as straightforward as initial assumptions might suggest. Should it be the individual on the ground? Should it be the individual pressing the button who is to be held responsible, if anyone is? Should it be those at the heart of the targeting process? Or should it be those at the heart of the decision-making process further up the chain of command? There was a developed sense among the fairly senior people who were engaged in the research that it tends to be lower level individuals who 'take the rap'. For example, the Iraq abuse cases were 'wretched', but 'the result of a lack of leadership'.[72] This leads to a suspicion that it is possible that the focus is on lower level troops, effectively covering up for senior personnel—about which some of the respondents apparently felt very uncomfortable. The system may be even better at covering up and protecting politicians. Military decisions may impact on political responsibility, but equally, there is a sense, not necessarily always clearly expressed by respondents, that because of political change, the nature of contemporary operations is actually the responsibility of politicians,[73] but that the latter do not take responsibility and are well protected, whatever happens.

Greater emphasis should be placed on responsibility at higher levels, and caution should be exercised while complexity and change interact. In one response, 'Politicians need to be more cautious, [to] allow time for training, education etc.'[74] There is a feeling that those 'who do the writing and training need "top-up" training'.[75] This is because:

What needs to be inculcated into us as military people is a greater sense of being culpable for our actions, especially officers. Training needs to be geared to what is reasonable.[76]

There is, then, a clear sense that part of the responsibility for war crimes issues has to be addressed by attention to education and training, making people aware, not just of basic law, or rules and some 'dos' and 'don'ts', but also of what is involved in often difficult and complex situations. That responsibility also goes up the command chain to their seniors. In one view:

Lethal authority has to be devolved to the lowest level. But they have to have the skills set. If not, then the chain of command is responsible for not training them. A subset of this is the language of officers. For example, a CO ... made a clear statement, stabbing his finger into the chest of a [faction-party] member that percolated to the troops and set [an unhealthy] atmosphere. Language is terribly important— otherwise, you can create an environment in which bad things can happen.

Broad assent to this included this statement:

The issue of language is important in creating 'atmosphere'. Soldiers need to be accountable for the ways in which they use their weapons. But the responsibility lies with the chain of command. The CO needs to be in charge.

Responsibility could also extend beyond the military chain of command to politicians. If political leaders and senior military figures are going to engage in contemporary operations, then there is a duty to ensure that that troops are properly prepared to go into whatever the relevant environment is. Although this was not said directly by anyone, one inference that could be drawn from the research is this: if someone lower down the chain of command gets into trouble, there might well be a case for saying that the real criminal responsibility lies somewhere further up the chain of command for not educating, training and preparing the troops properly, in the first place. In the end, whoever is responsible for any crimes committed, it is right and proper, and in the best interest of the military, to preserve professional ethos and good relations with society by welcoming judicial moves to hold wrongdoers accountable: 'Public accountability is important'. The conclusion was that: 'This is good for us in the end. It is short-term pain, for long-term gain'.

This chapter has shown various issues that have resulted in pressure on strategy, operations and morale regarding war crimes allegations from news media, societies and human rights activists—all part, or planes, of the *Trinity³(+)*—who might often have little understanding of military realities. It has also explored the impossibility of understanding issues of right and wrong (in some situations), or acceptability and unacceptability, in the conduct of warfare, without understanding the context and specific features of a decision. Aside from changes happening in strategy and justice, and their interrelationship, it is evident from this chapter's analysis that general principles of law and justice cannot always be applied generally. They can only be applied, in the view of professionals, with reference to and understanding of the context in which any particular action occurs. Thus, while accusations in relation to general principles will continue to be made by those with no experience of warfare itself, it is in the interest of the military to have these addressed, so long as the judgement of the professionals in the particular context is taken into account. This is the case, even though attention to war crimes adds to the pressures on service professionals. Issues of military judgement should be recognised when assessing actions.

There are three main points to conclude in this chapter. The first is that war crimes are changing, or rather, the character of war crimes is changing as part of the changing character of war. Shifts in approaches to justice and the legal markers of war constitute a measure of that change. The second is that the military face all of this with a considerable degree of developed responsibility and reflection. There can be no doubt that the armed forces have perhaps the strongest interest of all in having their actions scrutinised, however irritating such an examination might be, in the short term. Accountability for the armed forces' conduct is crucial to ensuring their long-term professional character and reputation, as well as to maintaining the public's support. The third is that the conceptualisation involved in strategy, transmitted to operations and tactical action, is all about context, that is, it is always part of the *Trinity³(+)*. It is imperative to ensure a good understanding of warfare as a context for allegations of war crimes. It is also essential to recognise that appropriate experience is necessary to passing informed judgement on charges relating to those allegations. This cannot free practitioners from the pressures that accusations of wrongdoing create. And the military cannot—nor should it—escape legal limitations. These factors are crucial to any notion of responsibility within military professionalism. Accountability to society—domestic, or international—is a *sine qua non* for the armed forces, but any legal process should be informed by suitable military understanding: in warfare, crimes are about context.

5

CONDUCT AND CASES

Greater attention to war crimes issues and the growth of prosecutions, particularly at the international level, represents a demand for stricter adherence to the law. However, while this might be the case at one level, at another, it is equally true that the emphasis on war crimes issues is a sign of change. It represents not only stricter application of the law, but also a greater degree of contest over both the law and, distinct from narrow legal interpretations, that which is acceptable in contemporary armed conflict. Most of the twentieth-century war crimes prosecutions concerned matters well outside any bounds of acceptability. Yet, increasingly, the attention to war crimes issues and sensitivities about the conduct of armed operations began to mean that almost any operation was likely to be subject to accusations of wrongdoing. This was an important shift. Allegations of war crimes attended the normal conduct of military business, in addition to instances of the mass murder of civilians, or similar actions beyond normal measures of acceptability.

Given the nature of warfare, the scope for accusations is great. It is the nature of war to be essentially contested (thus containing material ripe for accusations and disputes) and also to involve the salience of violent means (so that unpleasant incidents are inherent, with the rough edges of a blunt capability evident, much of the time). Yet, the only way properly to understand whether questions involving military judgement were justified, or not, is experience and expertise. Although the military must, in broad terms, be responsive to the standards of their parent societies, those societies are not always equipped to pass judgement on matters requiring expertise.[1] This is a finely balanced relationship, in which the military must both be reflective of society, but also different from that broader society. Without that difference, soldiers will not be able to behave as they are expected to when they are required to prosecute restrained coercive violence. In this sense, it is neither completely right, nor indeed fair, to military personnel to argue, as some do, that the armed forces must be completely bound by the mores of the society they represent, meaning that, in terms of values, the military 'has to conform to that of civil society, not vice versa'.[2] While the military must reflect society, there also needs to be some account of its necessary peculiarities. At a minimum, professional expertise should inform understanding where potentially wrongful military conduct or accusations of war crimes are considered.

The prosecutions of Generals Tihomir Blaškić (Croatia) and Stanislav Galić (Serbian) at the International Criminal Tribunal for the Former Yugoslavia (ICTY) for unlawful (disproportionate and indiscriminate)[3] bombardment raised the prospect of a soldier's being tried, probably for the first time, for doing what soldiers ostensibly do—in this case firing artillery.* However, I only note this as a matter of principle, notwithstanding other factors that will have been relevant in these cases, the detail involved in them and their final outcomes.[4] The purpose here is not—and could not be—to re-run those trials. And in no way is it a comment on them. I simply wish to emphasise that no soldiers had previously been charged for crimes connected with such a key part of their job. In a sense, this is an issue of 'mis-applying' their trade and either wilfully, or negligently, misusing artillery by firing without due discrimination (or, perhaps, with expressly unacceptable discrimination). This is a different question from deliberate mass murder, or the inhumane treatment of prisoners, and so forth. The allegations, in cases of unlawful attack, involved judgement about the use of artillery, as part of, and related to, the conduct of operations. The issue here was presented in a nutshell in the ICTY Appeals Chamber Judgement in the Blaskić case:

The Appellant [Blaškić] further submits that he never ordered attacks directed against a civilian population, and reiterates that civilian casualties were the unfortunate consequence of an otherwise legitimate and proportionate military operation, not an attack targeting a civilian population.[5]

---

* By 'ostensibly' I mean the actions soldiers perform, and are expected to perform. For example firing artillery is what gunners in the military do and are expected to do.

The case was not necessarily a matter of directly targeting or murdering civilians in an illegal manner—although the judgement in this case and others effectively concluded, in one interpretation, that 'indiscriminate and disproportionate attacks' might simply be construed to 'provide evidence of attack essentially directed against civilians'.[6] However, Blaškić alleged that he was doing his job and that civilian deaths were 'unfortunate' by-products of doing that job—unavoidable accidents. The Prosecutor alleged, *a contrario*, that the civilian deaths were criminal both because they involved deliberate targeting, and also because of 'unlawful, excessive and wanton destruction ... not justified by military necessity'.[7] It is on questions of this kind, irrespective of the detail of cases (but, where necessary, informing them), that what military personnel think must be taken into account—just as the opinions of medical or engineering experts are used in cases involving other practitioners' judgements in their fields. Starting from this understanding, and seeking to illustrate the need to take account of military voices as allegations of war crimes grow in the context of contemporary warfare, this chapter considers three situations, or scenarios, concerning the use of force: the killing of prisoners of war during a special forces mission; the use of cluster munitions in a humanitarian operation; and the use of artillery siege and bombardment.*

---

* As explained in Chapter 1, this analysis is based on empirical research, including data from focus group research with senior defence practitioners. Some of the information relating to this, as set out in Chapter 1, is repeated here (and again as it was in the previous chapter, which contains a note identical to the present note, this parenthetical connection aside). This was part of a wider programme of research, involving the War Crimes Research Group at King's College London, the Royal College of Defence Studies (RCDS) and the Joint Services Command and Staff College (JSCSC), in the UK, as well as the Humanitarian Law Center in Belgrade and the Center for Interdisciplinary Postgraduate Studies, University of Sarajevo. The bulk of the research used directly in this volume involved the RCDS, which embraces an international mix of defence practitioners, mostly at one star (Brigadier/Brigadier General) or equivalent levels. Those who took part in the research were an international mix from all continents and a variety of cultures. Participants were from all continents and roughly all parts of all continents. The research involved people from Middle Eastern countries, from all points of the African compass, from different Asian and Australasian countries, and from the Americas. There was a surprising degree of consistency. It is necessary to be careful when describing or referring to the group, because of the confidentiality involved, especially because some of them come from countries where if they could be identified, they might face censure, or punishment. All respondents volunteered freely, with no compulsion or obligation. The agreement to carry out the research with the RCDS involved sophisticated discussions with the Senior Directing Staff there.

Prisoners of War

Prisoners of war and their treatment have constituted a key leitmotif of armed conflict since the end of the Cold War. Sometimes they have even been the most important element in an engagement: the abuse identified at the Abu Ghraib prison in Baghdad became the single most decisive blow against the US-led expedition to Iraq.[8] Similar allegations of abuse were made against British soldiers and others, as discussed in Chapters 1 and 4. There were also concerns about the way in which Western prisoners were treated—and likely mistreated—from the UK airmen captured over Iraq in 1991, to the fourteen men and one woman of the Royal Navy and the Royal Marines kidnapped and paraded on television by Iranian Revolutionary Guards while operating inside Iraqi territorial waters during March 2007.[9] American attempts to struggle with a category of belligerents who did not necessarily fit existing legal templates, led to creating the highly controversial detention facility at Guantanamo Bay.[10] Thus, the treatment of POWs became a striking, if neither a novel, nor a unique, issue surrounding the conduct of contemporary warfare and the atmosphere of war crimes allegations that, in turn, surrounded it. The most extreme form of abuse, of course, would be killing. There was evidence that deaths had occurred in the allegedly abusive conditions of US custody at the Bagram Prison in Afghanistan,[11] but these were not deliberate. The US operation in which al-Qa'ida leader Osama bin Ladin was killed in May 2011 might present a different case. Although it was theoretically possible that those conducting the operation might have taken him prisoner, assumptions about operational security (and quite possibly other concerns, which would make the operation effectively a targeted killing) meant that the potential prisoner was killed, not captured. The possibility of the justifiable killing of

---

The type of research that was conducted has two particular strengths. First, it allows the generation of empirical data, simply through the discussion that takes place, with participants offering knowledge and information drawn from experience, as we well as giving expression to beliefs, values and attitudes. This provides the data for analysis. Secondly, in contrast to individual research interviews, the group process (especially when it involves the presentation of specific propositions or material—part of the research used in this volume draws on instances in which participants were shown visual material) allowed discussion and interaction between participants. As discourse developed, salient beliefs, values and attitudes were identified, as well as issues about which participants strongly agreed or diverged.

prisoners of war merits investigation as an extreme example with which to test understandings of where the boundaries of right and wrong in war can be placed, and against which differences of opinion between military personnel and human rights civilians might be particularly informative.

While the subsequent scenarios reflect actual cases, this first situation is hypothetical—although the research itself threw up one reported example, while other discussions have suggested other cases where something approximating this kind of situation occurred. The prompt for the hypothetical scenario was Telford Taylor, one of the prosecutors at the International Military Tribunal at Nuremberg. In passing, he posited a hypothetical scenario regarding circumstances in which it might be justifiable, in terms of necessity and proportionality, to kill prisoners of war, or more likely, those seeking to surrender as prisoners, where there was an issue of force protection:

Not uncommonly commandos encounter situations in which an enemy sentry is killed instantly to prevent his disclosing the proximity of the raiding party, or a captured enemy soldier is killed because the raiding party has no means of safeguarding him.[12]

In such a scenario, a unit has taken prisoners of war (or had enemies lay down arms and indicate surrender); yet, this unit cannot take the prisoners with the unit because it must conduct its mission, which is deemed to be of vital importance. The unit cannot afford to leave the prisoners behind because this would compromise the security of the force and so the operation. Likely, something of this kind occurred in relation to parachute operations in the Second World War and in many other uncharted cases.[13] Taylor pointed out that Article 23(c) of the Hague Convention—applicable even in the Second World War—would seem to prohibit such an action, perhaps more so than the particular references in the later Geneva Convention III.[14] Would the necessity of the mission make killing the prisoners an acceptable act? What 'necessity' would make such an act justifiable, if any? Is it reasonable to say, in line with the lawyers' view of the Hague Convention, that under no circumstances can it be acceptable and lawful to kill prisoners of war?

This scenario raises questions about prisoners of war and force protection. Everyone shares the general sense that 'you do not kill prisoners of war'. In the UK, for example, the army lawyers hold the view that it is never acceptable to kill a prisoner of war, and the troops are instructed accordingly.[15] However, it is not clear that Geneva Convention III actually makes such an explicit prohibition. Geneva Convention III, Article 13 provides that 'Any unlawful act or omission by the Detaining Power causing death or seriously endangering the health of a prisoner of war in its custody is prohibited, and will be regarded as a serious breach of the present convention'.[16] The key word in this is 'unlawful' and the stiff test, as a matter of fact, is whether or not the killing of prisoners can be justified by the circumstances of the mission. If so then it could be presented as a lawful act, whereas purely vindictive killing, including 'measures of reprisal', would constitute an unlawful act of murder.[17] As the participants in the research for this volume noted, this is, of course, a 'murky area'[18]—as the discussion of Henry V's order to kill prisoners at the Battle of Agincourt in Shakespeare's play, noted in Chapter 1, testifies.[19]

Soldiers understand that there might be, and might previously have been, tactical situations in which issues of force protection could require the killing of prisoners of war. However, if such a situation were to arise in the early twenty-first century, because of the tactical-strategic compression involved in contemporary conflict, it would be an extraordinarily difficult decision to make. A decision to kill, in those circumstances, would certainly have significant ramifications, which would lead to all kinds of accusations. Yet, in terms of the military professional's judgement, this action might well be deemed to be entirely defensible. Any decision of this kind would have to be measured in terms of the mission itself and on the scale of necessity and proportionality, in line with the approach to the key principle of necessity (discussed below) and in conjunction with ethical tests.

If the person in charge decided that there was no alternative other than to kill prisoners of war, then there would be an obligation to write that decision up and explain why it had been made. There was also a general sense among respondents that, if this were not done, such an absence would indicate that something wrong had taken place. Although this is an extreme, hypothetical case, which is unlikely to happen, it illustrates the point for other cases: it is vital to explain the rationale behind a decision at the time it was taken. In the course of discussion, one of the participants asked, 'If you killed prisoners of war, would you report it?' The emphatic and overwhelming answer, uttered in complete unison, was 'Yes!' This was supplemented by the comment that, 'If you don't, you don't believe you were right'.

Understandably, there was recognition that this was an 'incredibly difficult' area. One respondent described what he believed to be an actual case, where these issues had been confronted:

For example, SOE [Special Operations Executive] operatives in Yugoslavia in the Second World War were being harried by the Germans over the hill, they knew if they took prisoners, they would be a drain on resources if they kept them, but if they let them go, then they would reveal the operation.[20] Therefore, what they did was truss them up and leave them to die. Or they might have just killed them (or the Partisans, I'm not sure). It was a brutal set of circumstances, where ethics change.

While there is uncertainty over some detail (and, indeed, no clear evidence to locate the case as a matter of fact), the situation described clearly identifies the dilemmas involved. This confirmed that when 'you get into really brutal situations, ethics really do change', or rather—as noted above—that judgements made within ethical frameworks alter as 'a question of operational necessity'. There was a sense, despite the judgements involved (and contrasting with the case of artillery bombardment discussed below), that this would be a grave breach of the Geneva Convention, even if justified (although, as discussed above, the issue would be whether the necessity of the mission could render this action lawful, where it would not be, otherwise). Success would be one determinant in this respect. One participant asked meaningfully, without direct answer: 'If the mission doesn't succeed, would that pose greater questions?' The implicit answer to this is an affirmative and a successful mission would have a better chance of demonstrating its necessity, at the least, while one that failed would remain in the domain of contention and counter-factuality.[21] However, another question with even greater ethical and pragmatic salience concerned each military's self-interest in the matter. There was serious recognition that by killing prisoners of war, they would put their own soldiers at risk by setting up 'a precedent for tit-for-tat'. The conclusion, as far as one could be determined, is best expressed as follows:

You don't generally shoot prisoners, but there might be operational necessity in a tactical level decision. But, given contemporary strategic-operational-tactical compression, this could be difficult to define. In the World War Two setting, the question was clearer. Today it might not be.

Thus, it is hypothetically conceivable that the necessity of accomplishing a certain mission, coupled with issues of force protection, would justify the killing of prisoners. However, there could be no question of extrapolating anything that could lead to something like a charter for killing prisoners of war from this philosophical progression. A development of this kind would be inherently counter to general military interest. Moreover, the research respondents' unanimous and lucid insight was the recognition that contemporary strategic and empirical realities made it impossible to conceive of any situation where the kind of action explored in the scenario would occur, or could, as a matter of fact, be justified.[22] Even if it were conceivable that such an act could have been justifiably perpetrated in the past, it would not be accepted in the twenty-first century. The changing character of war has reduced, if not utterly removed, the already low probability that killing prisoners of war in any situation could be acceptably justified by claims of operational necessity *in extremis*. The nature of contemporary operations is such that the type of close contact that might result in prisoners' being taken and then posing a risk is extraordinarily rare and limited, though it could still occur. Were that kind of contact to occur, it would almost always be in a phase of operations where the nature of the mission did not embrace a degree of necessity that could warrant any suggestion that killing prisoners would be acceptable. Thus, investigation of this hypothetical scenario with seasoned practitioners suggests the following conclusions. First, it is generally understood to be both unacceptable and illegal to kill prisoners of war. Secondly, there could, theoretically, be extreme situations where the killing of prisoners of war might be tactically justifiable. However, thirdly, it is almost impossible to conceive of a situation, even theoretically, where such an action could be justified in contemporary operations.

Humanitarian Cluster Munitions

In 1999, NATO undertook aerial operations against Serbia in a 'humanitarian' action, with the stated aim to stop 'ethnic cleansing' by Serbian forces of the majority ethnic Albanian population in the southern province of Kosovo.[23] The lack of absolute and generalizable legal certainty (qualified by a variety of more or less confident understandings held by those carrying out the action)[24] regarding the *jus ad bellum* on NATO's side accentuated problems regarding the *jus in bello*.[25] Belgrade and other critics levied accusations of war crimes at the Alliance.[26] Given the extent of NATO's operations, involving some 38,004 sorties, of which 10,484 were strike missions, over seventy eight days, it was quite remarkable that there were so few serious errors:[27] Human Rights Watch produced a list of around eighty incidents.[28] Even if all of these merited investigation it would still only amount to a 0.8 percentage rate of mistake—by most standards a nearly perfect record. However, the number of incidents really worthy of anything approaching serious consideration was actually closer to a quarter of this figure. For example, the Prosecutor at the ICTY conducted a preliminary investigation into allegations of war crimes against NATO, including a list of twenty-two incidents.[29] However, the report concluded that, on the basis of the available evidence, there was no *prima facie* case to bring against anyone involved at whatever level in the NATO operations regarding the allegations made.[30] Some legal scholars in particular were not content with this finding.[31] However, the report offered sound bases for dismissing the charges.[32] Although the Prosecutor at the Tribunal had unquestionable legal authority, on one issue the Prosecutor's report was thin and weakly founded: the use of cluster munitions. The issue of cluster munitions might be worthy of further attention, even without research beyond the original the Prosecutor's report. It is far from entirely certain that there could be no case for the investigation of charges of military negligence. Despite the almost summary and superficial dismissal of any grounds for further investigation, or prosecution, by the Prosecutor, the *prima facie* case remains strong: the Alliance used a weapons system known to be inaccurate and indiscriminate against an airfield adjacent to a civilian residential area, without having the necessity and effect of military achievement considered and tested. Furthermore, the bomb in question malfunctioned.

Cluster munitions have up to perhaps two hundred separate missiles within one warhead. They are effective for battlefield use against concentrations of troops, tanks, or artillery, for example, dispersing multiple destructive devices over a widespread area. This makes them inaccurate and they also have a relatively high rate of redundancy—out of 200 devices, around 5 per cent fail at any time.[33] This means that for every cluster device, there will be around ten unexploded bombs in the dispersal zone. This then caused problems for the NATO-led ground forces of KFOR during their implementation mission in Kosovo after the air strikes. Both experienced soldiers and civilians were at risk if they accidentally detonated one, which they could by just stepping on it. This potential for civilian harm, both during and after the conflict, is compounded by the potential for damage to civilian objects at the time of use.

At Niš, cluster bombs were used in an urban, civilian populated area, where NATO targeted an airfield, which happened to lie inside the boundaries of the town. Zoran Živković, Mayor of Niš at the time, commented ironically, as an anti-Milošević activist and friend-in-waiting of the West: 'Their "humanitarian" intervention killed fifteen people in a day'.[34] Those deaths were unintentional. But, it is possible to accuse the Allies of negligence and unlawfulness if specific details of the situation are taken into account. The decision by the US not to persist in the use of cluster munitions after both this event and Human Rights Watch comments that questioned the legality of their use supports this. The White House issued a directive against using cluster weapons after this report, just at the time where the balance between precision and unguided munitions was shifting from ninety-to-ten to ten-to-ninety.[35] This suggests that the US decision to abandon cluster weapons could give reason to further interrogate the cluster-over-Kosovo issue. While the US dropped use of cluster munitions, the UK continued to deploy them, with all missions legally vetted prior to launch, not to be conducted in mixed civilian areas.[36] The discrepancy between the US and UK approaches could augment investigation of the *prima facie* case.

However, as in the preceding and subsequent scenarios investigated, the background realities of the Kosovo operations provided material and, furthermore, inspiration for the scenario presented and the subsequent discussion. Once again, it must be understood that the research was not an investigation of the actual use of cluster munitions in and around Niš, in the context of the Kosovo operations *per se*. Elements from that case simply prompted ethical discussion among professionals.

Thus, there are four considerations. First, there is the question of whether or not cluster munitions should be employed in any circumstance, given the potential harm to innocents at the time, or in a post-conflict situation (as well as to one's own forces).[37] Secondly, there is a more specific question over whether devices such as cluster bombs should be used in humanitarian operations. Thirdly, what are the implications of one partner's ceasing to use the munition in an operation, while others continue?[38] Finally, irrespective of the overall mission, should cluster munitions be used against any target in an urban area?

It is clear that, while cluster munitions retain some utility, defence professionals perceive them to be of limited, if any, use in contemporary operations. They are also seen as problematic in terms of their consequences, both immediately, with regard to potential contingent damage, destruction and death, and also in the longer-term, concerning the risks presented to civilians and the military by material that remains on the ground in the area of attack.[39] There was complete consensus in the research that cluster bombs could be useful and that respondents would use them: 'Yes, use cluster against tanks on battlefields, or airfields in the middle of nowhere'. However, the willingness to use such a weapons system was significantly mitigated by perceptions of reduced value.

Cluster is a good area munition. British ones have 147 devices. It was originally used for tanks, but tanks moved on and were hardened. Now it is used against troop concentrations and soft-skinned vehicles. They cover a wide area. Using them on an airfield would be effective, if the opposition is stupid enough to park all its planes in a row. It is not used against runways these days.

Because of this, a cluster bomb 'is not usually the weapon of choice' and has 'fallen out of favour':

There are two significant risks associated with the use of cluster munitions. First, cluster is a relatively indiscriminate area weapon, so, if employed in the wrong place, or if they go wrong, there is a risk of unintentional harm anywhere within range. Secondly, the risk, of course is that, 'Cluster bombs have a high dud rate'. This not only has implications for force protection. It also means that there are moral implications beyond their immediate use—children's legs, for example, down the line.[40]

Reduced value for cluster munitions stems, among other concerns, from issues of force protection, given the near certainty that one's own forces will move into the territory where these devices have been used.

The question is what are you trying to achieve in that area. And there is also a question of what the risks to one's own forces would be of using an alterative weapons system. It might be that using one cluster bomb with 200 devices might save making 200 separate missions, thereby reducing the risk to one's own forces.

Pragmatically, therefore, there is a dilemma. One aspect of force protection is that 'if you fly fewer sorties, there is less risk to the pilots'. Contrasting with this, there is a serious concern that the forces 'who use the munitions are increasingly responsible for clearing them up afterwards', which means that consideration of 'this aspect has to be part of the decision'. 'People', therefore, 'are worried about sowing seeds that they will have to clear up later'. The risky consequences of using cluster were evident with 'two UK dead after Kosovo, killed clearing up the cluster leftovers' reported by one respondent.

However, the more significant question is the contingent effect of these munitions on civilians, especially in the context of a purported humanitarian mission. The real issue is 'the innocents'. Whether by design, or accident, it is the 'civilian impact' that really counts. With cluster munitions, 'the issue is civilian impact, if a device does not disarm in time, or is not cleaned up afterwards'. These significant risks mean that the 'question should always be, should we prosecute this target this way?'[41]

The key question 'why prosecute this target this way?' presupposes that there are alternatives.[42] However, reasonable alternatives in operational terms are not always evident. Cluster bombs would certainly be useful when attacking an area, minimising the risk to those flying air operations. Alternatives might only be evident in terms of finding ways 'to invest more in different systems that will lower collateral damage'. Some voices might 'say to use PGM or some other munition'. Against this, there is clearly an element of rational use of resources that leads to the judgement that a commander 'wouldn't use laser for one soft-top truck'. However, there was no doubt that in situations where 'use is close to civilians' there will be questions about their suitability, meaning that, '[i]f you can achieve the aim with other munitions, then it would be better to do so'.

Participants had a fairly unanimous response to the decision of one partner to cease cluster operations, while another continued in face of alleged war crimes. The immediate assumption among respondents, given the Kosovo inspiration for, and background to, the scenario, was that the UK had ceased use, while the US continued. The initial view identified 'a fundamental psychological difference between the Americans and the Brits, the US is more ready to use a big hammer than is readily [acceptable] in the world'. This complemented the view that 'the Brits are always more conservative than the US'. Detailed specifics of the context and the decisions taken are thus necessary when judging the case: '[i]t is always a question of circumstances. Are they sharing targets? Or are the specifics different? Or are they exactly the same? Are they the same class of target?'

In addition to these questions there was confidence that 'UK targets always go through the system and UK collateral damage criteria', with the implication that American targets might not be so rigorously vetted.[43] This last view was also consistent with the judgement expressed once the facts of the case were clarified: that the UK is more thorough than other countries when vetting targets. Further, the explanation lay not only in this presumed thoroughness, but also in 'a greater ethos, and training and responsibility among the troops' when carrying out operations. In essence, British personnel could be relied upon not to exceed the bounds of acceptability, it was assumed, whereas the same might not be true of American ones. Ironically, this was evidently counter to the positions taken by the US and the UK, in practice, where the US was conservative about the boundaries of acceptability, and the UK continued with what might be seen as potentially risky actions.

In terms of using cluster munitions in a built-up area, there was a mixed sense. All agreed that it was probably wrong to use this weapons system against a target in a mixed area. One respondent used an example from operations in Iraq: '[T]here was an armoured concentration in a mixed area, but they didn't go near it, because of the chance of 10 per cent being duds, or going awry'. This decision offers a potential point of comparison with the Niš case regarding both use in a mixed area and possibly the decisions by one actor to cease use while another continued.

There was—perhaps unsurprisingly—consensus about NATO's use of cluster munitions during the 1999 Kosovo campaign, in general, and, in particular, around Niš among senior Serbian officers, who expressed strong views about these events in research conducted at a later stage.[44] They believed that the Main Post Office in Niš had been the target of a cluster munitions attack, in the middle of the town, in a built-up urban area. This was viewed as unacceptable and hypocritical, as the same NATO countries that had used cluster munitions against Niš condemned the forces of Colonel Qadaffi in Libya for using cluster weapons against civilian centres. Despite the possibility that the cluster bombs might have been intended for the nearby airfield at Niš and hit the town by mistake, many respondents still felt that cluster weapons had been deliberately used on an urban area because the main post office had been identified by NATO as a communications centre.[45] While this view was held by some members of the group, the discussion among the international group responding to the scenario already suggested that this was not the case. The earlier group revealed enough about the changing use of cluster munitions, as well as information on the types of situations and targets where they might be used, to show that NATO forces would not have used this type of weapon for a single-building target. That evidence did, however, point to the (possibly past) practice of using such munitions on airfields.

Whatever the case, there was a belief among the senior Serbian officers that the use of cluster munitions in this context had been 'illegitimate' and criminal, as the weapon was inherently indiscriminate and so should not be used in a populated area, if at all. One participant pointed out that an effect of the inherently indiscriminate character of cluster devices was that they killed civilians, even after the action had finished. All agreed that devices that did not detonate at the time they were dropped could later explode and kill or injure civilians: one participant noted that a device from a cluster bomb had remained on the post office roof in Niš, falling off and killing a woman at a later stage.

However, even outside the context of a humanitarian operation, there were concerns regarding use in a mixed area: responses included an awareness that it 'is a grey area issue because of the risk of collateral damage' and that '[i]t is all about the circumstances'. It was 'unlikely' that the circumstances would justify use. In such difficult circumstances, a view was expressed that anyone with serious concerns about use of cluster munitions ought to express those reservations clearly at the time: 'If they were in the chain of command, they should speak up. If not they should keep out'. Alternatively, it was felt, they 'should resign'. The bottom line was uncertainty, with the following comment summarising the general sense of the issue, taking account also of the perceived relative redundancy of cluster munitions and the contingent risks of using them: 'The problem is in a difficult area, the middle ground. Cluster seems close to something that should be banned'. This view was one likely to be welcomed by those campaigning to outlaw the use of cluster bombs, including the various governments who worked on a treaty agreement, almost a decade after the Kosovo action.[46]

Artillery Bombardment and Siege

Generals Tihomir Blaškić (Croatian) and Stanislav Galić (Serbian) were accused—and convicted—of indiscriminate and disproportionate bombardment.[47] The latter was charged in connection with the siege of Sarajevo during the armed conflict in Bosnia.[48] The Blaškić trial was the first to raise any serious questions of military conduct in terms of disproportionate attack, or bombardment. However, these charges were a smaller part of a case more directly and substantially focused on direct atrocities, including the deliberate targeting of civilians as a Crime Against Humanity, rather than war crimes involving wilful or negligent action that incidentally—though unjustifiably and unacceptably—brought civilian death and destruction. The Galić case highlights issues relating to the siege of Sarajevo from May 1992 to September 1995. The siege of Sarajevo offers a notional framework, or rather, the basis for a scenario, for considering questions of right and wrong and the principle of distinction—'the fundamental principle regulating targeting decisions in IHL [International Humanitarian Law]'.[49] It also aids judgement on matters of proportionality and discrimination when assessing war crimes, such as unlawful attack and (or) bombardment.

In the case of Galić, there were arguably constraints on the force available to him and his fellow commanders. This is not necessarily to suggest that strategic questions such as availability of forces would (or could) exculpate or mitigate in a trial, but simply to explore right-wrong boundary questions and the issues that would, hypothetically, affect judgement on these questions.[50] The case is only used as a cue for discussion, having identified the 'bombardment' element as constituting probably the first international trial ever conducted focused on what is, at first sight, purely a matter of military performance. It should be stressed that only one aspect of the case is the prompt for this study and that it is not the Galić case itself that is the focus of research; it merely functions as a cue for the research and material for the construction of hypothetical scenarios. This analysis is not meant to suggest that the General or others should be acquitted and released, indeed it could not legitimately do so, as it is in no way evaluates the case, or the volumes of evidence it produced.

However, the case does highlight issues to explore, given that these are not purely about definitively criminal actions that could never be seen as legitimate. The encirclement and shelling of Sarajevo, considering that there were hostile forces in the city, could be said, in theory, to have strategic logic. However, saying this does not justify it morally *per se*. Instead, it means looking at the issues around whether conduct can be ethically valid or not, and if it can, under what circumstances, or with what considerations. Serbian forces were short of manpower throughout Bosnia, but had abundant heavy artillery. Any attempt to capture the city through ground-force combat would likely have resulted in heavy losses and would probably have failed, given the general pattern of attempts to take urban areas through combat. There would also be the issue of force protection for the commander, which could be relevant when the military in question had significant manpower shortages, meaning it could not afford to take such losses in any circumstance. Any commander might, therefore, consider the same approach of standoff siege and bombardment, given the same calculation, to achieve the military objective and to preserve their own forces (a matter of priority and loyalty, key to the military ethos).[51] In addition to this, opposing forces defending the city under siege would fire artillery from a place of protection—such as positions either adjacent to, or inside, schools and hospitals. In these circumstances, proportionality becomes a concern and, in the conduct of the operation, it is not possible to judge whether ten shells are enough, but eleven too many, or twenty mortar rounds proportionate, while fifty rounds would be disproportionate (for the sake of argument).[52] Would the concern with force protection justify the approach taken? What conditions would it be appropriate to place on a commander regarding proportionality in such circumstances? To what extent must the reasonable prospect of civilian casualties, even when enemy forces are firing from, for example, hospitals, be a strong, or even an absolute, restraint? Leaving aside other potential issues, would a jury trial of peers acquit an equivalent of General Galić, on the basis of the scenario presented (a very much reduced and simplified version of those elements in the Galić case that prompted and shaped that scenario)?

Determining the most humane option and translating this into an operational decision is challenging when using area weapons in standoff bombardment and siege. It is especially complicated once considerations of proportionality and discrimination are introduced, in the context of action being seen as excessive and leading to allegations of war crimes. Issues of proportionality and discrimination are complicated—and its reduction to a numeric equation oversimplifies the case, as in the scenario proposition. But this does not mean that serious analysis is not possible, nor that investigation of the question is invalid. Indeed, this can help to discover the key issues to explore in such a scenario.

Three particular issues were identified in this study: effectiveness in comparison with using alternative means; knowledge of effect; and the nature of weapons systems. The first was the possibility of more subtle and complex approaches to numeric calculation. On one level, there can be 'a real question of judgement', in terms of whether a commander should 'use one shell a day for 200 days, or fifty on one and have the business done with?'[53] The second point was whether or not the commanding officer had knowledge of the effect being achieved—in particular, if the objective had been achieved. The judgement over whether fire was excessive would possibly turn on whether the commander 'could have been aware it was done' (that is, the objective achieved), or was 'unaware and kept firing in good faith'. Good faith is an essential factor, given the nature of warfare. The military view seems to be that a mistake made in good faith should not be a cause for conviction—or even, investigation or prosecution, in the first instance. Thirdly, in this context, there are non-quantitative concerns, which are perhaps more pertinent than counting shells (or similar measures) in many cases:

A. The number of shells can't be considered. The question is the nature of the weapons.

B. This is fine, providing that the message is crystal clear, that so long as you can justifiably say why you can use a particular system, you will get backing and protection from people who do not understand.

Thus, in seeking to locate culpability for possible criminal action regarding disproportionate bombardment, the appropriate focus might not be the number of times a particular device was fired at a particular area, but whether there could have been an alternative choice of weapon made, which would have offered a potentially more humane and less contingently damaging option than the one actually employed. The starting point for any assessment, though, would be a record of the reasoning behind a decision. The decision-making point over choice of weapon and target is where any responsibility lies.

This was confirmed in research with two sets of officers, which investigated a different kind of scenario—the use of precision-guided air munitions to target Ali al-Majid ('Chemical Ali') during the Battle for Basra by Coalition forces in spring 2003.[54] This was an attack in which one device failed, killing ten members of one family, over three generations, in an adjacent house, while the attack did not succeed in 'taking out' its prime target. Respondents in both groups questioned in detail the targeting and decision-making process. The group felt it necessary that the information on which the attack was based was checked and verified, and that appropriate caution had been shown through ensuring that the decision to attack was made only after its lawfulness had been established, and the proximity of civilian housing, the appropriateness of the munitions used, and similar issues had been addressed. There was particular concern about 'population densities around the target', in the second group, and the issue of whether the person on the ground relaying information had 'visual contact' in order to identify the collateral victims, with which to inform decisions involving collateral damage assessment.[55] An interview with the officer in command of the operation offers more insight into these issues: he stated that he did not actually know that 'Chemical Ali' was the target as such.[56]

As well as both locating responsibility with those who made decisions and selected targets, and considering the key options that would have to be considered in judging excessive use of force, the scenario raised issues of force protection and subterfuge by the enemy. Force protection provided another dimension to the issue of excessive detonations. This emerged in a discussion of reprisals, called 'preventive retaliation' by one participant. For example, if, for no clear 'military' aim, one side bombarded a town with no military facilities each day at the same time, using twenty-five to forty grenades, merely to intimidate and create disorder in the town, it was suggested that the 'only response was to send double'. A case was cited where this form of belligerent reprisal had occurred and the 'action stopped after one month of increment, ten grenades getting twenty back, thirty shells getting sixty in return'. These issues make it 'difficult for someone neutral to say if there is over use or not'—especially without appreciation of the situation and the calculations military commanders are constrained to make.

For example, if the US sends 50,000 troops, but loses 5,000 of them, but could send 100,000 and lose none, would 100,000 be excessive? There is a question of timing. And there is a question of intention. In the short-term, something might seem like too many grenades, but in the longer-term perspective, this might not seem excessive, with wider benefit.

Thus, what might seem inappropriate to outsiders on the surface and in the immediate circumstance might render a different interpretation once the wider perspective, including the strategic situation and issues of force protection, is taken into account. Force protection is a high-priority concern for any military and affects morale and cohesion as well as the military's relationship to its society. Most societies, if information is available, would be unlikely to countenance carelessness regarding their own troops: 'the moral responsibility to one's troops and one's own people is greater than to others, more than others'. Therefore, failing to protect one's own force would be 'equally negligent' to mis-employing armed force, even where there is a significant risk of collateral action through more extensive use of, for example, artillery. However, this might look like an inappropriate use of force and is the kind of issue that concerns some international lawyers.[57]

The issue of subterfuge drew particularly strong responses, for example, where the opponent used a hospital as cover for firing. This prompted a reaction that taking such an underhand step would actually change the parameters of what might be ethically justifiable. The cover of the hospital was used principally in order to draw incoming fire against a target that could then be used to demonstrate the supposedly callous disregard for the rules of war by those firing in. Despite the risks of collateral damage, in such a situation, it was felt that the duplicity of this aim might justify a response that would otherwise be inappropriate.[58] To some extent, the responses implicitly showed awareness of what would be required under law, even if, at times, they appeared also to see the necessity of action that would not respect the narrow legal parameters outlined by non-practitioners.

You would have to assess the damage from incoming fire, look at the position and decide whether, or how, to engage. Communications strategy would be an important issue. Do you look at using the media, for example, to say 'we will engage hospitals etc.' You could say that it is a crime to use civilians or a red cross as a shield. That could produce a response. Because of this, the communications strategy is very important. Then you have to consider how much information you can get on the weapons systems and then select systems to minimise collateral damage. The artillery recce might say to use laser guided air munitions. Could you flatten the hospital and make sure to take out the guns? Could you give them the option to move out? There is an important element of being seen to try to avoid using force, and only when this fails, to do so. You have to go through the process.

This thoughtful analysis of the question apparently reflects that which the law would require. Article 18 of Geneva Convention IV states that:

Civilian hospitals organised to give care to the wounded, sick, infirm and maternity cases, may in no circumstances be the object of attack, but shall at all times be respected and protected by the parties to the conflict.

The key to this lies in the last clause, which places responsibility for respecting the civilian hospital on all parties to the conflict, including the one on whose territory it is sited. If that side does not respect the hospital's protected status, then the situation can change. Hence, in Article 19:

The protection to which civilian hospitals are entitled shall not cease unless they are used to commit, outside their humanitarian duties, acts harmful to the enemy. Protection may, however, cease only after due warning has been given, naming, in all appropriate cases, a reasonable time limit, and after such warning has remained unheeded.

There is no explicit requirement to avoid using excessive force, or force at all, if possible, in contrast to the research response, noted above. However, the idea that misuse by the enemy changes the position, and that warnings should be communicated before any aggressive action, is entirely consistent with Geneva IV. However, the question is still not straightforward. It might not be possible to determine if the message was received. Or, if, having 'warned opponents about abuse of the hospital', then 'the [belligerent*] guys who use the hospital are aware that they are using it and are

---

* It is important to stress that the issue here is the illegal use of the hospital by belligerents—combat troops who are unlawfully and illegitimately conducting armed operations, firing out from the medical facility. This is clearly the thrust of the participant's comments here—although, technically, of course, everyone using the hospital would

wasting time'. Thus, the warning period is a complicated, potentially difficult and unknowable part of the equation:

The question for all of us is what happens to innocents, to third parties. Having given a warning .... Can't answer the question. If you are in a village, taking hits, if they go on, then the situation might result in more casualties than if you were to take them out [inflicting collateral casualties, as you did it]. But then, if you are in a village with civilians, are you negligent?

The view that emerges from participant's responses is that '[s]omeone using subterfuge and the shield of a red cross is an even more legitimate target because he is breaking the rules'.[59] However, the sense that an opponent using such subterfuge is an even more legitimate target suggests a strength of response that will, in practice, be counterbalanced by concerns for the ethical and practical complexity of the situation, given the likely presence of civilian sick, wounded, infirm and pregnant.[60]

Taking into account the points in this discussion, there was a general consensus that, based on the case presented, it would be hard for defence professionals to decide that the commander in question was guilty beyond reasonable doubt—meaning they would be acquitted. However, there was recognition that the scenario itself could not produce key evidence that would make a difference—notwithstanding completely separate issues of fact and evidence that might be pertinent, as in the Galić case. 'Operational logs and war diaries have to be kept' and examined. 'In some circumstances, you might convict, in others, you might acquit' was the understandable view. But the key would be the commander's personal approach: 'If he didn't care, then, guilty. But if it was a value judgement about lesser evil, then acquit'.

This sense of motivation in the particular context among an international group of senior military personnel in relation to the hypothetical scenario was more nuanced than a later focus group, in Belgrade, comprising only Serbian senior officers, albeit the latter group was not discussing the same scenario.[61] While elements of this discussion overlapped considerably with those in the initial group, some points were very sharply focused. This was perhaps a function of both experience and direct reference to cases, such as that of Galić, and the practitioners' familiarity with some of the issues.

---

know that they were using it—and those using it would include medical staff and patients.

'There are always two words for the same thing in international relations', said one participant, adding 'If it is one side, it is collateral damage, if it is the other, it is indiscriminate'. Others in the group agreed with this, though they questioned it further by noting that there was a fine line between collateral damage and negligence. In many situations, it was probably quite hard to judge. The problem, it was felt, was that mostly human rights lawyers without experience sought to judge, rather than those with experience of 'the fog of war' and an understanding of military operations.

Artillery bombardment was a particular focus of discussion, in relation to the 'fine line' between criminal negligence and acceptable error. This arose in relation to the verdict in the case of Croatian General Ante Gotovina and others, which had been delivered some days prior to the session. The group welcomed aspects of the verdict, and discussed it with some vigour; they agreed that the verdict did not support the Croatian Army's characterisation of the August 1995 'Oluja' campaign as a great military success, although the alleged crimes of which Gotovina had been accused had formed a part of it. He used Serbian military intelligence evidence to confirm that over 100,000 people, the overwhelming majority of Serbs in the area, had actually been evacuated according to a Serbian plan of withdrawal, both military and civilian as part of his defence. This meant that the Serbian side had actually withdrawn, so, in the respondents' view, there was no real Croatian victory, and nor was there a war crime in the 'Oluja' operation itself.* The judges' determination to 'convict' the dead political leaders Franjo Tudjman and Gojko Šušak for their aim to remove all Serbs from the region meant that the general, but flawed, interpretation of 'Oluja' as a success persisted.

What was salient in this context was the issue of indiscriminate bombardment. 'The gunners logs show everything', said one participant, '[y]ou have to keep a record, a grid reference for where you targeted and what your position is, that's international humanitarian law'. The group agreed that from the evidence it was clear that one person had particular responsibility: Ljutić** had a record that showed clearly, as the judges found, that civilian

---

* The participants' view on Operation 'Oluja' passes no comment on the subsequent murder and pillaging that occurred, once Croatian forces were in control of the region.

** An individual named Gojko Ljutić featured in the *Gotovina, et al.* judgement. However, this involved extensive information derived from Croatian criminal proceedings against Ljutić and others in relation to murder charges. It is not evident that an individ-

homes were targeted with the aim of 'driving people mad' and ensuring that, 'if not destroyed with their homes, they would leave'. One participant said that Ljutić had 'tried to conceal the gunner's books', hiding them. All agreed that this was also a sign of criminal action—and the absence of a log without good reason would not only be negligent, but also a crime, because by law the gunner's book has to be kept. This was judged to be a case of indiscriminate and criminal shelling. However, members of the group all qualified this by saying that the Ljutić shelling of Knin occurred only after the first two days of the 'Oluja' campaign, by which time, Gotovina had moved on, as the forces he was commanding swept forward through western Bosnia.

When prompted to consider the case of General Stanislav Galić, the Serbian artillery commander convicted of indiscriminate bombardment, among other offences, the group agreed that this constituted a war crime: 'Sarajevo? Without doubt!' said one participant to the strong agreement of the others. 'They fired out once, then there were hours of bombardment', said another participant, 'that's not proportionate, it's against the law'. There was complete agreement around this point. Some participants, however, raised the question of different definitions of 'proportionality' and stated that the US sense of proportionality, for example ('however much it takes to make absolutely sure with no doubt'), could be seen as inherently disproportionate, because it 'did not discriminate carefully', but simply applied overwhelming force.

Change in approaches to justice and the legal markers of war constitutes change in warfare itself. As in earlier analysis, this section has found that the conceptualisation involved in strategy and transmitted to operations and tactical action is affected by context. No particular measure is necessarily justified, or perceived as lawful—though many should not necessarily be regarded as unlawful. In most instances, lawfulness and unlawfulness will be a matter of debate. Law-war boundary issues signify change in the char-

---

ual named Ljutić played the role attached to him by the focus group participant. However, there were problems between the Gotovina defence and the Croatian authorities seeking to obtain evidence—in particular, on computers—that was material to the case, while some members of Gotovina's defence team were prosecuted for hiding and destroying official records. (*Sense Tribunal*, 19 March 2010, available at http://www.sense-agency.com/icty/gotovina-requests-for-certificate-to-appeal.29.html?cat_id=1&news_id=11622.)

acter of both war and law. These will shape the significant issues of any armed conflict, as the battle for legitimacy outweighs battlefield combat, in the realm of the *Trinity³(+)*. In the context of contemporary warfare, challenges of propriety can be expected to generate increasing pressures on the military in relation to their conduct within war, and on governments, regarding decisions to use armed force in the first place.

On both counts—decisions and conduct—it is clear that any use of force is likely to be surrounded by accusations about war crimes. These accusations add to the tests faced by Western troops in the conduct of warfare and constitute, to a considerable extent, the markers of success, or failure. It is vital that any discussion of accusations, and indeed any judicial prosecution, needs to take account of professional military perspectives. The evidence in this chapter has shown that only experienced military personnel can have a fully nuanced understanding of the context of a military action in terms of strategy and actions taken. While society, as a whole, must ultimately determine what is and is not acceptable, in order to foster a healthy civil-military relationship, a respect for military expertise and the difficulties of truly appreciating practical matters surrounding war crimes issues is required. At the same time, however, it seems evident that the remarkable and reflective character of defence professionals, evident in the research findings presented in this chapter, indicates that, in many respects, their thoughts on what constitutes an unacceptable wartime action might be ahead of the wider population. Certainly, military concerns about cluster munitions seem to be in advance of both campaigners and many governments. At the same time, the professional point of view might suggest alternative approaches to potentially simplistic views about standoff bombardment and siege—depending on the circumstances. It is, of course, the context that determines the empirical substance of whether an action is legitimate, or a war crime.

If one thing should emerge from the empirical research presented in this chapter, it is to persuade some of the people who make accusations against the armed forces to come to terms with, or at least be cautiously aware of, the issue of context, before launching such allegations. The detail of context and events determines whether actions committed constitute legitimate acts of war, or war crimes. Thus, the issue, in the end, can only be one of military motivation and judgement, both of which require direct experience of difficult situations and an awareness of the specifics of a case for a full understanding. This makes the opinions, values and beliefs of the armed forces vital in understanding detail and context.

6

WAR AND WAR CRIMES

Uncertainty came to dominate the spheres of war and war crimes in the early twenty-first century, and the fog and friction of warfare, described by Clausewitz, became more important than ever. The fog got denser and the friction had greater traction, despite—or even because of—the occasional moments of transparency and recorded glimpses from the heart of events. As warfare changed, its inherent ambiguities were magnified. The fog of war makes the principle of distinction in targeting decisions ever more difficult, amid the thick cloud of uncertainty enveloping contemporary armed conflict. Even the emergence of technical means, such as global satellite positioning and precision guided weapons, actually added to the murkiness. The armed forces using these tools gained unprecedented accuracy and, in some cases, the chance to strike accurately even where physical fog surrounded a target. Yet, public awareness of precision capabilities all too quickly translated into expectations that targets would always be clearly distinguished. Those greater expectations increased the opacity of war, while increased uncertainty and thicker fog meant that less could be distinct in the miasma of armed conflict. Greater certainty was expected, but military action was circumscribed by the ever more uncertain nature of war.

This chapter will focus on the uncertainty surrounding warfare and war crimes. The volume, as a whole, set out with the dual mission to consider how war and war crimes are mutually defining concepts, and how an understanding of this mutuality is important in the current context of change.

The preceding chapters have investigated this context through discussion of the multidimensional trinity, the *Trinity³(+)*, and the rapidly evolving changes around the prosecution of war crimes. This analysis has been informed by the perspectives of professionals, both on the strategic pressures that the emphasis on war crimes creates, and on the boundaries of wrong and right in the scope of contemporary warfare. The last chapter starts with the question of what constitutes war in an age dominated by 'terror'. It then considers, secondly, the uncertainty surrounding international criminal justice initiatives, as well as, thirdly, that generated by new trends that bring the web of civil justice into the realm of war. Following these three sections, the chapter continues by examining the power of wrongdoing—and conversely, that of 'rightdoing'—in contemporary warfare, arguing that legitimacy and success are determined by the perceived balance between wrong- and right-doing, in the age of the *Trinity³(+)*. Finally, the book concludes with an assessment of the inherent mutuality of war and war crimes.

Uncertainty and War in a Time of Terror

At the start of the twenty-first century, the certainties of the Cold War era had been replaced by uncertainty in a phase of historic change in warfare, leaving soldiers—especially those of the regular armed forces of the Western and advanced industrial world—in a confusing position. What war actually is had to be redefined in the twenty-first century to tackle effectively the threats, risks and challenges that marked international security. Debates surrounding the 'Global War on Terror' initiated by the US under President George W. Bush were often ideological, but they also reflected more material questions,[1] such as: was this really 'war'? When was a 'war' not a 'war'? Was it not simply a matter of dealing with 'terrorism', using the predominantly civilian and criminal law approaches that had served Western states well, in the past? And what happened to law and war in a time of terror? While many approached these questions from set positions, the debate was, at some level, evidence of change in the character of warfare—and, indeed, in that other form of politically calculated violence, terrorism. The problems that the US faced in coming to terms with the new context were also evidence of the change afoot, and showed that the environment was now dominated by uncertainty. This analysis will not pass moral judgement over whether or not one side was more 'right' than the other in these arguments.

Nor does it matter whether the US got some things wrong, in seeking to adjust to the new environment. Nor, again, does it matter here whether some of the errors made were also shaped in part by strains of ideology associated with the Bush Administration. Instead there are two key points to consider. First, the debates about and attempts to handle challenges were evidence of the change underway in the relationships between law, war and terrorism. These included the failure of President Barrack Obama's Administration to end practices, which, in opposition, it had attributed purely to 'wrong' Bush Administration ideology and vowed to end in office. Secondly, they revealed uncertainty about the very character of warfare.

Certainly, the international and territorially non-specific challenge of al-Qa'ida combined with the strategic manner in which it operated, using coordinated attacks, meant that conventional approaches to terrorism were inadequate and that the label 'war' was perhaps appropriate as more than just a metaphor for a major struggle. The initial approach to tackling al-Qa'ida's challenge also involved the commitment of traditional military means for operations in Afghanistan. However, the Global War on Terror generated many challenges and questions, both empirically, in terms of military conduct, and conceptually, provoking argument and debate.

Aspects of the law are central to this conceptual question. While both the era of internationalised and globalised international relations, on one hand, and the phase of networked non-state strategic environment, which it fosters, on the other, are governed by existing law, they point in some ways to the limits of that law and the need for additional measures. The realities of contemporary warfare are those of non-statehood: although states remain important actors, and individuals are increasingly held accountable both by states and by the international society of states for cases of misconduct in warfare, no state engages in twenty-first century warfare alone. While the possibility of residual twentieth-century state conflict remains—such as that between Ethiopia and Eritrea, for example—the wars of the twenty-first century are not likely to be purely those of one state against another. Even the most militarily powerful states, such as the United States, or China, must work with others in war—usually other states in coalition and partnership. However, working with others could also include alliances with non-state actors, such as non-governmental organisations, private companies, supra-state political communities, or sub-state political military groupings. John Donne's seventeenth-century description of human experience can be adapted for twenty-first century states: no state is an island. States, seeking to uphold their system and their privileges in it, as well as protecting their communities, cannot act alone for various reasons. Problems are transnational and require transnational perspectives. Resources are limited, so working with others is necessary. Legitimacy is difficult and, in contested times, tends to come from working in partnership with others.[2] Opponents could be a counter-grouping of states; or combinations of states and non-state actors in sometimes ambiguous relationships suggested by the realities of a networked world (for example, Serbia and the Bosnian Serbs; Iran, or Syria, and Hizbollah; or the Taliban in Afghanistan and al-Qa'ida); or sub-state or transnational groupings, with little or no state underpinning (while al-Qa'ida is the immediate example to spring to mind here, the realities of the twenty-first century world are those in which similar forms, mimicking the system that produces them, could develop, unnoticed, almost anywhere, at almost any point).[3]

The US-dominated conflict with al-Qa'ida, its effective offshoots and its allies, such as the Taliban, illustrated the potential need for a new calibration of law and war to meet the new circumstances. This process was inevitable, even if its precise form was not clear and, following the pattern shown earlier in Chapter 3, was likely to take decades, or centuries, to reach the point of being really settled. The issues of pre-emptive—and more controversially, preventive—self-defence,[4] and targeted killings and active self-defence,[5] which were prominent in the first decade of the twenty-first century, gained purchase, in this context, despite being contested.[6] However, the biggest example of the need for new law concerned the prisoners of 'non-war' held by the US at Guantanamo Bay, Cuba. While there was open public discussion about this, in terms of either existing international humanitarian law or domestic criminal jurisdiction, the heated debate surrounding these detainees is a marker of the lag between the changing character of warfare and the law to govern it, complicated further by assumptions derived from past handling of 'terrorism'. While many critics condemned these detentions for being in breach of the democratic and liberal principle of *habeas corpus* because prisoners were held for long periods without facing criminal charges, the reality was that the vast majority of those detained were not held as potential criminal suspects, but as soldiers of enemy armed forces—except, they were not formally described as soldiers.[7]

There were two reasons for this, both concerning status. The first was that traditional approaches to 'terrorist' action sought always to maintain the legality and legitimacy of the state confronted with a territorial claim by a group using political violence. One way to de-legitimate that group was to use domestic law to criminalise the group. Rather than combatants in legitimate struggle, they were to be treated as a criminal gang, engaged in conspiracies to commit murder and cause mayhem. The other side of the status question meant that the 'terrorists' were denied the privileges and protections afforded to lawful belligerents under international humanitarian law, specifically, Geneva Convention III. Traditionally, while groups such as the IRA (Irish Republican Army) sought to portray themselves as legitimate, they were never armed forces is the sense of being regulars, with recognisable symbols and open organisation, nor were they the troops of a state party to the Convention. In the early 1980s, IRA members interned by the UK under special provisions outside conventional criminal law, which appeared to give them quasi-prisoner of war status, sought to be treated as Prisoners of War (PoWs) under the Geneva Conventions. Among them was Bobby Sands, who became a highly symbolic figure, both through being elected from internment as a Member of the UK Parliament (never, of course, attending Parliament) and dying as a result of a hunger strike protest about the internees' status. While internment, in this context, raised issues, these were issues entirely within the domestic jurisdiction of the UK. The UK authorities also came to judge the internment policy as counter-productive, serving more to engender support for the IRA than prevent terrorist actions through the physical detention of those who might carry out such acts. This viewpoint informed criticism of the US approach in the 2000s.

There are contextual differences between Northern Ireland and the Global War on Terror though. First, one was purely a domestic issue, legally, where the other was a blend of international and transnational concerns and jurisdictions. Secondly, the IRA was a terrorist group focused on a limited political-territorial ambition against one state (the UK), whereas al-Qa'ida and its associates were acting in over sixty countries, against a range of local, transnational and international targets, through a transnational community of support across existing state boundaries, with the ultimate aim of destroying the prevailing state system. Thirdly, while the IRA used limited forms of political violence, they lacked the more developed, strategic character of al-Qa'ida, one of whose hallmarks was coordinated multiple attacks.[8]

Thus, conventional understandings of war and terrorism do not fit the global war focused around the transnational insurgency headed by al-Qa'ida, otherwise called 'international terrorism', that dominates the early twenty-first century. Following the watershed attack on the United States by al-Qa'ida on 11 September 2001, the terms 'war' and 'terror' became forever intrinsically linked in one category, which both marked and heralded change, as well as driving it. This reflected shifts in international politics, the nature of armed conflict and the scope and application of the rules of war. As the twenty-first century arrived, international politics, international law and strategy were all changing simultaneously, in rapid response to prevailing global conditions.

Law is central to gauging this change and to defining new boundaries. First, the law serves to mark war from non-war, as noted already. Secondly, the legal tensions surrounding various aspects of the Global War on Terror reflect change in the character of warfare. Those tensions emerge because new circumstances require new responses, meaning that the old legal frameworks are inadequate for the problems faced. This also means that some activities inevitably stretch, or extend beyond, established law. For example, the legal gap can be seen in the way that one of the main armed actors in the Global War on Terror, al-Qa'ida, is a type of armed force not covered by the Geneva Conventions. The latter cover armed conflict involving states party to the Treaties. To start with, al-Qa'ida is not a state, despite some quasi-state attributes and aspirations. As a non-state actor, it is not party to the Geneva Conventions. While as a non-state actor, laying claim to a transnational constituency, it could be argued that it is covered by the provisions under Common Article 3, those provisions, as stipulated in that article and generally interpreted, apply to non-state actors within a state, whether acting against the forces of the state, or in a mutual conflict of non-state actors irrespective of the state.[9] Those involved cannot necessarily be said to be subject to the law, in terms of their conduct, as they have not subscribed to that law, even if some elements of the law could be said to apply customarily.[10] Nor were the members of that transnational armed force necessarily protected persons under the law, which was framed to protect the members of regular armed forces, or civilians in the conduct of state actions.[11] This generates another set of problems, in terms of the Global War on Terror and its conduct, that can be captured by the label 'Guantanamo justice'—a shorthand form for US detention and interrogation policy, the prospect of war crimes trials, and the associated discourse.[12]

However, 'Guantanamo justice' was a misnomer, for the most part, as it was a label applied by critics who failed to grasp the changed circumstances. 'Justice' in the judicial sense was relevant only to the handful of captured persons whom the US authorities sought to bring to trial at Special Military Commissions (SMCs), including Sheik Khalid Mohammed, the self-confessed mastermind of the September 11 attacks—and the SMCs were even more questionable than the Guantanomo detention program itself.[13] For the hundreds of others, justice was not the reason for incarceration.[14] Rather, the majority could be said, arguably, to be equivalent to prisoners of war, yet without the formal status that would have meant protection under the Conventions.[15] The US struggled, in some ways, to invent a solution that met its needs and would fill the gap in the law, negotiating something of a grey area.[16] Among other legal contests, the US Supreme Court considered whether the US Constitution allowed the President to order indefinite detentions, although there was a differentiated approach to US citizens and non-nationals,[17] as well as recognition of the need for military and security precautions. US courts also considered the relevance of the Geneva Conventions, finding that minimal standards were applicable, forcing serious revisions of the plan to try a small number of detainees for alleged crimes.[18] In a Global War on Terror, which was a war in terrain beyond existing legal provision, as already noted, these were the equivalent of prisoners of war, but could not be labelled as such.[19] Therefore, their detention had more to do with the provisions available in wartime for the detention of those deemed to be enemy combatants, or civilians deemed to represent a security risk on territory under control by a party to the Conventions. However, there was no explicit category pertaining to the 'unlawful' in 'unlawful combatant'. This reflected the fact that al-Qa'ida forces and their affiliates (and others like them) were not belligerents in the sense of Geneva III, and so not 'protected persons' under that Convention. 'Unlawful' did not, therefore, mean 'criminal'; it meant 'unprotected', or 'not covered by the law'. In a sense, if these combatants were not protected as military personnel, under Geneva III, they would technically be civilians, according to the Geneva regime. As such, provisions for the detention of civilians as a security measure in Geneva IV might have been relevant, although they were never explicitly referenced. In any case, the key matter was the ambiguous position of al-Qa'ida combatants, perhaps covered by 'Common Article 3' of the Geneva Conventions, which is applicable in non-international as well as international armed conflicts.[20]

The simple division in the Geneva system between combatants and civilians is increasingly hard to sustain in many contemporary contexts. It presents problems not only in terms of detention, whether as prisoners of war, as quasi-prisoners of war, or as civilians constituting a security threat—none of which would completely satisfactorily cover members of al-Qa'ida, the Taliban, Hamas or any number of other groups. It also presents problems in terms of targeting questions and the core principle of international humanitarian law, that of distinction between lawful and unlawful targets, which translates broadly as discriminating between military and civilian targets. Bill Fenrick has expressed one version of this problem in discussing the need to develop the notion of direct (civilian) participation in hostilities: 'it conjures up visions of terrorists attacking civilians, or soldiers, and then claiming exemption from direct attack by an abuse of civilian status'.[21] The reality is that a civilian 'who belongs to a like minded group' and 'is ... for all practical purposes engaged in combatant style activities of a particularly reprehensible type, attacks directed exclusively at civilians or indiscriminate attacks',[22] is effectively a combatant. Yet, while potentially a lawful target, such a combatant's formal protection as a prisoner of war remains, at best, a murky issue.

Because they were detained as combatants and as a security measure, issues raised in highly critical reports by the non-governmental organisation Human Rights Watch were not wholly appropriate to the challenge being addressed (even if their attention to humanitarian questions of conscience was, as ever, in the right spirit).[23] One example was the two-year detention without charge of these combatants, a fallacy because there was no question of their ever being charged. However, it took the US courts to force judicial review of detainees, as the Geneva Conventions on the detention of civilians as a security measure, or as a prisoner, would require at least once a year. After initial difficulties and some mistakes at the original temporary detention facility, Camp X-ray (replaced by Camp Delta, once improved facilities had been constructed), it seemed that the detainees had relatively good, though basic, conditions—not that this was the widely shared perception of the Camp, which continued to be both a source of, and focus for, complaint. The International Committee of the Red Cross/Red Crescent (ICRC) had been permitted access to ensure good conditions. Such visits are normally conducted without public fanfare and with the responsible authorities quietly responding to any criticisms and adjusting arrangements accordingly.[24] Only if a significant problem emerges, such as failure to adjust arrangements in line with past ICRC visits, would there be a public statement (leaving the reasonable assumption to be made by observers that, if the ICRC had access and was saying nothing, conditions were reasonable). That the ICRC raised grave concerns about the detention of three children under the age of fifteen and an undisclosed number aged between thirteen and seventeen, including three in the age range thirteen to fifteen, is therefore indicative of major problems.[25] The reality was that new bearings in law were needed to match those in the character of armed conflict, whatever misgivings critics might have regarding the Bush Administration's approach.[26] Among those critics was Bush's successor, Obama, whose own sharp criticism of Guantanamo arrangements was tempered severely in office, when he found that the practical difficulties (as well as the political ones in Congress) of changing the arrangements confirmed that there was a need for change in the law.

Whatever the details of the ins and outs, and rights and wrongs, Washington's struggle to reconcile the strategic context and the law is important in illustrating issues for the focus of this book. Change in the strategic context ran ahead of change in the law. But, with the GWOT signalling the contemporary and future character of warfare, it also highlighted the need to bring the law into line. If there is a war, but the armed forces of one side are not covered by that law, or only weakly covered by it, then the law must be revised. If the armed forces of one side cannot be treated as prisoners of war, but are not to be treated as criminals, then acknowledging some legitimacy in their status and devising legal arrangements under which they become protected—other than as a type of civilian classified as an 'unlawful combatant' or 'illegal', or 'unprivileged belligerent'[27]—is a *sine qua non* of twenty-first century warfare. The conflict between al-Qa'ida and its affiliates and imitators, on one side, and Western states and those regarded by Osama bin Ladin and his supporters as 'apostate' in the Islamic realm, on the other, is a harbinger of future armed conflict. The participants in this and other armed conflicts will have similar characteristics. If war is the instrument with which to engage against these forces, the laws of war have to be applicable and appropriate. But, as the ICRC major study on customary international law noted, the 'wealth of treaty law does not regulate a large proportion of today's armed conflicts in sufficient detail'[28]—to which, it might be added, nor does the wealth of ever-developing customary law, or its interpretation. If there is a war, then prisoners of war must be a possibility. Until this possibility and other changes are legally effectuated, the pressures on those involved in armed action will be great, reflecting the dissonance between public expectations and the actual content of war crimes law.

Understandable, though not always justified, criticism focused on legal issues was at the heart of a process of re-conceptualisation and re-definition. In the context of change, as always the case, it was the interaction of legal and political issues that marked the boundary of 'war' and 'non-war'. It also marked the core of growing pressures on those engaged in the conduct of warfare, with allegations of unlawfulness made, as armed forces were deployed in novel circumstances that some deemed illegitimate, as well as charges of criminality over how those forces acted in those situations. The growing pains of change were marked by challenges regarding the law. These, in themselves, heralded the possible need for new approaches to law and strategy, embedded in each other, to meet the demands of the new wars in the new environment. The tension between, and within, law and war in this period of rapid change highlighted the significance of the boundary between wrong and right, legitimate action and war crimes, and war and non-war—confirming that it is this boundary, wherever it sits precisely, in any given temporal, or cultural, context, that separates war crimes from war.

Uncertainty and International Criminal Justice

International justice has come to be a prominent feature of the international scene since the end of the Cold War and will remain so. But, from high ambitions and aspirations, governed by certainties of legality and prosecution, as well as those of peace and justice theory, significant limitations have emerged on that which can be achieved. With that sense of limitation, uncertainty about the benefits, practice and purpose of international criminal law have come to the fore. Whereas Chapter 3 charted the rapid evolution in the sphere of prosecuting war crimes, in the late twentieth century and the start of the twenty-first, the present section is, in effect, a stocktaking exercise. Its purpose is to reflect on some of the implications of that rapid evolution, the types of international judicial body that have come into existence and the doubts, ambiguities and uncertainties that it has produced, as well as its achievements.

Some of the sharp dilemmas confronting those engaged with peace, justice and security were apparent in the different fates that met the two most wanted 'war criminals' in the spring of 2011. Both General Ratko Mladić and Osama bin Ladin (UBL) were found within a few weeks, the former after sixteen years on the run, the latter after almost a decade in hiding. Mladić was detained and transferred to face trial at the International Criminal Tribunal for the former Yugoslavia. UBL was killed as he was detected in Pakistan. The immediate killing of the al-Qa'ida leader—irrespective of the fact that there were only the most limited of circumstances in which he would have been taken alive—could be said to have given some sense of justice. Yet, there was undoubtedly unease about this course of action. The absence of a due process and fair trial made notions of justice questionable. Yet, there was also no doubt that a trial, however, fair, would have become a platform, one way or another, for bin Ladin, and a focal point for his followers.

The trials of Saddam Hussein and, especially, Slobodan Milošević were testimony to the ways in which attempts to render justice through fair trials could be manipulated politically by the accused. Mladić's detention, however, brought the prospect of another necessarily long trial, with the accused exploiting the emphasis on holding fair trials to delay and undermine that very process, only to end with an unsatisfactory outcome that would leave victims feeling that justice had not been done—as had been the case with Milošević's death before the end of his trial and Saddam's hanging in connection with his first trial (a small case, almost open and shut) before his second, for genocide, had finished the prosecution stage. As with the debates, in the 1940s, about summary execution of senior Nazis, or the holding of trials, and the subsequent doubts about sentences and the completeness of the trial, there was no guaranteed, easy or completely satisfactory approach (although the Mladić trial, at least, offered the theoretical chance of a trial in which prosecution discipline might lead to an efficient trial and an outcome that could be widely recognised and accepted as justice's being done).

When the Rome Statute of the International Criminal Court came into effect, in July 2002, it was the starting point for a new phase of international criminal justice. It was also the culmination of almost a decade of rapid development in this sphere. International co-operation at the end of the Cold War and the extensive reporting of mass atrocities in the Yugoslav wars at the start of the 1990s gave rise to the International Criminal Tribunal for the former Yugoslavia, as shown in Chapter 3, the first of a new wave of bodies associated with international justice. This was an *ad hoc* body, formed under the authority of the UN Security Council, with a status and a statute that overrode other elements of international and national law, formally. Another *ad hoc* body, with the same status as the ICTY, followed in response to the Rwandan genocide of 1994—the International Criminal

Tribunal for Rwanda. Subsequently, a range of bodies emerged: the Special Court for Sierra Leone (SCSL); the International Criminal Court (ICC); and the UN Special Tribunal for Lebanon (UNSTL). In addition, the Bosnian War Crimes Court (BWCC), the Iraqi Higher Criminal Court (often referred to as the Iraqi High Tribunal—IHT) and Extraordinary Chambers in the Courts of Cambodia (ECCC), were established as judicial bodies with responsibility for war crimes and international crimes, but under municipal jurisdiction with significant international involvement, while the UN Transitional Administration in East Timor set up a Serious Crimes Investigations Unit, with a view to holding trials under municipal jurisdiction. None of these bodies is the same as any other—each has its own statute and rules of procedure.

There are three broad types of court here—each marked by its own limitations, each contributing to uncertainty about the merits and direction of that which might be called the international justice 'project'. First, there are fully international judicial bodies. The ICTY and ICTR were established under Chapter VII of the UN Charter by the UN Security Council, formally giving those bodies binding authority in international law and a status overriding all other aspects of international law. As subsidiary bodies of the UN Security Council, they operate as part of the UN system. The ICC is also an international body, but in contrast to the Security Council mandate of the *ad hoc* bodies, it was established by treaty agreement among the signatory and ratifying states, having been negotiated in Rome in 1998. It has complementary jurisdiction with municipal courts and is only allowed to deal with matters if the state in question is party to the treaty, has proved itself unwilling or unable to deal with a matter, or either the state itself, or the UN Security Council, has referred business to it.

Secondly, so-called 'hybrid' courts have emerged. The SCSL, for example, was created as a joint enterprise between the UN and the authorities in Sierra Leone. In part, this was to address criticism that the Yugoslavia and Rwanda tribunals had been geographically distant (as well as, perhaps, philosophically and legally) from the communities in whose interests they were supposed to operate. Its statute combined elements of the law of Sierra Leone with elements of international humanitarian law. A similar approach was adopted for the UNSTL, with the difference that while the SCSL was embedded as a domestic venture with UN assistance, the Lebanon Tribunal was given 'an international character' and established under Chapter VII authority—although the criminal law to be applied was municipal.

Lastly, 'internationalised' courts have emerged. The IHT was initially intended as an international body—criminal investigations and work on a prospective international statute had begun a year ahead of the 2003 US-led military action against Iraq. However, a variety of factors led to the establishment of a municipal body with significant international input and support: the trend towards 'local ownership' of international justice; the deeply contested circumstances in which the operations against Iraq were conducted and the associated difficulties of gaining UN authority; and the insistence of the new Iraqi government on inclusion of the death penalty, which the EU could not support. The BWCC was created as a municipal court that would deal with the great number of lower-level war crimes cases that would not go to the ICTY, but with strong international support and assistance. The emergent ECCC has support from a dedicated international body—UN Assistance for the Khmer Rouge Trials.

Each type of body has both reflected and contributed to the limitations of international criminal justice. These various forms of international justice share a set of purposes, derived from understandings of the 'Nuremberg Legacy' with regard to Nazi war crimes during the Second World War and the prosecution of senior war crimes suspects by the International Military Tribunal at Nuremberg, following that war. However, in several respects, post-Cold War international courts have been a disappointment.

First, there is disenchantment in terms of the retributive justice mission to punish war criminals—and the primary purpose of war crimes prosecutions is held (by prosecutors, at least) to be the exercise of retributive justice upon the perpetrators of war crimes and Crimes Against Humanity. This is understood as an end in itself, as well as serving the interests of those in future conflict by providing a deterrent. However, the record here has been patchy—some major figures, such as Slobodan Milošević, ultimately escaped conviction because they died in custody (and he would have been acquitted, on many counts, had he lived), or, as in the case of General Ratko Mladić for many years, were not captured. Alongside the costs and difficulties of gaining custody in the first place, the outcome of most trials has left victims and observers dissatisfied.

Secondly, a key attribute of international criminal justice among proponents is the capacity to create an authoritative historical record, which will help to foster post-war reconciliation. One of the great achievements of Nuremberg was the creation of a largely indisputable history about Nazi mass murder and other crimes. This historical record is said to have made it impossible for Germans and others who might have doubted what had happened to argue against it. Yet the evidence and procedure in each instance has been contested politically, away from the courtroom, and even though significant evidence has emerged, neither this, nor the proceedings and outcomes, have been well communicated or understood. In Sierra Leone, where contact with the population is widely seen as the 'Jewel in the Crown' as Chief Prosecutor David Crane put it, emerging evidence shows disaffection with and little understanding of the SCSL, which is seen as expensive and out of touch.[29]

Thirdly, as suggested already, the rendering of justice is believed by many to offer a route to reconciliation, removing the grounds for grievance and revenge, and making further armed conflicts on the same lines less likely in the future. The principal basis for this, aside from opinion and theory, is the post-Second World War transformation of Germany into a democratic country in which the wrongs of the past were acknowledged and a determination to ensure that there should be no repetition was evident. Yet, the radically different circumstances of the 1990s and 2000s are stark—continuing political contest, rather than Germany's complete occupation and control, and liberal civilian criminal courts with due process, including extensive defendant's rights, rather than the military tribunals with questionable procedures and rules of evidence of 1945 (issues that reappeared in the context of Special Military Commissions at Guantanamo in recent years). In almost every case, an initially positive welcome has given way to disillusion among victims and observers, on all sides, who feel that justice has neither been done, nor seen to be done.[30]

Despite the failings and disappointments of the international justice era, all generating uncertainty, there have been notable achievements—themselves adding to uncertainty about the direction of international justice. The various post-Cold War international courts have had significant accomplishments. These include their very creation and the generation of a new field—international criminal law. They also include success, against all initial expectations, in bringing accused into custody and conducting prosecutions—the biggest of these operations, the ICTY, had dealt with (or was dealing with at this writing) 161 individuals it had indicted: many cases continued, the majority had been completed, though some were at the appeals stage, while a handful had been closed because the accused had died, or charges were dropped. Moreover, the ICC, which many assumed might never become involved in any cases, began a series of proceedings, including issuing indictments against Libyan dictator Muammar Qadaffi, his son Saif Islam Qadaffi, and the head of Qadaffi's intelligence and security service, Abdullah al-Sanussi (who, according to the ICC indictment personally commanded attacks against civilians). With the successful overthrow of Qadaffi by rebels backed by NATO in the course of 2011, it seemed very likely, for a while, that one of these, at least, would actually appear before an ICC trial chamber by the end of the year. That was bypassed, however, as Qadaffi senior was killed by his over-throwers and the new regime sought to hold trials itself, rather than allowing prosecution in The Hague, and claiming the Court's backing for this. However, the ICC continued to assert its jurisdiction and made no commitment of any sort.[31] This put the onus on the new authorities in Tripoli to prove that they could mount effective and fair investigations and prosecutions—a considerable challenge for a new regime, emerging from the shadow of authoritarian dictatorship. As consultations continued, it seemed likely that the judges at the ICC would insist on holding a jurisdictional hearing, at least, about whether Libya could deliver fair trials, perhaps with ICC and other international assistance, or not. If not, the cases of Qadaffi junior, who was imprisoned in Libya, and Sanussi, who was held in Mauritania, would go to The Hague. A Libyan trial would be a remarkable achievement, if it were to happen, especially if Saif Qadaffi were to appear there. This would bring the Court the attention, and perhaps status, that the first case it actually got to handle did not—the case of DRC (Democratic Republic of Congo) warlord Thomas Lubanga. Cooperation between the DRC government, which had referred cases to the ICC as part of its peace process, and the Court, resulted in Lubanga's first appearing in The Hague in January 2009 and being found guilty of recruiting child soldiers in March 2012.[32] In light of this, it is important to recognise that, despite the sobering sense that difficulties have outweighed success, international justice has important achievements and the imperatives for justice make further developments likely. Whatever their precise character, those developments will add to the clouds of uncertainty surrounding both international attempts to end impunity and the impact of these on contemporary warfare.

Uncertainty and Civil Justice

In addition to the uncertainty international criminal justice prompted about the conduct, nature and future of warfare, a relatively new phenomenon also characterised the first decade of the twenty-first century: the ever-increasing impact of civil justice. The rapid evolution in the sphere of international humanitarian law and the growth of its offshoot, international criminal law), charted in Chapter 3, was accompanied by swift developments in the field of human rights law. As Guglielmo Verdirame has commented, in a crucially important analysis, the conventional boundary between international humanitarian law and international human rights law was permeated in the first decade of the twenty-first century. The relationship between these two bodies of law 'was understood on the basis of the classic distinction between the law of war and the law of peace', he noted, but a series of cases after 1998 in various human rights courts established that 'human rights protection does not cease in wartime'. This meant a redefinition of the 'law of war to include under certain conditions and with some qualifications aspects of human rights protection'.[33] While those making the law of war were perhaps always motivated by the desire, encapsulated in the UN Charter, to rid the world of 'the scourge of war', as Verdirame notes, they were always grounded in reality and accepted 'war as a social phenomenon' that could 'at best, be contained' and 'its inherent inhumanity constrained'.[34] As noted throughout this book, it was the presence of rules, including those codified in the nineteenth and twentieth centuries, that defined war—and distinguished it from unlawful violence.

The focus of international humanitarian law as it developed was at the international level, seeking to regulate state actions in a phenomenon mostly occurring between states. In contrast, human rights law is 'an invention of political philosophy and constitutional law'[35] with absolute presumptions. Unlike the laws of war, human rights law has no doctrine of necessity and proportionality to be applied to evaluate cases. There is no principle of distinction. This cannot, in practice, mean the end of all war, or the somewhat absurd notion of completely applying human rights standards in times of war. As Verdirame notes, 'the law is mandatory, but full respect for it is an impossibility' and so, 'while human rights may not be extinguished by war, they can never be fully enjoyed during it'.[36] However, the 'coordination' of the two bodies of law,[37] in which the more developed, appropriate, or applicable of them will have precedence, significantly adds to the concerns and friction affecting those responsible for conducting warfare, when that is deemed to be necessary.

Thus, the claim of the defence counsel in a major UK case (Jocelyn Cockburn) that judicialisation was not 'the end of our ability to go to war' was flawed.[38] He was speaking with reference to one particular judgement, where he represented the family of a British serviceman who died in Iraq. The Court of Appeal in London made a landmark ruling that the British Human Rights Act (2000) protected UK soldiers, wherever they were serving. On 18 May 2009, the UK Ministry of Defence (MoD) lost its appeal against an April 2008 High Court judgement that the Human Rights Act (HRA—2000) applied to all serving personnel, regardless of location or role.[39] The original case had been brought by Mrs. Catherine Smith, whose son Private Jason Smith had been found dead from heatstroke in 2003, on the floor of his room at the King's Own Scottish Borders' base in Basra. The case was brought because Andrew Walker, the Oxfordshire Assistant Coroner, who sat for the inquest into Private Smith's case, found that the solider had died because of 'serious failure' on the Army's part to deal with the difficulties Smith had found in adjusting to temperatures in excess of 50°C—his body temperature was 41.1°C when it was discovered. A significant additional factor was the MoD's refusal to release relevant medical records to the inquest, which spurred Mrs. Smith's petition to the courts. The High Court ruled in her favour, judging that, under the HRA, military lives were protected wherever they were and that families had the right to more information than the MoD provided on deceased personnel. A new inquest would be held and the Court of Appeal judgement instructed the coroner to investigate the possibility of systematic failings by the army. The MoD accepted responsibility under the HRA because Private Smith had been on a British military base, but it appealed against the ruling that the Act applied away from British authority on the battlefield and elsewhere. The Appeals Court upheld the High Court decision, although it gave the Secretary of State for Defence the right to take the case to the House of Lords, providing that the MoD paid all the costs involved, irrespective of whether it won, or lost, the case.

Although no immediate decision was announced, the MoD had almost no alternative to taking the case to the Lords. The Secretary of State would have to take the case to the House of Lords because the Appeal Court's decision that Human Rights protections apply to soldiers anywhere has extraordinarily serious ramifications for the armed forces and the MoD. First, the ruling meant that a swathe of other cases could, and probably would, be brought, dating back to 2000 when the HRA came into force. Wherever the families of deceased believed that the military failed to safeguard the lives of their lost ones—the requirement under Article 2 of the

Act—and was deficient in ensuring that personnel had adequate equipment or medical treatment, or in providing information relating to the deaths, they had the right to sue the Secretary of State. This would embroil the MoD in numerous legal cases, each one of which would involve large legal bills, as well as tying up officials and lawyers in the ministry. Each could also finish with the MoD liable to make large compensation payments.

The Court of Appeal decision added to the problems besetting UK defence and security policy, particularly after Gordon Brown became Prime Minister. Jocelyn Cockburn's statement that the Smith judgement would not affect the UK's ability to go to war reflected a significant misunderstanding of the realities of military operations. These often only succeed because of the spirit and capacity of personnel to 'make do', despite inadequate resources, and to act swiftly and reflexively in difficult situations. Although officers might prefer to think that decisions would not be affected by what is, in effect, an extension of the law into momentary decision-making in the heat of operations, the reality is that some will hesitate, or not act in the most appropriate way for a particular situation, thus diminishing their capability. There could be no doubt that the Appeals Court ruling might have an impact on future operations.

A ruling of this kind and any confusion it spread within the armed forces could have a seriously damaging effect on morale, a key factor in military success, and a resource already badly affected by recent difficulties and poor performance, particularly arising from the campaign in Iraq.[40] It might also affect morale and cohesion in operations, where it opened up the possibility of soldiers invoking the HRA—irrespective of whether claims would be justifiable—and questioning orders at crucial moments. In the world of the *Trinity*[3](+), this was a potential problem in the context of coalition operations.[41] As one deeply experienced practitioner, former Chief of the Defence Staff and *inter alia* commander of forces in Kosovo, General Sir Michael Jackson reflected: 'I cannot imagine that this is what Parliament had in mind when it voted for the Human Rights Act [...] It's potentially very dangerous and could damage operational effectiveness because commanding officers will be concerned that they run the risk of being taken to court over decisions they have had to make'.[42] Developments of this kind only added to problems of morale among British defence professionals, which, in any case, had been in decline since the perceived insult of Prime Minister Brown's appointing Des Browne as both the Secretary of State for Defence and Secretary of State for Scotland, at the same time. Browne's successor,

John Hutton, although known to have a genuine interest, was able to do little to inspire confidence.

There was no reason to suppose that trends affecting the UK armed forces, one of the most robust forces in the world and among those most likely to be engaged in operations, would not affect the military in other countries—in Europe and beyond. The escalating problems of civil action are not unique to the United Kingdom, as the extension of human rights law into the field of warfare spreads through various courts.[43] The most developed set of cases and case law at the European Court of Human Rights relates to Russian military action, particularly in Chechnya.[44] The Iraq expedition that started in March 2003 was another focus for action concerning the application of international human rights law in different courts and countries.[45] The case of Nuhanović and Mustafić v. The Netherlands, noted in Chapter 1, was also part of this pattern of development—and had important implications for a parallel criminal case.[46] In the United States, while the language used was not necessarily 'international', government and military action was challenged through the courts in civil action cases, forcing the authorities to change their policies and practices, or to introduce legislation.[47] Moreover, whereas criminal law requires confirming action by an appropriate judicial body or criminal authority, the application of international human rights law, whether applied municipally or internationally, is a matter of civil action. Anyone who finds a lawyer believing that there is a case to be made can bring legal action. Various national—and whenever national options are exhausted—international courts (most noticeably the European Court of Human Rights) have keenly accepted cases where applying international human rights law in armed conflicts is in question. The parallel and enmeshed tracks of both criminal and human rights international law, while not quite making the use of armed forces impossible, made decisions to engage harder, and conduct of operations more difficult. As change occurred apace, the context for those decisions and actions was ever more uncertain, placing an increasing emphasis on getting things right—and not making mistakes.

Uncertainty and the Power of Wrongdoing

In many respects, conducting war became harder than ever, at least in the Western world, in the early twenty-first century. Although situations continued to arise that had to be addressed through military means, decisions to use force were severely complicated by the potential for accusations of wrongdoing to inhibit action, or spawn failure. The difficulties of using force were multiplied by examples of proven wrongdoing, The rapid pace of strategic, political and legal change—above all, legal change—at times seemed almost to make it impossible to use armed force.

Necessity and proportionality inform the laws of war, but how these principles work in modern warfare, as argued in this book, is far from straightforward. This is especially true when, as shown in the previous section, the laws of war and their traditional acknowledgement of the realities of war are complemented by the way that the domain of the laws of war has been permeated by human rights law—which has no realist grounding in principles of necessity and proportionality. The practitioners of war face unprecedented pressures in light of rapid changes in strategy and policy, communications, and, above all, of an increasing emphasis on ethics and legality. Wars waged in fluctuating environments make the legitimacy of armed force harder to establish than ever before, especially among diverse international and transnational publics. More than ever, strategy has come to embrace justice and law as crucial components of military success. However, legitimacy is fragile and easily contested, and today's militaries struggle to respond positively, consistently, and legally to an ever-shifting dynamic. Yet, legitimacy, framed around these issues, is the test of success.

Success, in the context of contemporary warfare, is not gauged in terms of decisive victory—and neither is defeat. Success and failure are not defined simply in terms of the traditional Clausewitzian triad of government, armed forces and people; although this conceptual framework is still relevant changing contexts have demanded its adaptation. Success is determined by strategic effect on, or within, what should be conceived as a multidimensional trinity cubed-plus—the *Trinity³(+)*.

The *Trinity³(+)* is the context for considering strategy and for considering war crimes. The honeycombed triangles and multiple three-dimensional diamond rhomboids provide a framework for both. The questions of wrong and right were once primarily, if not exclusively, the privilege of one triangular set of relationships—the political leadership, armed forces and political community of one actor in a war. In the world of the *Trinity³(+)*, this home front triad is multiplied not only by those of opponents, but also by myriad audiences around the globe: not only those of particular states and political communities, but also those of transnational communities, as well as cosmopolitan networks of commentators, human rights activists and lawyers. In a world where success and failure are determined by perceptions and judgements of wrong and right, the exponential expansion of the trinity refracts the conduct of military personnel and political leaders. The *Trinity³(+)* creates an environment where misdeeds, or even merely accusations of war crimes, can have multiple reverberations in multiple contexts, determining failure. The *Trinity³(+)* magnifies the power of wrongdoing.

Not only does the *Trinity³(+)* magnify the power of wrongdoing, but it also allows the rapid enlargement, as noted above, of the province of law. Not only is the effect of wrongdoing potentially multiplied, but so too are the possibilities of wrongdoing as the multidimensional webs of laws, values and communications work to complicate the world of war beyond anything in the past. They expose conduct and inspect it away from the fog of war, requiring careful consideration of the law and its different aspects within the realm of the *Trinity³(+)*. Wrongdoing is more likely to be noticed because of this closer attention and the greater volume of applicable law. Allegations of war crimes and confirmed cases are ever more likely, therefore, and the use of armed force will be ever more complicated. Although war will not, and cannot, be eliminated, its practice will be harder—perhaps contributing to the fulfilment of the dream underpinning the development of the laws of war: the elimination of war's worst excesses and, perhaps, a reduction in the frequency with which armed force is used. However, the reality is that the world of the multidimensional *Trinity³(+)* is one where the use of armed force will still be present, even necessary, while at the same time harder to get right and achieve success, as any engagement will be scrutinised for wrongdoing.

Though the spread of law through the multiple pathways of the *Trinity³(+)* has generated new demands on the military professionals, making success in their business harder, there are also clearly positive aspects to these developments. At the same time as complicating the use of force in many cases, one final innovation in the legal-strategic domain has been the instrumentalisation of the laws of war, and judicial authorisation, to spur often highly successful war crimes detentions. These can have a significant impact on the strategic environment, as was the case in Bosnia and Hercegovina, and Serbia, where they were the catalyst for peace processes and transition, removing obstacles to peace and inducing cooperation.[48]

The importance of law and justice can be seen in a few examples of this action, whether the approach was under UN authority in the former Yugoslavia, or the capture and trial of Saddam Hussein, the capture and trial of

Charles Taylor by the joint hybrid Special Court for Sierra Leone, or, perhaps, the pivotal case of Osama bin Ladin and his accomplices. Even if bin Ladin and many in his operation were killed in action, or subject to (questionable, in some regards) forms of summary justice, it was the language of war crimes and justice that dictated the campaigns to pursue them as individuals. This was evident from the outset with the CIA and the US Department of Justice dropping matchbooks offering first US$5 million and later US$25 million for information leading to bin Ladin's capture. It was also clear in President George W. Bush's famous—and provocative—use of old 'Wild West' posters' saying 'Wanted—Dead or Alive!' It was that language, and its contingent values, that meant that finding bin Ladin and dealing with him, in terms of rendering justice (even if the detail could be debated by specialists and the merits of different approaches contested) would reverberate as a success in the prism of the $Trinity^3(+)$.

In their own way, these operations, at the nexus of law and strategy, make vital contributions to legitimacy. They do so not only because they offer the possibility of judicial means contributing to the restoration, or maintenance, of peace and security through processes of catharsis and rendering justice. They also serve strategically as a means to affect opponents' behaviour—whether inducing surrender, as in the case of Kosovo, or paving the way to consolidated peace, as in Bosnia and Hercegovina.

Where does this leave us, then? Legitimacy is a function of the interaction of political, legal and strategic elements. All of these will be the focus for the discussion that surrounds events. Where the *jus ad bellum* is questioned, then conduct, the *jus in bello*, is going to be all the more fragile. This means that legitimacy, overall, is going to be more fragile. That is going to be the case, inevitably, in just about any military operation, or any military-political mission in the twenty-first century. There is unlikely to be any more of the old-fashioned, clear-cut, type of situation—at least, until a new era dawns.

Trust and legitimacy are vital qualities for any decision to use force and for the conduct of armed hostilities. This is not only true in terms of international socio-political legitimacy. It is acutely true in each domestic context, where a decision of that kind is taken and armed forces are committed. In terms of the Clausewitzian trinity of political leaders, armed forces and people, harmony among the three elements is an essential condition of success. But, that trinity is now a multidimensional phenomenon, making the whole globe relevant. The $Trinity^3(+)$ is the core of success.

However, a loss of confidence, trust and legitimacy in government (and other social institutions) makes the decision to use armed force and the subsequent application of force that much harder, impacting on the success of any operation. Where decisions are taken and action follows, public trust is necessary—both in the governments making the decisions and in the news media, which report, discuss and interpret them. Moreover, while suitable scrutiny by human rights organisations, international humanitarian lawyers and international prosecutors is always appropriate, in principle, this needs to be leavened by a developed sense of the fragility affecting the right-wrong boundary in the context of simultaneously changing strategy and law. The military's inherent need to be within the law and, where the law is less clear, ethically to be in the right, must be better understood.

War Crimes Define War

This volume has explored the relationship of war crimes to war at the start of the twenty-first century and has located the important place of law, in particular, and ethical restraint in the definition of war, in general. It has identified the increasing relevance of the strategy-law-politics nexus beyond the contemporary era. The exploration of the definition that law gives war aids analysis of the salience of legitimacy in determining success in the complex circumstances of twenty-first century military operations. On this basis, this concluding section identifies the essential place of law and the notion of war crimes in relation to strategy and war. This is a matter of defining change, continuity and success in twenty-first century warfare.

This analysis has defined and conceptualised war and war crimes in a changing environment; established the relationship between the two, including the necessary importance of law, or rules, as the unifying definitional element; and explored the content of each in relation to their shifting character in the twenty-first century. It has placed war crimes, conceptually, in the context of warfare. And it has developed the concept of the *Trinity³(+)* as the framework for understanding how war crimes issues affect the success of military operations in the contemporary world—the multidimensional version of Clausewitz's original triangulation of political leaders, agents of violence and political community. It has also explored both the conduct of military operations and the increasing relevance of justice and war crimes issues, while developing understanding of the importance of the nature and realities of warfare, in order to examine the character of potential war crimes. It has used empirical research with defence professionals to investigate the boundaries and content of certain potentially criminal actions, encouraging understanding of that which defence professionals regard as acceptable and unacceptable.

Drawing on that empirical research, both focus groups and interviews with seasoned military professionals, this volume has explored how militaries can work successfully within the politics-law-strategy nexus to foster legitimacy and success in war. That is, how they can manage the *Trinity*^{3}(+). This involved identifying the mutual relationship between war and war crimes, therein pinpointing the moment in which a war act becomes a war crime, especially within the murky mists of multidimensional combat. By attempting to reconcile different aspects of contemporary war and war crimes, and treating sometimes troubling and taboo issues, the book has provided both empirical material and a conceptual framework to help strategists, policymakers and also lawyers and others, as they work at the boundaries of war and war crimes and, in their own worlds, to tackle issues of success.

War crimes define war. Axiomatically, war defines war crimes. Neither exists without the other. At the heart of warfare lie rules. These distinguish war from other forms of violence. They separate that which is acceptable, within an otherwise blunt and brutal activity, from that which is not. War crimes have always defined war and continue to do so, but definitions have become increasingly uncertain.

War crimes give war a bad name, or, perhaps it would be better to say, a worse name than it has normally. While warfare is never to be desired, it is sometimes needed—as the brilliant account by Sir Michael Howard makes regretfully clear—and often when the momentum to reject it as an option has been strongest.[49] In this context, it is the armed forces who need war to remain as acceptable as possible, because giving war a bad name gives them a bad name too. It is they who need war crimes issues to be addressed. However, this should be based on balanced and realistic understanding of that which should really be seen as a war crime and that which should not.

Regarding this question, four crucial conclusions have emerged from this analysis. First, there are many aspects of warfare on which the attention of those seeking to make or enforce the law—and so define criminality—is not focused, or which they only come to consider at a relatively late stage. In this study, empirical research among an international group of practitioners revealed significant questioning of cluster munitions and support for stopping their use—some way ahead of the decision by 109 states (not including the US), in May 2008, to agree on a draft treaty on banning such weapons. The views of military personnel suggest very limited utility for cluster munitions and question their use in anything approaching a mixed situation, whether immediately involving civilians, civilian areas, or indirectly involving them in post-conflict situations. Outlawing the use of cluster munitions seems to be largely endorsed by practitioners—although some use, in both narrow and major combat situations, might still be regarded as appropriate. Irrespective of an emerging mix of norm and law against the use of cluster munitions, it seems reasonable to infer from professional values and perceptions that, while new law might be welcome for the clarity it brings, the use of these weapons quite probably fell foul of the traditional limitations of necessity and proportionality under the existing laws and customs of war in the contemporary era. As noted in Chapter 5, this raises doubts about the ICTY Prosecutor's cursory and unreflective consideration, and dismissal, of concerns about NATO's use of these devices over Kosovo and Serbia in 1999. The research in this volume has also highlighted how military personnel are aware of 'unnoticed' areas, such as naval and submarine warfare, where existing constraints may not apply, or where there are specific issues of concern.

Secondly, no issue of criminality relating to the conduct of military operations can, or should, be understood without reference to the specifics of the context in which an issue arose. The traditional principles of necessity and proportionality were developed in recognition of this. While certain actions will never be justified—murdering civilians, massacring prisoners, or using chemical weapons, for example—many other questions lie closer to the boundary between war and war crime. These must be judged in terms of detail, decisions and records pertinent to the situation—and the degree to which relevant rules, or moral and ethical standards, were at stake. Necessity and proportionality should be the guide to reconciling these different elements. Even where civil action and human rights law are involved, it is likely that judgements will have to be informed by some version of this traditional approach found in the laws of war.

Thirdly, in exploring particular situations and questions of necessity and proportionality, it was clear that the judgement of military professionals should be salient. The views of professional peers on the judgement exercised should be a determinant in criminal cases, including defining the level at which criminal accountability should be exercised, if necessary. In a world where, for the first time, soldiers have been tried ostensibly for doing their job, and others come under pressure, as they conduct apparently normal operations, the judgement of military command personnel is vital—albeit appropriately related to values in society at large. No issue of criminality relating to the conduct of military operations can, or should, be understood without reference to the specifics of the context in which an event occurred. The judgement of military professionals at relevant levels of decision-making is the appropriate way to determine the point at which issues of criminality should be assessed. Understanding how soldiers view difficult cases is imperative.

Finally, lawfulness is essential to the military. It is also vital to strategy and the conduct of operations. It is in the interest of the armed forces to ensure that war crimes allegations are dealt with, and seen to be dealt with, both internally and externally, for the sake of professional ethos and also to ensure wider legitimacy and public support for the armed forces, generally, and for the particular operations they undertake. Clearly defined laws of war are in the interest of military personnel. But the views of military personnel are largely ignored in the understanding of war crimes. This study has made an initial step towards addressing this by considering the empirical evidence of how war crimes issues affect the armed forces and strategy, as well as how soldiers view both the ways in which war crimes issues should be understood, and how they regard particular issues and cases. Strategy inherently embraces issues of justice and law; the armed forces recognise the increasing importance of this more than anyone.

There is therefore an imperative for those engaged at the legal-political interface of research on international peace and security to understand the pressures on government and military practitioners as they confront decisions on launching and conducting military operations. This is a necessary complement to understanding aspects of the law and the ethics of warfare, as well as the concerns of legal and human rights practitioners. However, there is also an imperative for those in government and the armed forces to be conscious of the relevant law, and the problems of not erring on the side of doubt and not exercising due caution, where there may be legal lacunae—something that military personnel participating in research for this book made clear. The power of wrongdoing must be recognised—and so, too of 'right-doing'—in defining outcomes in contemporary warfare. The values of 'wrongdoing' and 'right-doing' are intrinsic to any sense of justness in warfare, and also to any developed notion of war. 'Right' and 'wrong', whether understood ethically, socially, or legally, are essential to the mutually reinforcing definitions of war and war crimes. They mark the boundary between the two—a boundary that, combined with politics, distinguishes war from any other form of collective violence.

ANNEXES

SELECTED EXTRACTS FROM
INTERNATIONAL CRIMINAL STATUTES

ANNEX A

STATUTE OF THE INTERNATIONAL CRIMINAL TRIBUNAL FOR THE FORMER YUGOSLAVIA (EXTRACT)

Article 2

Grave Breaches of the Geneva Conventions of 1949

The International Tribunal shall have the power to prosecute persons committing or ordering to be committed grave breaches of the Geneva Conventions of 12 August 1949, namely the following acts against persons or property protected under the provisions of the relevant Geneva Convention:

(a) Wilful killing;
(b) Torture or inhuman treatment, including biological experiments;
(c) Wilfully causing great suffering or serious injury to body or health;
(d) Extensive destruction and appropriation of property, not justified by military necessity and carried out unlawfully and wantonly;
(e) Compelling a prisoner of war or a civilian to serve in the forces of a hostile power;
(f) Wilfully depriving a prisoner of war or a civilian of the rights of fair and regular trial;
(g) Unlawful deportation or transfer or unlawful confinement of a civilian;
(h) Taking civilians as hostages.

Article 3

Violations of the Laws or Customs of War

The International Tribunal shall have the power to prosecute persons violating the laws or customs of war. Such violations shall include, but not be limited to:

(a) Employment of poisonous weapons or other weapons calculated to cause unnecessary suffering;

(b) Wanton destruction of cities, towns or villages, or devastation not justified by military necessity;

(c) Attack, or bombardment, by whatever means, of undefended towns, villages, dwellings, or buildings;

(d) Seizure of, destruction or wilful damage done to institutions dedicated to religion, charity and education, the arts and sciences, historic monuments and works of art and science;

(e) Plunder of public or private property.

Article 4

Genocide

1. The International Tribunal shall have the power to prosecute persons committing genocide as defined in paragraph 2 of this article or of committing any of the other acts enumerated in paragraph 3 of this article.

2. Genocide means any of the following acts committed with intent to destroy, in whole or in part, a national, ethnical, racial or religious group, as such:

(a) Killing members of the group;

(b) Causing serious bodily or mental harm to members of the group;

(c) Deliberately inflicting on the group conditions of life calculated to bring about its physical destruction in whole or in part;

(d) Imposing measures intended to prevent births within the group;

(e) Forcibly transferring children of the group to another group.

3. The following acts shall be punishable:

(a) Genocide;

(b) Conspiracy to commit genocide;

(c) Direct and public incitement to commit genocide;

(d) Attempt to commit genocide;

(e) Complicity in genocide.

Article 5

Crimes against Humanity

The International Tribunal shall have the power to prosecute persons responsible for the following crimes when committed in armed conflict, whether international or internal in character, and directed against any civilian population:

(a) Murder;

(b) Extermination;

(c) Enslavement;

(d) Deportation;

(e) Imprisonment;

(f) Torture;

(g) Rape;

(h) Persecutions on political, racial and religious grounds;

(i) Other inhumane acts.

ANNEX B

STATUTE OF THE INTERNATIONAL CRIMINAL TRIBUNAL FOR RWANDA

Article 2

Genocide

1. The International Tribunal for Rwanda shall have the power to prosecute persons committing genocide as defined in paragraph 2 of this Article or of committing any of the other acts enumerated in paragraph 3 of this Article.
2. Genocide means any of the following acts committed with intent to destroy, in whole or in part, a national, ethnical, racial or religious group, as such:

(a) Killing members of the group;
(b) Causing serious bodily or mental harm to members of the group;
(c) Deliberately inflicting on the group conditions of life calculated to bring about its physical destruction in whole or in part;
(d) Imposing measures intended to prevent births within the group;
(e) Forcibly transferring children of the group to another group.

3. The following acts shall be punishable:

(a) Genocide;
(b) Conspiracy to commit genocide;
(c) Direct and public incitement to commit genocide;

(d) Attempt to commit genocide;

(e) Complicity in genocide.

Article 3

Crimes against Humanity

The International Tribunal for Rwanda shall have the power to prosecute persons responsible for the following crimes when committed as part of a widespread or systematic attack against any civilian population on national, political, ethnic, racial or religious grounds:

(a) Murder;

(b) Extermination;

(c) Enslavement;

(d) Deportation;

(e) Imprisonment;

(f) Torture;

(g) Rape;

(h) Persecutions on political, racial and religious grounds;

(i) Other inhumane acts.

Article 4

Violations of Article 3 Common to the Geneva Conventions and of Additional Protocol II

The International Tribunal for Rwanda shall have the power to prosecute persons committing or ordering to be committed serious violations of Article 3 common to the Geneva Conventions of 12 August 1949 for the Protection of War Victims, and of Additional Protocol II thereto of 8 June 1977. These violations shall include, but shall not be limited to:

(a) Violence to life, health and physical or mental well-being of persons, in particular murder as well as cruel treatment such as torture, mutilation or any form of corporal punishment;

(b) Collective punishments;

(c) Taking of hostages;

(d) Acts of terrorism;

(e) Outrages upon personal dignity, in particular humiliating and degrading treatment, rape, enforced prostitution and any form of indecent assault;

(f) Pillage;

(g) The passing of sentences and the carrying out of executions without previous judgement pronounced by a regularly constituted court, affording all the judicial guarantees which are recognised as indispensable by civilised peoples;

(h) Threats to commit any of the foregoing acts.

ANNEX C

ROME STATUTE OF THE INTERNATIONAL CRIMINAL COURT

Article 5

Crimes within the Jurisdiction of the Court

1. The jurisdiction of the Court shall be limited to the most serious crimes of concern to the international community as a whole. The Court has jurisdiction in accordance with this Statute with respect to the following crimes:

(a) The crime of genocide;
(b) Crimes against humanity;
(c) War crimes;
(d) The crime of aggression.

2. The Court shall exercise jurisdiction over the crime of aggression once a provision is adopted in accordance with articles 121 and 123 defining the crime and setting out the conditions under which the Court shall exercise jurisdiction with respect to this crime. Such a provision shall be consistent with the relevant provisions of the Charter of the United Nations.

Article 6

Genocide

For the purpose of this Statute, 'genocide' means any of the following acts committed with intent to destroy, in whole or in part, a national, ethnical, racial or religious group, as such:

(a) Killing members of the group;
(b) Causing serious bodily or mental harm to members of the group;
(c) Deliberately inflicting on the group conditions of life calculated to bring about its physical destruction in whole or in part;
(d) Imposing measures intended to prevent births within the group;
(e) Forcibly transferring children of the group to another group.

Article 7

Crimes against Humanity

1. For the purpose of this Statute, 'crime against humanity' means any of the following acts when committed as part of a widespread or systematic attack directed against any civilian population, with knowledge of the attack:

(a) Murder;
(b) Extermination;
(c) Enslavement;
(d) Deportation or forcible transfer of population;
(e) Imprisonment or other severe deprivation of physical liberty in violation of fundamental rules of international law;
(f) Torture;
(g) Rape, sexual slavery, enforced prostitution, forced pregnancy, enforced sterilisation, or any other form of sexual violence of comparable gravity;
(h) Persecution against any identifiable group or collectivity on political, racial, national, ethnic, cultural, religious, gender as defined in paragraph 3, or other grounds that are universally recognised as impermissible under international law, in connection with any act referred to in this paragraph or any crime within the jurisdiction of the Court;
(i) Enforced disappearance of persons;

(j) The crime of apartheid;

(k) Other inhumane acts of a similar character intentionally causing great suffering, or serious injury to body or to mental or physical health.

2. For the purpose of paragraph 1:

(a) 'Attack directed against any civilian population' means a course of conduct involving the multiple commission of acts referred to in paragraph 1 against any civilian population, pursuant to or in furtherance of a State or organisational policy to commit such attack;

(b) 'Extermination' includes the intentional infliction of conditions of life, inter alia the deprivation of access to food and medicine, calculated to bring about the destruction of part of a population;

(c) 'Enslavement' means the exercise of any or all of the powers attaching to the right of ownership over a person and includes the exercise of such power in the course of trafficking in persons, in particular women and children;

(d) 'Deportation or forcible transfer of population' means forced displacement of the persons concerned by expulsion or other coercive acts from the area in which they are lawfully present, without grounds permitted under international law;

(e) 'Torture' means the intentional infliction of severe pain or suffering, whether physical or mental, upon a person in the custody or under the control of the accused; except that torture shall not include pain or suffering arising only from, inherent in or incidental to, lawful sanctions;

(f) 'Forced pregnancy' means the unlawful confinement of a woman forcibly made pregnant, with the intent of affecting the ethnic composition of any population or carrying out other grave violations of international law. This definition shall not in any way be interpreted as affecting national laws relating to pregnancy;

(g) 'Persecution' means the intentional and severe deprivation of fundamental rights contrary to international law by reason of the identity of the group or collectivity;

(h) 'The crime of apartheid' means inhumane acts of a character similar to those referred to in paragraph 1, committed in the context of an institutionalised regime of systematic oppression and domination by one racial group over any other racial group or groups and committed with the intention of maintaining that regime;

(i) 'Enforced disappearance of persons' means the arrest, detention or abduction of persons by, or with the authorisation, support or acquiescence of, a State or a political organisation, followed by a refusal to acknowledge that deprivation of freedom or to give information on the fate or whereabouts of those persons, with the intention of removing them from the protection of the law for a prolonged period of time.

3. For the purpose of this Statute, it is understood that the term 'gender' refers to the two sexes, male and female, within the context of society. The term 'gender' does not indicate any meaning different from the above.

Article 8

War Crimes

1. The Court shall have jurisdiction in respect of war crimes in particular when committed as part of a plan or policy or as part of a large-scale commission of such crimes.

2. For the purpose of this Statute, 'war crimes' means:

(a) Grave breaches of the Geneva Conventions of 12 August 1949, namely, any of the following acts against persons or property protected under the provisions of the relevant Geneva Convention:

(i) Wilful killing;

(ii) Torture or inhuman treatment, including biological experiments;

(iii) Wilfully causing great suffering, or serious injury to body or health;

(iv) Extensive destruction and appropriation of property, not justified by military necessity and carried out unlawfully and wantonly;

(v) Compelling a prisoner of war or other protected person to serve in the forces of a hostile Power;

(vi) Wilfully depriving a prisoner of war or other protected person of the rights of fair and regular trial;

(vii) Unlawful deportation or transfer or unlawful confinement;

(viii) Taking of hostages.

(b) Other serious violations of the laws and customs applicable in international armed conflict, within the established framework of international law, namely, any of the following acts:

(i) Intentionally directing attacks against the civilian population as such or against individual civilians not taking direct part in hostilities;

(ii)   Intentionally directing attacks against civilian objects, that is, objects which are not military objectives;

(iii) Intentionally directing attacks against personnel, installations, material, units or vehicles involved in a humanitarian assistance or peace-keeping mission in accordance with the Charter of the United Nations, as long as they are entitled to the protection given to civilians or civilian objects under the international law of armed conflict;

(iv)   Intentionally launching an attack in the knowledge that such attack will cause incidental loss of life or injury to civilians or damage to civilian objects or widespread, long-term and severe damage to the natural environment which would be clearly excessive in relation to the concrete and direct overall military advantage anticipated;

(v)   Attacking or bombarding, by whatever means, towns, villages, dwellings or buildings which are undefended and which are not military objectives;

(vi)   Killing or wounding a combatant who, having laid down his arms or having no longer means of defence, has surrendered at discretion;

(vii) Making improper use of a flag of truce, of the flag or of the military insignia and uniform of the enemy or of the United Nations, as well as of the distinctive emblems of the Geneva Conventions, resulting in death or serious personal injury;

(viii) The transfer, directly or indirectly, by the Occupying Power of parts of its own civilian population into the territory it occupies, or the deportation or transfer of all or parts of the population of the occupied territory within or outside this territory;

(ix)   Intentionally directing attacks against buildings dedicated to religion, education, art, science or charitable purposes, historic monuments, hospitals and places where the sick and wounded are collected, provided they are not military objectives;

(x)   Subjecting persons who are in the power of an adverse party to physical mutilation or to medical or scientific experiments of any kind which are neither justified by the medical, dental or hospital treatment of the person concerned nor carried out in his or her interest, and which cause death to or seriously endanger the health of such person or persons;

(xi)   Killing or wounding treacherously individuals belonging to the hostile nation or army;

(xii)   Declaring that no quarter will be given;

(b)   Other serious violations of the laws and customs applicable in international armed conflict, within the established framework of international law, namely, any of the following acts:

(xiii) Destroying or seizing the enemy's property unless such destruction or seizure be imperatively demanded by the necessities of war;

(xiv)   Declaring abolished, suspended or inadmissible in a court of law the rights and actions of the nationals of the hostile party;

(xv)   Compelling the nationals of the hostile party to take part in the operations of war directed against their own country, even if they were in the belligerent's service before the commencement of the war;

(xvi)   Pillaging a town or place, even when taken by assault;

(xvii) Employing poison or poisoned weapons;

(xviii) Employing asphyxiating, poisonous or other gases, and all analogous liquids, materials or devices;

(xix)   Employing bullets which expand or flatten easily in the human body, such as bullets with a hard envelope which does not entirely cover the core or is pierced with incisions;

(xx)   Employing weapons, projectiles and material and methods of warfare which are of a nature to cause superfluous injury or unnecessary suffering or which are inherently indiscriminate in violation of the international law of armed conflict, provided that such weapons, projectiles and material and methods of warfare are the subject of a comprehensive prohibition and are included in an annex to this Statute, by an amendment in accordance with the relevant provisions set forth in articles 121 and 123;

(xxi)   Committing outrages upon personal dignity, in particular humiliating and degrading treatment;

(xxii) Committing rape, sexual slavery, enforced prostitution, forced pregnancy, as defined in article 7, paragraph 2 (f), enforced sterilisation, or any other form of sexual violence also constituting a grave breach of the Geneva Conventions;

(xxiii) Utilising the presence of a civilian or other protected person to render certain points, areas or military forces immune from military operations;

(xxiv) Intentionally directing attacks against buildings, material, medical units and transport, and personnel using the distinctive emblems of the Geneva Conventions in conformity with international law;

(xxv) Intentionally using starvation of civilians as a method of warfare by depriving them of objects indispensable to their survival, including wilfully impeding relief supplies as provided for under the Geneva Conventions;

(xxvi) Conscripting or enlisting children under the age of fifteen years into the national armed forces or using them to participate actively in hostilities.

(c) In the case of an armed conflict not of an international character, serious violations of article 3 common to the four Geneva Conventions of 12 August 1949, namely, any of the following acts committed against persons taking no active part in the hostilities, including members of armed forces who have laid down their arms and those placed hors de combat by sickness, wounds, detention or any other cause:

(i) Violence to life and person, in particular murder of all kinds, mutilation, cruel treatment and torture;

(ii) Committing outrages upon personal dignity, in particular humiliating and degrading treatment;

(iii) Taking of hostages;

(iv) The passing of sentences and the carrying out of executions without previous judgement pronounced by a regularly constituted court, affording all judicial guarantees which are generally recognised as indispensable.

(d) Paragraph 2 (c) applies to armed conflicts not of an international character and thus does not apply to situations of internal disturbances and tensions, such as riots, isolated and sporadic acts of violence or other acts of a similar nature.

(e) Other serious violations of the laws and customs applicable in armed conflicts not of an international character, within the established framework of international law, namely, any of the following acts:

(i) Intentionally directing attacks against the civilian population as such or against individual civilians not taking direct part in hostilities; Rome Statute of the International Criminal Court 14;

(ii) Intentionally directing attacks against buildings, material, medical units and transport, and personnel using the distinctive emblems of the Geneva Conventions in conformity with international law;

(iii) Intentionally directing attacks against personnel, installations, material, units or vehicles involved in a humanitarian assistance or peacekeeping mission in accordance with the Charter of the United Nations, as long as they are entitled to the protection given to civilians or civilian objects under the international law of armed conflict;

(iv) Intentionally directing attacks against buildings dedicated to religion, education, art, science or charitable purposes, historic monuments, hospitals and places where the sick and wounded are collected, provided they are not military objectives;

(v) Pillaging a town or place, even when taken by assault;

(vi) Committing rape, sexual slavery, enforced prostitution, forced pregnancy, as defined in article 7, paragraph 2 (f), enforced sterilisation, and any other form of sexual violence also constituting a serious violation of article 3 common to the four Geneva Conventions;

(vii) Conscripting or enlisting children under the age of fifteen years into armed forces or groups or using them to participate actively in hostilities;

(viii) Ordering the displacement of the civilian population for reasons related to the conflict, unless the security of the civilians involved or imperative military reasons so demand;

(ix) Killing or wounding treacherously a combatant adversary;

(x) Declaring that no quarter will be given;

(xi) Subjecting persons who are in the power of another party to the conflict to physical mutilation or to medical or scientific experiments of any kind which are neither justified by the medical, dental or hospital treatment of the person concerned nor carried out in his or her interest, and which cause death to or seriously endanger the health of such person or persons;

(xii) Destroying or seizing the property of an adversary unless such destruction or seizure be imperatively demanded by the necessities of the conflict;

(f) Paragraph 2 (e) applies to armed conflicts not of an international character and thus does not apply to situations of internal disturbances and tensions, such as riots, isolated and sporadic acts of violence or other acts of a similar nature. It applies to armed conflicts that take place in the territory of a State when there is protracted armed conflict between governmental authorities and organised armed groups or between such groups.

3. Nothing in paragraph 2 (c) and (e) shall affect the responsibility of a Government to maintain or re-establish law and order in the State or to defend the unity and territorial integrity of the State, by all legitimate means.

NOTES

1. STRATEGY, WAR AND LAW

1. *The Guardian*, 21 January 2004.
2. See, for example, Karen J. Greenberg, Joshua L. Dratel and Anthony Lewis, eds, *The Torture Papers: The Road to Abu Ghraib*, New York: Cambridge University Press, 2005; Philippe Sands, *Law Less World: America and the Making and Breaking of Global Rules*, London: Penguin, 2005; and Sands, *The Torture Team: Deception, Cruelty and the Compromise of Law*, London: Penguin, 2008.
3. The classic modern discussion of 'Just War' theory is Michael Walzer, *Just and Unjust Wars: A Moral Argument with Historical Illustrations*, Harmondsworth: Penguin, 1978. This was written in response to the United States' Vietnam War in the 1960s and 1970s (see also his later *Arguing About War*, New Haven and London: Yale Nota Bene, 2005). Walzer drew on the Western tradition founded in the Christian Roman Catholic thinking of St. Augustine and later expanded by Thomas Aquinas, which developed an ethical framework that has continuing relevance for evaluations to the two major axes of wrong and right in warfare—whether the reason for going to war is just (the *jus ad bellum*) and whether the way in which warfare is conducted is just (the *jus in bello*): just cause and just conduct. For a brief survey of Just War thinking in the tradition of St. Augustine through history written by two of Britain's preeminent practitioners (one was Chief of the Defence Staff; the other was Permanent Under Secretary at the Ministry of Defence and one of the most elegant of thinkers and writers) in the late twentieth century, see Charles Guthrie and Michael Quinlan, *Just War: The Just War Tradition: Ethics in Modern Warfare*, London: Bloomsbury, 2007. See also Alex J. Bellamy, *Just Wars: From Cicero to Iraq*, Cambridge: Polity, 2006; David Fisher, *Morality and War: Can War Ever Be Just in the Twenty-first Century?*, Oxford: Oxford University Press, 2011.

4. Various 'revolutions' in military affairs have been noted in the history of warfare. For a brief survey, for example, see Williamson Murray, 'Thinking About Revolutions in Military Affairs', *Joint Forces Quarterly*, Summer, 1997; for a fuller investigation in relation to strategy, see Colin S. Gray, *Strategy for Chaos: Revolutions in Military Affairs and the Evidence of History*, with a forward by Williamson Murray, London: Frank Cass and Co., 2002. The Oxford University program *The Changing Character of War* was established in relation to the latest bout of change; but by involving prominent historians and through the direction of Huw Strachan (one of the most eminent historians of warfare) the program also captured the sweep of change comparatively throughout history. See http://ccw.modhist.ox.ac.uk/ (accessed 10 March 2011).

5. The changing character of warfare is discussed more extensively later in this chapter, and in the context of its implications for strategy in Chapter 2.

6. James Gow, *The Serbian Project: A Strategy of War Crimes*, London: Hurst and Co., 2003.

7. Gerard Prunier, *The Rwanda Crisis: History of a Genocide*, London: Hurst and Co. 1995; Alain Destexhe, *Rwanda and Genocide in the Twentieth Century*, London: Pluto Press, 1995; Linda Melvern, *A People Betrayed: The Role of the West in Rwanda's Genocide*, London: Zed Books, 2000; Human Rights Watch, *Leave None to Tell the Story: Genocide in Rwanda*, New York; Human Rights Watch, 1999; Jessica Lincoln, *Transitional Justice, Peace and Accountability Outreach and the Role of International Courts After Conflict*, London: Routledge, 2011.

8. See Mary Kaldor, *New and Old Wars*, Cambridge: Polity, 1999; and Martin Shaw, *The New Western Way of War*, Cambridge: Polity, 2005.

9. Human Rights Watch, *Civilian Deaths in the NATO Air Campaign*, 12, 1(D), February 2000; Human Rights Watch; *Ticking Time Bombs: NATO's Use of Cluster Munitions in Yugoslavia*, 11, 6(D), June 1999.

10. Amnesty International, *NATO/Federal Republic of Yugoslavia 'Collateral Damage' or Unlawful Killings? Violations of the Laws of War by NATO during Operation Allied Force*, EUR 70/018/2000, 6 June 2000.

11. These cases are discussed later.

12. Radio Netherlands Worldwide, 5 July 2011; BBC News, 5 July 2011.

13. Elspeth Guild, 'The Judicialisation of Armed Conflict: Transforming the Twenty-First Century', in Jef Huysmans, Andrew Dobson and Raia Prokhovnik, *The Politics of Protection: Sites of Insecurity and Political Agency*, London: Routledge, 2006, pp. 122–35.

14. Gerry Simpson, *War, Law and Crimes: War Crimes Trials and the Reinvention of International Law*, Cambridge: Polity, 2007.

15. Milena Michalski and James Gow, *War, Image and Legitimacy: Viewing Contemporary Conflict*, London: Routledge, 2007, Chapter 6.

16. William Shakespeare, *King Henry V*, ed. J. H. Walter, *The Arden Edition of the Works of William Shakespeare*, London: Methuen, 1954, Act IV, Scs. *vi–vii*.

17. Michalski and Gow, *War, Image and Legitimacy*; Andrew Hoskins and Ben O'Loughlin, *War and Media: the Emergence of Diffused War*, Cambridge: Polity, 2010; Donald Matheson and Stuart Allan, *Digital War Reporting*, Cambridge: Polity, 2009.

18. This footage of the Serbian Scorpions and that involved in the UK case of Baha Mousa, discussed below, are examples investigated in research during 2010 and 2011 for the 'Pictures of Peace and Justice' project. The Milošević trial was never completed because the accused died of natural causes (albeit connected, in all probability, with not taking medication as prescribed) in prison around two months before his self-run defence case was scheduled to complete.

19. Transcript, *Prosecutor v. Slobodan Milosevic* ICTY, 40277–81, June 2005, p. 40218, available at http://www.icty.org/x/cases/slobodan_milosevic/trans/en/050601IT.htm (accessed 14 March 2011).

20. Judith Armatta, *Twilight of Impunity: the War Crimes Trial of Slobodan Milošević*, Durham: Duke University Press, 2010, p. 424.

21. See Ivan Zveržhanovski, 'Watching War Crimes: The Srebrenica Video and the Serbian Attitudes to the 1995 Srebrenica Massacre', *Southeast European and Black Sea Studies*, Vol. 7, No. 3, September 2007.

22. *International Criminal Court Act 2001*, Explanatory Note 6, available at http://www.legislation.gov.uk/ukpga/2001/17/notes/division/2 (accessed 22 March 2011).

23. See Rachel Kerr, *The Military on Trial: The British Army in Iraq*, Nijmegen: Wolf Legal Publishers, 2008.

24. Opening statement, Mr. Julian Bevan for the prosecution, *R v. Payne and others*, 19 September 2007, pp. 91–2. Another of the Iraqi victims suffered renal failure as a result of injuries to his kidneys while in the care of 1st QLR.

25. Four of these were acquitted at the same time that the judgement on Payne was reached; the other two were acquitted a month later. See James Gow and Rachel Kerr, 'Law and War in the Global War on Terror' in Aidan Hehir, Natasha Kuhrt and Andrew Mumford, eds, *International Law, Security and Ethics: Policy Challenges in the post-9/11 World*, London: Routledge, 2011.

26. The Baha Mousa Public Inquiry, Day 103, 10 June 2010, Afternoon Session.

27. In light of the trial's outcome, a formal independent inquiry was established. In the context of the inquiry, the film evidence was shown in public for the first time on the day that former Secretary of State for Defence Geoff Hoon was giving evidence. This, and the admission of one of those involved that he had lied to the Court Martial and that others had done so, made it possible, if not probable, that there would be further prosecutions, this time by the Crown, not the military, once the inquiry had reported. This was certainly the view of some following the inquiry closely. *Panorama*, BBC1, 27 September 2010.

28. This was in breach of embed pool agreements to share material and not to broad-

cast 'scoops' ahead of the pool, even if it was understandable that he did so. Jennifer Glasse, Interview, Strand C, Shifting Securities Project.

29. It is worth noting that research among both military and non-military focus groups questioned what was seen on film and suggested that the context was important and that more needed to be known, so as to interpret the images. Military practitioners were worried that no context was given in news reports as to the type of operation or the rules of engagement, and that this would add to the mounting negative reporting on military operations in Iraq. Research with mainly Muslim British civilians also evoked some scepticism, though less worry about impact. Participants did not exclude the possibility that a criminal act had been committed, given that they did not know the precise detail. However, the general sense was that the presentation of the incident, without any attempt to understand what was happening, was likely to be unfair and wrong, and was certainly damaging. This is discussed more extensively in Michalski and Gow, *War, Image and Legitimacy* and in Marie Gillespie, James Gow, Andrew Hoskins, Ben O'Loughlin and Ivan Zveržhanovskii, 'Shifting Securities: News Cultures, Multicultural Societies and Legitimacy', *Ethnopolitics*, Vol. 9, No. 2, June 2010, pp. 239–53.

30. Notable exceptions here include Mark Osiel, *Mass Atrocity, Collective Memory and the Law*, New Brunswick: Transaction, 1997, and Rachel Kerr, *The Military on Trial: The British Army in Iraq*. In addition, Bill Fenrick, as a military lawyer, has written articles consistently informed by an understanding of military realities, as well as international humanitarian law: 'A First Attempt to Adjudicate Conduct of Hostilities Offences: Comments on Aspects of the ICTY Trial Decision of the Prosecutor v. Tihomir Blaskic', *Leiden Journal of International Law*, Vol. 13, No. 4, 2000, pp. 931–47; 'The Law Applicable to Targeting and Proportionality After Operation Allied Force: A View From the Outside', *Yearbook of International Humanitarian Law*, Vol. 3, 2000; 'The Prosecution of Unlawful Attack Cases Before the ICTY', *Yearbook of International Humanitarian Law*, Vol. 7, 2004; 'Targeting and Proportionality During the NATO Bombing Campaign Against Yugoslavia', *European Journal of International Law*, Vol. 12, No. 3, June 2001; 'The Targeted Killings Judgment and the Scope of Direct Participation in Hostilities', *Journal of International Criminal Justice*, Vol. 5, No. 2, May 2007.

31. Much of the focus of this debate has been centred on its various contributions to the broadening and deepening understanding of international criminal law through its practice and jurisprudence in the field of international law (Kelly Dawn Askin, *War Crimes Against Women: Prosecution in International War Crimes Tribunals*, The Hague: Kluwer, 1997; M. C., Bassiouni and P. Manikas, *The Law of the International Criminal Tribunal for the Former Yugoslavia*, New York: Transnational Publishers, 1996; Theodor Meron, 'War Crimes in Yugoslavia

and the Development of International Law', *American Journal of International Law*, Vol. 88, 1994; Guenael Mettraux, *International Crimes and the Ad Hoc Tribunals*, Oxford: Oxford University Press, 2005; W. Schabas, *The UN International Criminal Tribunals: Former Yugoslavia, Rwanda and Sierra Leone*, Cambridge: Cambridge University Press, 2006) and, in the field of politics and international relations, on the politics of war crimes prosecutions and the relationship between justice and peace (Payam Akhavan, 'The Yugoslav Tribunal at a Crossroads: the Dayton Peace Agreement and Beyond', *Human Rights Quarterly*, 18, 1996; 'Justice in the Hague, Peace in the former Yugoslavia?: A Commentary on the UN War Crimes Tribunal', *Human Rights Quarterly*, Vol. 20, 1998; 'The Contribution of the Ad Hoc Tribunals to International Humanitarian Law: The Dilemmas of Jurisprudence', *American University International Law Review*, Vol. 13. No. 6, 1998, 'Beyond Impunity: Can International Criminal Justice Prevent Future Atrocities?', *American Journal of International Law*, Vol. 95, No. 1, 2001; Gary Bass, *Stay the Hand of Vengeance: The Politics of War Crimes Tribunals*, Princeton: Princeton University Press, 2000; Antony D'Amato, 'Peace vs. Accountability in Bosnia', *The American Journal of International Law*, 88, 1994; Rachel Kerr, *The International Criminal Tribunal for the Former Yugoslavia: An Exercise in Law, Diplomacy and Politics*, Oxford: Oxford University Press, 2004; Rachel Kerr and Eirin Mobekk, *Peace and Justice*, Cambridge: Polity, 2007; James Meernik, 'Victor's Justice or the Law? Judging and Punishing at the International Criminal Tribunal for the Former Yugoslavia', *The Journal of Conflict Resolution*, Vol. 47, No. 2, 2003, and 'Justice and Peace? How the International Criminal Tribunal Affects Societal Peace in Bosnia', *Journal of Peace Research*, Vol. 42, No. 2, 2005; Victor Peskin, *International Justice in Rwanda and the Balkans: Virtual Trials and the Struggle for State Cooperation*, New York: Cambridge University Press, 2008; Jack Snyder and Leslie Vinjamuri, 'Trials and Errors: Principle and Pragmatism in Strategies of International Justice', *International Security*, Vol. 28, No. 3, 2004, and Vinjamuri and Snyder, 'Advocacy and Scholarship in the Study of International War Crime Tribunals and Transitional Justice', *Annual Review of Political Science*, Vol. 7, 2004; Eric Stover, *The Witnesses: War Crimes and the Promise of Justice in the Hague*, Philadelphia: University of Pennsylvania Press, 2005; Stover and Harvey M. Weinstein, eds, *My Neighbor, My Enemy: Justice and Community in the Aftermath of Mass Atrocity*, Cambridge: Cambridge University Press, 2005; Chandra Lekha Sriram, *Confronting Past Human Rights Violations: Justice vs. Peace in Times of Transition*, London and New York: Frank Cass, 2004; Paul Williams and Michael Scharf, *Peace with Justice? War Crimes and Accountability in the Former Yugoslavia*, Boulder: Roman and Littlefield, 2002). Notwithstanding the contributions that the ICTY has made on both of these fronts, there is doubt about the extent to which a retributive approach to transitional justice, such as that practised by the international tribunals (and by national courts now dealing with war crimes cases) has proved adequate enough for the goal of societal reconciliation. In this connection, there is a need, it is argued, to go beyond criminal trials (Zoran Pajic, 'Rethinking War-Crimes Trials', *Transitions Online*, March 2006, and 'Restorative Justice: Victim's Needs and Compensation Policy Potentials', *Forum for Transitional Justice*, Vol. 2, March 2009). However, nothing in this literature has attempted to understand war crimes in the context of war.

32. A. C. Grayling, *Among the Dead Cities: Was the Allied Bombing of Civilians in WWII a Necessity or a Crime?*, London: Bloomsbury, 2006.

33. Telford Taylor, *The Anatomy of the Nuremberg Trials: a Personal Memoir*, New York: Bloomsbury, 1993, p. 640.

34. This is in line with the principle of *nullum crimen sine lege*—there can be no criminal offence (or punishment) where a legal offence does not already exist. Aly Mokhtar, 'Nullum Crimen. Nulla Poena Sine Lege: Aspects and Prospects', *Statute Law Review*, Vol. 26, No. 1, 2005.

35. Marco Roscini, for example, points out that there was reference to the principle of distinction in Article 24 (1) of the 1923 Hague Rules, stating that aerial bombardment was 'legitimate only when directed at a military objective'. Marco Roscini, 'Targeting and Contemporary Aerial Bombardment', *International and Comparative Law Quarterly*, Vol. 54, No. 2, 2005, pp. 412; see also William J. Fenrick, 'Targeting and Proportionality', especially notes 11 and 12 and the discussion around them. However, Roscini also notes that even at the time of his writing (2005) the law of air warfare remained a long way from being 'completely codified' (p. 411).

36. Eric Markusen and David Kopf, *The Holocaust and Strategic Bombing: Genocide and Total War in the Twentieth Century*, Boulder: Westview Press, 1995, p. 246.

37. *Ibid.*, p. 250.

38. *Ibid.*, p. 168.

39. Grayling, *Dead Cities*, p. 272.

40. Bradley F. Smith, *Reaching Judgement at Nuremberg*, London: Andrew Deutsch, 1977, p. 304.

41. Smith, *Reaching Judgement*, p. 303.

42. Similarly, noting that the Soviet Union was responsible for mass murder and gross human rights abuses on a massive scale does not mean that Russians were not justified either in fighting a war of self-defence using all the means they had, or in liberating the Nazi extermination camps they uncovered in the East, or in forming part of the victorious 'United Nations' and the four-power prosecution at Nuremberg. On the term 'United Nations' and its relevance to the Tribunal, see Dan Plesch, *America, Hitler and the UN: How the Allies Won World War II and Forged a Peace*, London: I.B. Tauris, 2010.

43. Smith, *Reaching Judgement*, p. 303.

44. Grayling.

45. See Max Hastings, *Bomber Command*, London: Pan Macmillan, 3rd edn, 1999.

46. While Grayling is troubled by the saturation bombing of German cities, Walzer uses the concept of 'supreme emergency' to distinguish that action, which he sees as justifiable, from the unjustifiable use of nuclear bombs over Hiroshima and, more particularly, Nagasaki. Walzer, *Just and Unjust Wars*, p. 259. Against this, it might be argued that the deployment of the atom bomb against Hiroshima was an action calculated to bring a swifter end to the war in the Pacific, saving more American and Allied lives, as a protracted invasion and land campaign lasting several months was avoided. In this context, the use of the hydrogen bomb at Nagasaki appears more flimsy, given that Hiroshima had achieved the desired effect and this second attack has a possible air of simply wanting to try out the different device (although some would argue that it was equally necessary to reinforce the message of inevitable defeat delivered by the Hiroshima attack). It might also be reflected, as one reader of the present MS did, that Walzer's 'supreme emergency' argument might be stronger if the Allies had attempted to do more directly to end the murder and misery of Auschwitz sooner—an issue around which a lively debate exists. (See Michael J. Neufeld and Michael Berenbaum, eds, *The Bombing of Auschwitz: Should the Allies Have Attempted It?* (Lawrence, KS: University Press of Kansas, 2003).

47. I have discussed these changes in Gow, *Defending the West*, Cambridge: Polity, 2005.

48. UN Document S/23200, 31 January 1991.

49. Bobbitt, *The Shield of Achilles: War, Peace and the Course of History*, London: Penguin, 2003, pp. *xxiv* and 8.

50. Field Marshal Lord Inge and General Klaus Naumann, 'The Moral and Practical Challenges Facing the Armed Forces of Our Liberal Democracies in this Present Security Environment', Inaugural Bagnall Lecture, in memory of the late Field Marshal Sir Nigel Bagnall, British-German Association, British-German Officers' Association (BGOA) and Royal Institute of International Affairs, Chatham House, 26 October 2004. This was a joint lecture (see note 53 etc. below). Inge was the most senior officer in the British military in 1994–7, during which time he was significantly involved in operations concerning Bosnia and Hercegovina. Naumann's career was also shaped by the war in the Western Balkans, including his being part of the NATO military delegation sent directly to meet Serbian President Slobodan Milošević and his military leaders in the months preceding the conflict over Kosovo in 1999, which later resulted in Naumann's being a key witness at the trial of the Serbian leader at the ICTY. Their involvement with the Yugoslav War clearly provided a context, as well as the then current operations over Iraq, for their lecture.

51. See note 3 above.

52. Inge and Naumann, 'The Moral and Practical Challenges Facing the Armed Forces of Our Liberal Democracies in this Present Security Environment', Inaugural Bagnall Lecture, in memory of the late Field Marshal Sir Nigel Bagnall, British-German Association, British-German Officers' Association (BGOA) and Royal Institute of International Affairs, Chatham House, 26 October 2004. See note 51 above for clarification.

53. Fenrick, 'A First Attempt to Adjudicate Conduct of Hostilities Offences'.

54. For example, see Ewen MacAskill, 'UK Should Face Court for Crimes in Iraq, Say Jurists', *The Guardian*, 21 January 2004.

55. Anna Blundy, *The Review Show*, BBC2, 5 March 2010. Blundy was one of a panel reviewing films about the conflict in Iraq, mostly focused on atrocities. Having been a journalist and written an autobiography of her journalist father, she then wrote a series of novels about a female war correspondent, which perhaps explains her enhanced understanding of warfare. Blundy, *The Bad News Bible*, London: Headline, 2004.

56. Inge and Naumann, 'The Moral and Practical Challenges …'.

57. Roscini, 'Targeting', pp. 420 and 441; Ken Roberts has noted the need—and the practice of the ICTY—to modernise the grave breaches regime of the Geneva Convention, similarly reflecting the mismatch between contemporary conflict and the law in place. Ken Roberts, 'The Contribution of the ICTY to the Grave Breaches Regime', *Journal of International Criminal Justice*, Vol. 7, No. 4, 2009, p. 753.

58. Morale is one of the most significant factors in warfare. It has often been judged to be the most important by thinkers and writers of diverse backgrounds. One author of particular interest in the context of the present discussion is Nazi propaganda chief Joseph Goebbels. In a speech on 7 August 1943, as the tide in the Second World War was turning with regard to discussion of the Allied bombing campaign, he made this statement: 'None of us would want to gloss over the air war against the German Homeland. It presents our people with a stiff test. But, we must pass this test'. In this speech, Goebbels also asserted the Western Allies' 'acceptance of heavier and more debilitating losses against us, in trying to break our morale'. Joseph Goebbels 'Die Moral als Kriegsentscheidender Faktor', in Geobbels, *Der Steile Aufstieg*, Munich: Zentralverlag der NSDAP, 1944, pp. 406–413. On the other side of this, the high morale of bomber crews, despite incredibly high risks and statistics that suggested they were not likely to return from missions, is regarded as a key factor in the eventual success of the Allied bombing campaign, in particular, and, as a consequence of this, the overall Allied victory in the Second World War. See 'Introduction' by Sebastian Cox to Sir Arthur T. Harris, *Despatch on War Operations*, London: Frank Cass, 1985; Hastings, *Bomber Command*; Mark H. Wells, *Courage and Air Warfare: The Allied Aircrew Experiences in the Second World War*, Frank Cass, 1995.

For a concise, more general, overview of morale, see Huw Strachan, 'Training, Morale and Modern War', *Journal of Contemporary History*, Vol. 41, No. 2, April 2006.

59. See Philip Bobbitt, *The Shield of Achilles*.

60. Michael Bothe, 'The Protection of the Civilian Population and NATO Bombing on Yugoslavia: Comments on a Report to the Prosecutor of the ICTY', *European Journal of International Law*, Vol. 12, No. 3, 2001, p. 535.

61. For example, Amnesty International, *Killings of Civilians in Basra and al-'Amara*, May 2004.

62. Military experts have been called as witnesses at international trials to offer testimony on matters such as this. In theory, the testimony offered could be personal or even anecdotal. However, the assumption has to be that professional judgement is being exercised—hence, their being called as 'expert' witnesses. For example, two British ex-serviceman, Captain Jonathan Hinchcliffe and Quartermaster Sergeant Instructor Richard Higgs, were used as experts by the Office of the Prosecutor at the ICTY in several cases, including the *Prosecutor v. Stanislav Galic* case, where both gave evidence. The former testified on the use of snipers around Sarajevo in the 1992–4 period and the latter on the use of artillery, in particular, mortars. Although Higgs held a non-commissioned rank, he testified that he was the 'the senior advisor' so any rulings or instructions he gave 'had to be acted upon' and that his 'appointment was such' that senior officers would carry out his instructions. He further testified that the 'rank did not bear any resemblance to my appointment as senior mortar officer' and that he 'worked on an appointment far higher than my rank as I supported the British government and the British Army at very senior levels' (*Prosecutor v. Stanislav Galic*, Transcript 070423IT, pp. 4993–4). The standing of both as experts was questioned in the Galić proceedings, with the Trial Chamber suggesting that it 'might feel the need to test whether the evidence could be admitted as expert evidence' (*Prosecutor v. Stanislav Galic*, Transcript 070423IT, p. 11323). Examples of military experts for both the Prosecution and the Defence can be seen in *Triumph of Evil* (Dir. Mirko Klarin, 2001). This is an exemplary visual summary of all aspects of the initial trial of General Radislav Krstić made by Sense Agency/Tribunal TV, under the helm of the remarkable Mirko Klarin. It includes extracts from the evidence of both General Richard Dannatt (later head of the UK Army), giving evidence as a military expert for the prosecution, and General Radovan Radinović, a retired Belgrade general lecturing at Serbia's highest military schools, giving evidence for the defence.

63. Bothe, 'Protection of the Civilian Population', p. 535.

64. Professor A. J. W. Gow and Dr. R. C. Kerr, 'Pictures of Peace and Justice'; Professor Gow, 'War and War Crimes'; Dr. M. L. Gillespie, Professor Gow and Dr. A. D. Hoskins 'Shifting Securities'. Reference to the focus group empirical

research in the present book is indicated as follows: Pictures of Peace and Justice, Focus Group 1, etc.; War and War Crimes Focus Group 1, etc.; Shifting Securities Project Focus Group 1, etc.

65. Under King's College London ethical policy, all audio recordings are normally deleted once research reports or transcripts are completed, unless they have been made with a specific release agreement for use as part of educational provision, or audio-visual research presentation.

66. It perhaps could not go without saying that this type of research relies on collaboration, and not only with those organisations such as the RCDS, which provide access, facilities and support in helping to recruit research participants. The conduct of such research is deeply collaborative, for the most part, with focus groups normally involving a facilitator, observers and, on occasions, technical support. In this context, although already acknowledged generally in the preface, the roles played by Zoran Pajić, Milena Michalski, Rachel Kerr, Ann Lane, Ben O'Loughlin, Ivan Zveržhanovski, Ernst Dijxhoorn and Inara Khan must be fully recognised as making the research and its findings possible. That said, as also noted already, but perhaps requiring emphasis in this context, the responsibility for the presentation of those findings and the interpretations offered in the present volume is entirely my own.

2. STRATEGY AND THE MULTIDIMENSIONAL TRINITY

1. Although originally developed in the context of the present volume, this formulation first appeared in Milena Michalski and James Gow, *War, Image and Legitimacy: Viewing Contemporary Conflict*, London and New York: Routledge, 2007, Ch. 7.

2. James Gow, *Defending the West*, Cambridge: Polity, 2005.

3. Philip Bobbitt, *The Shield of Achilles: War, Peace and the Course of History*, Penguin: London, 2003.

4. Lieutenant General Sir Rupert Smith, *The Utility of Force: The Art of War in the Modern World*, London: Allen Lane, 2005, Ch. 7.

5. William S. Lind, 'Understanding Fourth Generation War', *Military Review*, September-October 2004, pp. 12–16; Thomas G. Hammes, *The Sling and the Stone: On War in the 21st Century*, St. Paul: Zenith Press, 2004, and 'War Evolves into the Fourth Generation', *Contemporary Security Policy*, Vol. 26, No. 2, 2005.

6. Gen. Charles Krulak, 'The Strategic Corporal: Leadership in the Three Block War', *Marines Magazine*, January 1999.

7. Margaret S. Bond, *Hybrid War: A New Paradigm for Stability Operations in Failing States*, Carlisle, PA: US Army War College, 30 March 2007; Frank G. Hoffman, *Conflict in the 21st Century: The Rise of Hybrid Wars*, Arlington, VA: The Potomac Institute, December 2007.

8. Lawrence Freedman, *The Transformation of Strategic Affairs*, Adelphi Paper 379, London: Routledge for the International Institute of Strategic Studies (IISS), 2006.

9. See Joseph P. Nye, *The Paradox of American Power: Why the World's Only Superpower Can't Go It Alone*, Oxford: Oxford University Press, 2002, and 'US Power and Strategy After Iraq', *Foreign Affairs*, Vol. 82, No. 4, July-August 2003.

10. Joseph P. Nye, 'Soft Power and the Struggle Against Terrorism', Lecture, The Royal Institute of International Affairs, Chatham House, London, 5 May 2005.

11. Of course, it should be noted that this phenomenon of warfare was new in terms of new technical means and in relation to that which had gone immediately before it, but that it was not an entirely new feature of strategy that factors other than decisive battle could contribute to victory, and that the purpose of battle itself was to create a set of strategic conditions. Indeed, this was a dominant mode of strategy in the era of Frederick the Great that was outmoded by the advent of Napoleonic mass armed forces. For a guide to Frederick's life and thinking, see Ludwig Reiners, *Frederick The Great: An Informal Biography*, translated and adapted from the German by Lawrence P. R. Wilson, London: Oswald Wolff (Publishers) Limited, 1960.

12. Carl von Clausewitz, *On War*, trans. J. J. Graham, 'Introduction' and 'Notes' by Colonel F. N. Maude, C. B (Late R. E.) and 'Introduction to the New Edition' by Jan Willem Honig, New York: Barnes and Noble, 2004. All subsequent references are to this edition, unless otherwise indicated.

13. This is Clausewitz's secondary trinity, which is a reflective derivative of the primary trinity of reason (linked mainly to government), chance (linked mainly to the military) and passion (linked mainly to the people). See Beatrice Heuser, *Reading Clausewitz*, London: Pimlico, 2002,: pp. 53–4.

14. Mary Kaldor, *New and Old Wars*, Cambridge: Polity, 1999; Martin van Creveld, *On Future War* London: Brassey's, 1991.

15. Creveld, *On Future War*, p. 58.

16. Smith, *Utility of Force*, p. 278.

17. Clausewitz, *On War*, p. 529.

18. Creveld, *On Future War*, pp. 6–18 and 33–49.

19. CNN, 2 May 2003. It might be noted that the USS Abraham Lincoln was off the coast of California when President Bush was flown aboard—not, as might have been assumed, somewhere off the coast of Iraq.

20. Adam Woods, 'So where does strategy fit in?', *MediaWeek*, 8–15 November 2005, p. 22. Another business and management version of strategy (Henry Mintzberg, 'Crafting Strategy', *Harvard Business Review*, July-August 1987, p. 66) emphasises the creative aspect of strategy over planning, but loses sight of what strategy really is: first, by suggesting that strategy can be an *ex post facto* rationalisation of a previous pattern of behaviour, rather than problem-solving

conceptualisation (even if that conceptualisation, in the time-honoured tradition of genius, might include creative, intuitive, unreasoned insight); and, secondly, by quite clumsily and erroneously proposing that 'managers are craftsmen and strategy is their clay', where clay clearly would be the material and strategy, even sidelined for use in arts and crafts, would be the approach to shaping the material and making something out of it, just as, in war, the general officer uses strategy to craft success out of the material of war.

21. Key texts in the evolution of strategy include the following: Clausewitz, *On War*, (cit.); Edward Mead Earle et al, eds, *The Makers of Modern Strategy from Machiavelli to Hitler*, Princeton, N. J.: Princeton University Press, 1943, and its update, Peter Paret, ed., *Makers of Modern Strategy from Machiavelli to the Nuclear Age*, Princeton, N. J.: Princeton University Press, 1986 (although the latter is less even and sometimes weaker); Thomas C. Schelling, *The Strategy of Conflict*, Cambridge, Mass.: Harvard University Press, 1960; Williamson Murray, MacGregor Knox and Alvin Bernstein, *The Making of Strategy: Rulers, States, and War*, New York: Cambridge University Press, 1994 (see also the review of this volume by Jan Willem Honig in *Survival*, Vol. 39, No. 4, Winter 1997–8, pp. 188–90); Azar Gat, *A History of Military Thought from the Enlightenment to the Cold War*, Oxford: Oxford University Press, 2001 (which compends three important earlier volumes; Michael Howard, *War in European History*, Oxford: Oxford University Press, 1976; Creveld, *On Future War*; Lawrence Freedman, ed., *War*, Oxford: Oxford University Press, 1994); Joe Maiolo and Thomas Mahnken, eds, *Strategic Studies: A Reader*, London: Routledge, 2008; Colin S. Gray, *Modern Strategy*, Oxford: Oxford University Press, 1999; John Stone, 'Politics, Technology and the Revolution in Military Affairs', *Journal of Strategic Studies*, Vol. 27, No. 3 (September 2004), pp. 408–27; John Stone, 'Clausewitz's Trinity and Contemporary Conflict', *Civil Wars*, Vol. 9, No. 3 (September 2007), pp. 282–96; Gerard Chaliand, ed., *The Art of War in World History: from Antiquity to the Nuclear Age*, Berkeley: University of California Press, 1994; Bruce D. Porter, *War and the Rise of the State: the Military Foundation of Modern Politics*, New York: Free Press, 1994; David Kaiser, *Politics and War, European Conflict from Philip II to Hitler*, Cambridge, Mass.: Harvard University Press, 1990; David A. Welch, *Justice and the Genesis of War*, Cambridge: Cambridge University Press, 1993; Richard K. Betts, 'Is Strategy an Illusion?', *International Security*, Vol. 25, No. 2, Fall 2000, pp. 5–50, and Betts, 'The Trouble with Strategy: Bridging Policy and Operations', *Joint Force Quarterly*, Autumn/Winter 2001–2, pp. 23–3; Huw Strachan and Andreas Herberg Rothe, eds, *Clausewitz in the Twenty-first Century*, Oxford: Oxford University Press, 2007. Lastly, and with special mention, see Beatrice Heuser, *The Evolution of Strategy: Thinking War from Antiquity to the Present*, Cambridge: Cambridge University Press, 2010, which offers a remarkable and com-

pelling sweep over the history of ideas of strategy, including some of the lesser (or un-)known figures, who none the less had interesting things to say (she is particularly fond of the very little known Mathew Sutcliffe); the only weak point of this book is that she does not engage with contemporary thought—for example, there is only one passing reference to the vitally important work of Rupert Smith.

22. There has been notable attention to the hyper-version of strategy, or grand strategy, in which the whole economic, social and political wherewithal of a state (or other form of political community) is considered as part of the strategic equation, both under conditions of war and those of peace. Indeed, peacetime, as much as wartime, is time in which political aims and the resources available to the political community and (therefore, if judged necessary) its military are to be developed, nurtured, harnessed and protected. For one of the more prominent examples of this fashion, see: Paul Kennedy, ed., *Grand Strategies in War and Peace*, New Haven: Yale University Press, 1991.

23. Clausewitz, *On War*, p. 129.

24. See, for example, Michalski and Gow, *War, Image and Legitimacy*.

25. Martin van Creveld, *On Future War*, pp. 98–116.

26. Clausewitz, *On War*, p. 127.

27. Clausewitz, *On War*, pp. 128–9.

28. In many ways, the evolution of nuclear strategy is the epitome of this high conceptual and philosophical understanding of strategy, where the most rational interpretations of the means and ends involved entailed embracing apparent paradoxes. (Lawrence Freedman, *The Evolution of Nuclear Strategy*, 2nd edn, Basingstoke: Macmillan for the International Institute of Strategic Studies, IISS, 1989).

29. Earle, *Makers of Modern Strategy From Machiavelli to Hitler* and Paret ed., *Makers of Modern Strategy From Machiavelli to the Nuclear Age*.

30. Smith, *Utility of Force*, Chs. 6. 7 and 8, especially.

31. This is an awkward point for an academic to make, given that it is our very purpose and profession to discuss these matters—and I have certainly made my own public comments, both seeking to understand and to expand the scope of strategic discussion on the Yugoslav War. I also note that there are times when such public discussion might lead to better and more elegant conceptualisation, as well as to improvements in practice. However, my research and experience also leaves me acutely aware of the immense frustration that those actively seeking to solve very difficult equations and get them 'right' feel when the chorus of commentators creates a din, which becomes part of the strategic equation, or applies friction so as either to distort it, or to make it harder to implement.

32. Sun Tzu, *The Art of War*. Transl. Thomas Cleary, Boston and London: Shambhala, 2005.

33. Smith, *Utility of Force*, p. 327.

34. The CIA's apparent failure to have an accurate and up-to-date map of Belgrade, in 1999, when the Chinese Embassy there was seen by one reader of this manuscript as a good illustration of this point.

35. Steve Jermy refers to the 'military cliché and truism' coined by Field Marshall Helmuth von Molkte (or Molkte the Elder) that 'no plan survives first contact with the enemy'. Steven Jermy, *Strategy for Action: Using Force Wisely in the 21st Century*, London: Knightstone Publishing, 2011, p. 58.

36. Baron de Jomini, *The Art of War*, trans. Capt. G. H. Wendell and Lt. W.P. Craighill, Westport: Greenhill Press, 1971; Clausewitz, *On War*.

37. Earle, ed., *Makers of Modern Strategy from Machiavelli to Hitler*; Michael Howard, *War in European History*, Oxford: Oxford University Press, 1976, and 'The Influence of Clausewitz' in Carl von Clausewitz, *On War*, edited and translated by Michael Howard and Peter Paret, Introductory Essays by Peter Paret, Michael Howard and Bernard Brodie, Princeton: Princeton University Press, 1976 (revised 1984); Heuser, *Strategy*.

38. Basil Liddell Hart, *The Strategy of Indirect Approach*, London: Faber, 1941; *Strategy: The Indirect Approach*, London: Faber, 1954, and; *Memoirs*, Vol. 2, London: Cassell, 1965.

39. Lawrence Freedman, *Deterrence*, Cambridge: Polity, 2004.

40. These are my own core questions. For an extended range of questions that inspired my own, see Smith, *Utility of Force*, pp. 384–5.

41. Smith, *Utility of Force*, p. 318.

42. James Gow and Christopher Dandeker, 'Strategic Peacekeeping: Military Culture and Defining Moments', in S. D. Gordon and F. H. Toase, eds, *Aspects of Peacekeeping*, London: Frank Cass and Co., 2001. This was the final and most complete instalment of this analysis. It evolved through a set of articles published on this theme, in the 1990s: James Gow, 'Strategic Peacekeeping: UNPROFOR and Diplomatic Assertion', in Espen Barth Eide, ed., *Peacekeeping in Europe*, Peacekeeping and Multinational Operations Series No. 5, Oslo: NUPI,1995; James Gow and Christopher Dandeker, 'Peace-support Operations: the Problem of Legitimation' *The World Today*, Vol. 51, Nos. 8–9, August-September 1995; Christopher Dandeker and James Gow, 'The Future of Peace Support Operations: Strategic Peacekeeping and Success', *Armed Forces and Society*, Vol. 23, No. 3, Spring 1997. The last of these is perhaps the most recognised of the series, although it was not the final iteration of this evolving discussion.

43. This treatment of legitimacy draws on: James Gow, *Legitimacy and the Military: The Yugoslav Crisis*, London: Pinter, 1992; Gow and Dandeker, 'Strategic Peacekeeping'; Michalski and Gow, *War, Image and Legitimacy*, where Ch.7 includes a discussion of legitimacy, as used in the present context and in the context of

contemporary military affairs and armed conflict, and where directions to the wider literature can be found.

44. Smith, *Utility of Force*, p. 289.

45. Bobbitt, *Shield of Achilles*, pp. 5–7 and 355–6.

46. Notions of 'will', 'hearts and minds' and, ultimately, in effect, legitimacy, were recognised as relevant to counter-insurgency operations in the twentieth century; the same types of issues are relevant to the dominant forms of warfare, reflecting the nature of all types of conflict, in the contemporary era. On counter-insurgency and its evolution see, for some of the better examples, John MacKinlay, *The Insurgent Archipelago*, London and New York: Hurst/Columbia University Press, 2010; Thomas Rid and Thomas Keaney, eds, *Understanding Counterinsurgency: Doctrine, Operations and Challenges*, London: Routledge, 2010; and David Kilcullen, *Counterinsurgency*, London: Hurst and Co., 2010. For an unusual and particularly reflective account of the issues see M. L. R. Smith, 'Whose Hearts and Whose Minds: The Curious Case of Global Counter-insurgency', *Journal of Strategic Studies*, February 2010.

47. John Stone's subtle analysis of technology and the trinities casts useful light on the latter and their relevance to contemporary armed conflict; see Stone, 'Clausewitz's Trinity and Contemporary Warfare'.

48. Krulak, 'Strategic Corporal'.

49. Terry Terriff, Frans Osinga and Theo Farrell, eds, *A Transformation Gap?: American Innovations and European Military Change*, Stanford: Stanford University Press, 2010.

50. Gray, *Modern Strategy*, p. 273.

51. Smith, *Utility of Force*, pp. 317–8.

52. Gow and Dandeker, 'Strategic Peacekeeping'.

53. James Gow, *The Serbian Project and Its Adversaries: a Strategy of War Crimes*, London and Montreal: Hurst/McGill-Queen's University Press, 2003, Ch. 7.

54. This part of the book was originally presented at the Woodrow Wilson School, Princeton University, in November 2010, marking the tenth anniversary of the Liechtenstein Institute on Self-Determination there. 'Crisis Diplomacy: 10 (or 20) Years of Pictures, Prosecutions and Political Will', 12 November 2010.

55. Michalski and Gow, *War, Image and Legitimacy*.

3. PROSECUTING WAR CRIMES

1. 'Deuteronomy', Chapter 20, *The Bible, Authorized King James Version with Apocrypha*, Oxford: Oxford University Press, 1999. These clearly stated laws, while wholly out of kilter with twenty-first century assumptions about that which is and is not acceptable in warfare, certainly pre-date the injunctions of Sun Tzu to wise command (500 BC); or the Indian Code of Manu (200 BC), cited among

the earliest examples of the rules of war by Yves Beigbeder, *Judging War Criminals: The Politics of International Justice*, London: Macmillan, 1999; or, the agreed limitation on the use of projectile missiles in the War of the Lelantine Plain (700 BC), cited by Josiah Ober, 'Classical Greek Times' in Michael Howard, George I. Andreopoulos, and Mark R. Shulman, eds, *The Laws of War: Constraints on Warfare in the Western World*, New Haven: Yale University Press, 1994, p. 12.

2. *Instructions for the Government of Armies of the United States in the Field* ('*Lieber Code*'), 24 April 1863, http://www.icrc.org/ihl.nsf/73cb71d18dc4372741256 739003e6372/a25aa5871a04919bc12563cd002d65c5?OpenDocument; this set of rules for the US Unionist army was drafted by Francis Lieber, Professor of Law at Columbia University, whose name is associated with them (Richard S. Hartigan, *Lieber's Colde and the Law of War* Chicago: Precedent, 1983). The Declaration Respecting Maritime Law, Paris, 16 April 1856, could be seen as the first chronological point in the modern evolution of the law relating to war, but it was quite limited and it does not contribute to the subsequent evolutionary canon in the same manner as the Lieber Code.

3. ICRC, *Resolutions of the Geneva International Conference*, 26–9 October 1863, available at http://www.icrc.org/ihl.nsf/FULL/115?OpenDocument,. *Convention for the Amelioration of the Condition of the Wounded in Armies in the Field*, Geneva, 22 August 1864, available at http://www.icrc.org/ihl.nsf/FULL/120? OpenDocument.

4. Adam Roberts and Richard Guelff, *Documents on the Laws of War*, 3rd edn, Oxford: Oxford University Press, 2000, and 2nd edn, Oxford: Oxford University Press, 1989.

5. See Yves Beigbeder, *Judging War Criminals: The Politics of International Justice*, London: Macmillan, 1999, pp. 39–49.

6. See James Gow, *Defending the West*, Cambridge: Polity, 2005, pp. 51–2; and 'A Revolution in International Affairs?', *Security Dialogue*, Vol. 30, No. 3, September 2000.

7. This is not to say that there was not a truly legal dimension to war crimes in earlier ages—there was. However, it was only at the end of the nineteenth century that the laws of war really began to be codified in international treaty agreements. See Roberts and Guelff, *Documents*, 2nd edn, n.p., p. 3. (NB this appears in the 2nd edition but not in the 3rd, hence the 2nd edition is quoted here, but the 3rd is referenced elsewhere).

8. Geoffrey Best, *Law and War Since 1945*, Oxford: Oxford University Press, 1994.

9. '1977 Geneva Protocol II Additional to the Geneva Conventions of 12 August 1949, and Relating to the Protection of Victims of Non-International Armed Conflicts', in Roberts and Guelff, *Documents*, 3rd edn.

10. International Committee of the Red Cross (ICRC), 'How is the Term Armed

Conflict Defined in International Humanitarian Law? Opinion Paper, March 2008.

11. The ICRC defines customary international law as 'a general practice accepted as law'. Customary international law is identified as a major source of international law in Article 38 of the Statute of the International Court of Justice. It is broadly thought to require two elements—general practice (including inaction) by states and *opinio juris* (evidence that a state or actor believes that there is a legal obligation associated with a particular course of action). There is contention over the status of persistent objections, with the ICRC study on customary international humanitarian law explicitly taking no position on whether it is legally possible to be a persistent objector, noting that commentators would say this cannot be available where there is a *jus cogens* principle involved, but recognising that, as a matter of fact, such objectors must express their objections consistently from the earliest stage. *Statute of the International Court of Justice*, Article 38, p. xlv, in Jean-Marie Henckaerts and Louise Doswald-Beck, *Customary International Humanitarian Law*, Vol. 1, Rules, Cambridge: Cambridge University Press for the ICRC, 2005, Reprinted with Corrections, 2009; Jean-Marie Henckaerts and Louise Doswald-Beck, eds, *Customary International Humanitarian Law*, Vol. 2, Practice Parts I and II, Cambridge: Cambridge University Press for the ICRC, Reprinted with Corrections, 2005.

12. Article II, 'The 1948 United Nations Convention on the Prevention and Punishment of the Crime and the Genocide', in Roberts and Guelff, *Documents*. The definition of genocide was initially wider in its original coinage by sociologist Raphael Lemkin. (Lemkin, *Axis Rule in Occupied Europe: Laws of Occupation, Analysis of Government and Proposals for Redress*, New York: Carnegie Endowment for Peace, 1944, p. 7). Martin Shaw has led the way in arguing for a return to the social understanding pioneered by Lemkin, with a compelling analysis for moving beyond the narrow and limited technical limitations of the legal definition in the Convention. (Shaw, *What is Genocide?*, Cambridge: Polity, 2007). See also Dominik J. Schaller and Jürgen Zimmerer, eds, *The Origins of Genocide: Raphael Lemkin as a Historian of Mass Violence*, Abingdon and New York: Routledge, 2009. For a solid introduction to the field, see Adam Jones, *Genocide: A Comprehensive Introduction*, New York: Routledge, 2006.

13. http://www.icc-cpi.int/Menus/ASP/ReviewConference/Resolutions+and+Declarations/Resolutions+and+Declarations.htm.

14. International Criminal Law, distinct from International Humanitarian Law, is a field concerned primarily with the jurisprudence and prosecution of individuals at the international level for international crimes (although, given that the concept of 'international crimes' is relevant to both and applies in both international and domestic jurisdictions, there is inevitably overlap—see David Armstrong, Theo Farrell and Hélène Lambert, *International Law and International*

Relations, Cambridge: Cambridge University Press, 2007, Chapter 6). Among the markers of this emerging field, the creation of a chair in International Criminal Law at Flinders University in Adelaide was a significant step. This was specifically focused on the handling of war crimes and their cognates in prosecutions at the international level—that is in bodies requiring the cooperation of more than one state to establish and disestablish them—in contrast to the establishment of a similarly titled chair at the University of Edinburgh, which focused on the international and transnational dimensions of essentially domestic crimes, such as organised crimes and drug trafficking. Another milestone was the appearance of a new journal, in 2001, dedicated to this emerging field—*The Journal of International Criminal Justice*—under the stewardship of Antonio Cassese, one of the most prominent figures in international humanitarian law, and, *inter alia*, the first president of the International Criminal Tribunal for the former Yugoslavia. For authoritative surveys of this newly emerged field, see: Robert Cryer, Håkan Friman, Darryl Robinson and Elizabeth Wilmshurst, *An Introduction to International Criminal Law and Procedure*, Cambridge: Cambridge University Press, 2007; William Schabas, *The UN International Criminal Tribunals: Former Yugoslavia, Rwanda and Sierra Leone*, Cambridge: Cambridge University Press, 2006; and Antonio Cassese, ed., *The Oxford Companion to International Criminal Justice*, Oxford: Oxford University Press, 2009.

15. Lyal S. Sunga, *Individual Responsibility in International Law for Serious Human Rights Violations*, Dordrecht: Martinus Njihoff, 1992, pp. 18–19. Georg Schwarzenberger, *International Law as Applied by International Courts and Tribunals, Vol. II, The Law of Armed Conflict*, London: Stevens and Sons, 1968, pp. 462–6.

16. The trial of Wallace was certainly an earlier example of a war crimes prosecution, although its 'international' credentials are not nearly so strong; while twenty-eight countries were represented in the Breisach process, that of the Scottish leader was a matter between two countries—and even, given the position of the English, a domestic matter, given that Wallace was accused of treason, though other parts of the indictment presented a more confusing picture of war and invasion. I am grateful to Gavin Ruxton, who first brought the otherwise seemingly unnoticed case of Walllace to my attention.

17. Edward's brutality and 'crimes against humanity' were not restricted to the Scots. His forces slaughtered the 'Welsh Bards', in action that would certainly not have been condoned in eras later than the thirteenth century. The Bards were professional poets and singers, whose role was to praise their king and to inspire troops in battle, a vital component of Welsh morale. In a sense, they could be associated with the 'media' of the twentieth century and beyond. Their physical elimination is elegiacally captured in a painting by nineteenth-century painter John Martin, *The Bard* (in the Laing Art Gallery, Newcastle-upon-Tyne).

The picture shows Harlech Castle, the symbolic home of the Welsh—the 'Men of Harlech' in the famous song of that name—in an Alpine setting, with the 'last Bard' cursing the English troops below him, before plunging into the river, rather than suffer the murderous fate of his fellow poet-singers.

18. Quoted in William Power, *Wallace Monument: the Official Guide*, Stirling: Stirling Town Council, n.d.

19. On the history of Nuremberg and Tokyo, see Bradley F. Smith, *Reaching Judgement at Nuremberg*, London: Andrew Deutsch, 1977; Telford Taylor, *The Anatomy of the Nuremberg Trials: a Personal Memoir*, New York: Bloomsbury, 1993; Ann Tusa and John Tusa, *The Nuremberg Trial*, London: BBC Books, 1995; Beigbeder, *Judging War Criminals*, Chs 2 and 3; Madoka Futamura, *The Tokyo Trial and the Nuremberg Legacy*, London: Routledge, 2007; B. V. A. Roling, and Antonio Casese, *The Tokyo Trial and Beyond*, Cambridge: Polity, 1993; B. V. A. Roling, and C. F. Ruter, eds, *The Tokyo Judgement: The International Military Tribunal for the Far East (IMTFE)*, Amsterdam: APA University Press, 1977.

20. Tony Millett, *The Political and Public Discourse Surrounding the Development of British Policies on War Crimes from 1918 to Nuremberg and Beyond*, Unpublished Ph.D. Dissertation, King's College London, 2005.

21. M. Cherif Bassiouni, for example, notes that in negotiations on the Charter, 'The Subject of CAH [Crimes Against Humanity] Only Appeared as an Outgrowth of War Crimes'. *Crimes Against Humanity: Historical Evolution and Contemporary Application*, Cambridge: Cambridge University Press, 2011, p. 126.

22. *Agreement for the Prosecution and Punishment of the Major War Criminals of the European Axis, and Charter of the International Military Tribunal*, London, 8 August 1945.

23. For a concise discussion of the issues surrounding the IMTs' legal frameworks, see Yves Beigbeder, *Judging War Criminals: The Politics of International Justice*, London: Macmillan, 1999, Chs. 2 and 3. On the different perspectives of, and differences between, the quadripartite victors, see Smith, *Reaching Judgement*.

24. Count 2 in the London Charter, the statute, of the IMT charged individuals with 'crimes against peace', a charge based on an 'evolutive' or 'adaptive' interpretation of international law, where individuals carrying out a policy held clearly to be in breach of an international legal agreement between states must have known that, in launching attacks, they were doing something wrong. Beigbeder, *Judging War Criminals*, pp. 42–3.

25. The principle was first set down by Paul Johann Anselm Ritter von Feuerbach in the Bavarian Criminal Code, 1813. Aly Mokhtar, '*Nullem Crima. Nullem Poena Sine Lege*: Aspects and Prospects', *Statute Law Review*, Vol. 26, No. 1, 2005.

26. Quoted in Cryer, et al., *International Criminal Justice*, p. 18.

27. Taylor, *Anatomy*, pp. 399–401.

28. Although frequently addressed as criticism of the Nuremberg process, 'victor's justice' was an issue faced head on and dealt with by the Justice Robert Jackson (who used the singular possessive adopted here, while others use the plural—victors') in his opening statement to the IMT. See Taylor, *Anatomy*, pp. 167–8; see also Michael Blindiss, '"Victors'" Justice at the Nuremberg Tribunal?', *History Today*, May 1995.

29. Beigbeider, *Judging War Criminals*, pp. 55–6.

30. Only one of the judges was American at the time of the judgement.

31. See Futamura, *The Tokyo Trial*, Chapters 4–6.

32. *International Criminal Court Act*, 2001, Chapter 17, 11 May 2001. See Dominic McGoldrick, Peter J. Rowe and Eric Donnelly, *The Permanent International Criminal Court: Legal and Policy Issues*, Portland, OR: Hart Publishing, 2004.

33. *The Observer*, 1 May 2005. The later-ennobled Lord Boyce subsequently asserted that the 'armed forces are under siege'. Quoted in Christopher P. M. Waters, 'Is the Military Legally Encircled?' *Defence Studies*, Vol. 8, No. 1, 2008, p. 26. The Iraq expedition was surrounded with legal contention (see most notably, Philippe Sands, *Law Less World: America and the Making and Breaking of Global Rules*, London: Penguin, 2005). These issues would be evaluated as part of The Iraq Inquiry, officially launched by the UK on 30 July 2009 under the Chair of Sir John Chilcot (and commonly known as the Chilcot Inquiry). Among other things, it was not impossible to imagine that the Inquiry would even find that internally there had been legal authorisation for, and explanation of, regime change added to the rules of engagement, perhaps serving as complete reassurance to Boyce. If something of this kind were to emerge, it would go some way beyond the existing contestation, almost certainly opening up a new era of debate at the political-legal nexus of these events.

34. Although 'aggression' appeared in the ICC statute, it had no definition until the Kampala Review Conference of the ICC in August 2010. ICC doc. RC/WGCA/1/Rev. 2.

35. Andrea Birdsall, *The International Politics of Judicial Intervention: Creating a More Just World*, Abingdon: Routledge, 2009, p. 142.

36. *Statute of the International Criminal Tribunal for the former Former Yugoslavia* (available at www.un.org/icty), Article 1 and *Statute of the International Criminal Tribunal for Rwanda* (available at www.ictr.org), Article 1; see also Futamura, *The Tokyo Trial*, pp. 17–24; Rachel Kerr, *The International Criminal Tribunal for the Former Yugoslavia: An Exercise in Law, Diplomacy and Politics*, Oxford: Oxford University Press, 2004; Paul R. Williams and Michael P. Scharf, *Peace With Justice? War Crimes and Accountability in the Former Yugoslavia*, Boulder: Rowan and Littlefield, 2002; Victor Peskin, *International Justice in Rwanda and the Balkans: Virtual Trials and the Struggle for State Cooperation*, New York: Cambridge University Press, 2008.

37. *Statute of the International Criminal Tribunal for the former Yugoslavia*, Art.1.

38. *Statute of the International Criminal Tribunal for Rwanda*, Art. 1.

39. *Statute of the International Criminal Court*, Arts. 1 and 12.

40. Jessica Lincoln, *Transitional Justice, Peace and Accountability: Outreach and the Role of International Courts After Conflict*, London: Routledge 2011.

41. *Prosecutor* v. *Taylor*, Decision on Immunity from Jurisdiction, SCSL-2003–01-I, SCSL Appeals Chamber 31.5.2004; Schabas, *The UN International Criminal Tribunals*. It was especially significant that the SCSL determined itself to be international, as this gave it the authority to override any consideration of sovereign immunity in the case of Liberian President Charles Taylor, who claimed that, despite accepting exile in Nigeria under an immunity arrangement whereby he would no longer be involved in Liberian politics (a condition he persistently breached, in any case), he was a serving head of state and therefore could not be prosecuted; the court found that, as established by precedent in the jurisprudence of international tribunals (and irrespective of status in relation to Chapter VII of the UN Charter), international courts had the right to try sovereigns, overriding any claims to sovereign immunity. For discussion of this and its implications, see Cryer, et al., *International Criminal Law*, pp. 442–3. The Special Court for Sierra Leone is 'international', but not entirely in the same sense as the *ad hoc* tribunals established for the former Yugoslavia and Rwanda. Each of the latter bodies has UN Security Council authority under Chapter VII of the UN Charter, giving them overriding international status. However, the SCSL also blends the domestic and the international, involving formal agreement between the UN and Sierra Leone, intentionally bringing elements of local ownership to the court and, in aspiration at least, bringing it closer to the communities it is meant to serve. On 'internationalised' judicial bodies, including the Special Court, see Rachel Kerr and Eirin Mobekk, *Peace and Justice: Seeking Accountability After War*, Cambridge: Polity, 2007, Chapter 4.

42. Richard Goldstone notes that when he first arrived as Chief Prosecutor, in the middle of August 1994, there were twenty-three Americans and five Australians among the forty-strong staff gathered in the first short phase of operation—he does not record the British contingent, however, which was also notable and gave the impression that the Tribunal was an American-Australian-Anglo conspiracy (with the technical exception, of course, that Gavin Ruxton was a Scot—the Senior Legal Advisor and later Chief of Prosecutions, remained in the Office of the Prosecutor until June 2010). Goldstone, *For Humanity: Reflections of a War Crimes Investigator*, New Haven: Yale University Press, 2000, p. 80.

43. Goldstone, *For Humanity*, pp. 74–6.

44. 'Statement of Heads of State and Government of the United Nations Security Council', UN doc. S/23200, 31 January 1992.

45. It is important to register that this was a matter of making something completely clear—as noted elsewhere, the authority for the UN Security Council to take action contrary to conventional protections of sovereignty had been 'generally unnoticed for forty years', even though the founders of the UN had allowed for this provision in Article 2 (7) of the UN Charter. (Gow, *Defending the West*, p. 56).

46. Paul Fifoot, 'Functions and Powers, and Inventions: UN Action in Respect of Human Rights and Humanitarian Intervention', in Nigel Rodley, ed., *To Loose the Bands of Wickedness: International Intervention in Defence of Human Rights*, London: Brassey's, 1992.

47. Gow, *Defending the West*, pp. 56–8.

48. Taylor, *Anatomy*, p. 641.

49. The Special Court for Sierra Leone was, nonetheless, ultimately, an international body—see above.

50. For example, Col. Charles Garraway, a UK military lawyer, attached to the Coalition Provisional Administration in Baghdad. Garraway, contributed significantly to the Statute of the High Tribunal. Charles Garraway, 'The Iraqi Special Tribunal and the "New Trial of the Century"', King's College London, 30 November 2005.

51. The UK and the US had been preparing for a tribunal, initially expected to be an international body—either under the UN Security Council alone, or a 'hybrid' on the lines of Sierra Leone. Months before the operations against Iraq were launched, even, lawyers and investigators from the two countries met in London to consider files against around twenty individuals. Cherif Bassiouni, in what appears to be an authoritative account (based, in part, on personal involvement in the evolving process) suggests that it was September 2003 when concepts cohered and momentum began for 'the idea of an Iraqi national tribunal bolstered by international support'. M. Cherif Bassiouni, 'Post-Conflict Justice in Iraq: An Appraisal of the Iraqi Special Tribunal', *Cornell International Law Journal*, Vol. 38, No. 327, 2005. For further discussion of the Iraqi High Tribunal, see: Michael P. Scharf 'The Iraqi High Tribunal: A Viable Experiment in International Justice?', *Journal of International Criminal Justice*, Vol. 5, No. 2, 2007; Guénaël Mettraux, 'The 2005 Revision of the Statute of the Iraqi Special Tribunal', *Journal of International Criminal Justice*, Vol. 5, No. 2, 2007; Sylvia de Bertodano, 'Were There More Acceptable Alternatives to the Iraqi High Tribunal?' *Journal of International Criminal Justice*, Vol. 5, No. 2, 2007.

52. On the remarkable development of the International Criminal Court, especially the swiftness with which it emerged and came to the brink of existence, see Vesselin Popovski, 'The International Criminal Court', *International Relations*, Vol. XV, No. 3, December 2000.

53. Kerr, *International Criminal Tribunal for the Former Yugoslavia*, Chapter 3.

54. The UN organisation as a global and inclusive body operates a 'representative' policy in filling formal positions, seeking an international spread of employees that reflects all the countries in the world, rather than recruiting purely on merit. Added to this, the UN organisation has established bureaucratic procedures for its operations. As it was, the ICTY could well have operated more effectively and cheaply had the UN organisation not been so deeply involved—as, initially, it was not. As a broad comparative point of reference, neither private legal practices, nor the organisation of prosecution and trial in domestic jurisdictions, require a bureaucracy that takes up around half the personnel on the payroll, which, as an approximation, was the case with the ICTY.

55. Goldstone, *For Humanity*.

56. The last person on the 'wanted' list, Goran Hadžić, was arrested on 20 July 2011. For an overview of all indictees and their fates, see: 'Key Figures of ICTY Cases', available at www.un.org/icty/glance-e/index.htm, accessed 24 August 2011.

57. See www.sc-sl.org/Taylor.html at 11 August 2008; see also the short advocacy, rather than analytical, film *Charles Taylor and Justice for Liberia*, Amnesty International, 2006, which makes a case for prosecuting Taylor for alleged crimes committed in Liberia, as well as those he was charged with committing in Sierra Leone.

58. Relevant extracts appear for reference in the Annex to the present volume.

59. With regard to the ICC, one commentary has suggested that the treatment of crimes in the Rome Statute has 'contributed to the development of customary law'—but this has been a broad characteristic of the processes surrounding all of the various international tribunals or courts. Cryer, et al., *International Criminal Law*, p. 126; see also *Decision on the Defence Interlocutory Appeal on Jurisdiction, Prosecutor v. Dusan Tadic*, IT-94-1-AR72, which discusses many of the issues associated with evolving international criminal law in relation to the ICTY statute and jurisdiction—and, in effect, contributes to the evolutionary process as it does so.

60. For some of the impact of ICTY jurisprudence on customary law, see Robert Cryer, 'Of custom, treaties, scholars and the gavel: the influence of the international criminal tribunal on the ICRC customary law study', *Journal of Conflict and Security Law*, Vol. 11, No. 2, 2006.

61. Minna Schrag has indicated that this was the case, probably strongly influenced by the 'advocacy' of those who saw particular opportunities to advance international law. 'Lessons Learned from ICTY Experience', *Journal of International Criminal Justice*, Vol. 2, No. 2, 2004, p. 431.

62. An introductory guide to some of the issues here can be found in Chapters 7, 8, 10, 11 and 12 of Cryer, et al., *International Criminal Law*. It might also be assumed that the *Decision on the Defence Interlocutory Appeal on Jurisdiction*,

Prosecutor v. Dusan Tadic, cited in note 60 above, had some influence on the ICTR Statute, given that, *inter alia*, this made clear that, outside of Article 5 of the ICTY Statute, custom had established that no nexus with armed conflict was required when dealing with Crimes Against Humanity.

63. Personal assistance was given to the court in this respect, introducing empirical detail with which the Prosecutor could argue for subject matter jurisdiction regarding each article. A summary of this experience is offered in James Gow, *The Serbian Project and Its Adversaries: a Strategy of War Crimes*, London and Montreal: Hurst/McGill-Queen's University Press, 2003, pp. 26–30.

64. The detail provided relating to war crimes in the ICC Statute provided 'certainty', as well as reflecting 'the principle of legality', and also helping 'to limit unexpected exposure to prosecution' according to Cryer, *et al.*, *International Criminal Law*, p. 125. This might be taken as a fairly authoritative assessment, given that one of the authors, Elizabeth Wilmshurst, was at the heart of the drafting process as Deputy Legal Advisor at the UK Foreign and Commonwealth Office—and her erstwhile boss, Sir Franklin Berman, asserted that there was 'not a paragraph' of the Statute that did not bear her touch. (Said at a conference discussing 'UK Perspectives on the Laws of Armed Conflict', held under the Leverhulme-funded *Changing Character of Warfare* program at Oxford University, 1 July 2004).

65. On the significant evolution in law and interpretation relating to Crimes Against Humanity, see: Bassiouni, *Crimes Against Humanity*; Cryer, et al., *International Criminal Law*, Chapter 10; Geoffrey Robertson, *Crimes Against Humanity: the Struggle for Global Justice*, London: Penguin, 2008; Lindsay Moir, 'Towards the Unification of International Humanitarian Law' in Richard Burchill, Nigel D. White, and Justin Morris, eds, *International Conflict and Security Law: Essays in Honour of Hilaire McCoubrey*, in association with the McCoubrey Centre for International Law, Cambridge: Cambridge University Press, 2005; *Convention on the Non-Applicability of Statutory Limitations to War Crimes and Crimes Against Humanity*, UN General Assembly, Resolution 2391 (XXIII), UN doc. A/7218, Art. 1(b).

66. The nexus with armed conflict was probably inserted to address the conservative and state protective concerns held by the framers of the Statute. The extent to which this creation of the Tribunal was an innovation, and to which there were profound sensitivities among states to ensure that there were limits on this peculiar body, meant that those designing the ICTY were probably keen not to be too radical. This is discussed in the *Decision on the Defence Interlocutory Appeal on Jurisdiction, Prosecutor v. Dusan Tadic* (cit.).

67. It should be noted that the requirement is widespread, or systematic, not widespread and systematic—jurisdiction did not require both conditions.

68. Rape had been alleged as an element of Crimes Against Humanity at the Yugo-

slavia Tribunal, although not explicitly noted as an element or crime itself. (*Prosecutor v. Dragoljub Kunarac*, IT-96-23). The ICTR took the handling of rape further, identifying it as an offence under Crimes Against Humanity and Article 3, common to the Geneva Conventions in the Statute, while the Trial Chamber went beyond even the arguments of the Prosecution to find rape to be a constitutive act of genocide. (*Prosecutor v. Jean-Paul Akayesu Judgement*, ICTR-96-4-T 2, September 1998, paras 507–8).

69. Martin Shaw has made a particularly interesting call for 'genocide' to be given a more sociologically defined interpretation, including recognition of the victims' experience (and recalling the sociological origins of the term in the work of Raphael Lemkin, who, as noted above, coined the term), rather than the narrow definition focused on the perpetrators' intent, as is found in the Genocide Convention. (Shaw, *What is Genocide?*)

70. Vesselin Popovski, 'Terrorizing Civilians as a "Counter-terrorist Operation": Crimes and Impunity in Chechnya', *Journal of Southeast European and Black Sea Studies*, Vol. 7, No. 3, 2007.

71. Rachel Kerr, *The Military on Trial: The British Army in Iraq*, Nijmegen: Wolf Legal Publishers, 2008.

72. Elspeth Guild, ed., *War or Crime?: National Legal Challenges in Europe to the War in Iraq*, Nijmegen: Wolf Legal Publishers, 2009.

73. *Isayeva* v. *Russia*, No. 57950/00, Judgment, 24 February 2005; *Isayeva, Yusupova and Bazayeva v. Russia*, Judgment, of 24 February 2005; Douwe Korff, *The Right to Life: A Guide to the Implementation of Article 2 of the European Convention on Human Rights*, Human Rights Handbooks No. 8, Strasbourg: The Council of Europe, 2006, pp. 34–5.

74. *Akhmadov et al.* v. *Russia*, No. 21586/02, Judgement, 14 November 2008, para. 97.

75. Guglielmo Verdirame, 'Human Rights in War: A Framework for Analysis', *European Human Rights Law Review*, No. 6, 2008.

4. STRATEGY AND JUSTICE

1. Christopher P. M. Waters, 'Is the Military Legally Encircled?', *Defence Studies*, Vol. 8, No., 1, 2008, p. 26.

2. Ministry of Defence, *Claims Annual Report 2005/2006* London: Ministry of Defence, 2006.

3. Waters, 'Is the Military', p. 27.

4. Edward Garnier MP, *Hansard*, Standing Committee D, 10 April 2000, ICC Bill (Lords), http://www.publications.parliament.uk/pa/cm200001/cmstand/d/st010410/pm/10410s01.htm accessed 3 July 2011.

5. W. G. L. Mackinlay, *Perceptions and Misconceptions: How Are International and*

UK Law Perceived to Affect Military Commanders and Their Subordinates on Operations?, Defence Research Paper, Shrivenham: Joint Services Command and Staff College, July 2006, p. 3.

6. Libya accused NATO's airmen of committing war crimes as they prosecuted an air campaign against the Qadaffi regime in 2011. For example, a Qadaffi-loyalist Libyan diplomat, Mustafa Shaban, accused the Alliance of 'crimes against humanity, crimes of war and crimes of aggression', (*Reuters*, 9 June 2011). Disturbingly for the Alliance and its airmen, it was clear that some among the Allies were uncomfortable with the conduct of operations, or even the overall idea of Operation Odyssey Dawn itself, especially when NATO had to concede errors, such as the 'weapons system failure' that resulted in the highly publicised deaths of two babies among nine civilians in one attack on Tripoli. This enhanced concerns about the operation within NATO and outside it, adding to the pressures on the aircrews conducting operations. (*BBC News*, 20 June 2011).

7. Mackinlay, *Perceptions and Misperceptions*, pp. 16–19.

8. Mackinlay, *Perceptions and Misperceptions*, p. 19.

9. Waters asserts that 'legal misinformation is rife in the armed forces'. The basis for this is assertion is not evident, but personal experience suggests that it is a reasonable comment. 'Is the Military', p. 41.

10. For example, *The Guardian* published an article by Ewen MacAskill under the title 'UK should face court for crimes in Iraq, say jurists', *The Guardian*, 21 January 2004.

11. Confidential author interviews with three officials from NATO countries, Washington and London, April 1999, September 2005 and November 2005.

12. The notion of the '3-block war' was first introduced by the commander of the US Marine Corps in the 1990s, General Charles 'Chuck' Krulak. He explained that his forces had to plan increasingly to be involved in operations where, in one city or neighbourhood, the troops might be engaged in full combat on one block; conducting a struggle against insurgents with a need for judicious use of force and to win 'hearts and minds' on the next block; and guarding a peace support and humanitarian operation on the next. Krulak, 'The Strategic Corporal: Leadership in the Three Block War', *Marines Magazine*, January 1999.

13. War and War Crimes Project, Focus Group 2 (hereafter, Focus Group references will appear as, e.g., 'FG2').

14. War and War Crimes Project, FG2.

15. War and War Crimes Project, FG1.

16. *Ibid.*

17. *Ibid.*

18. *Ibid.*

19. *Ibid.*

20. Milena Michalski and James Gow, *War, Image and Legitimacy: Viewing Contemporary Conflict*, London: Routledge, 2007.

21. War and War Crimes Project, FG3.

22. War and War Crimes Project, FG5.

23. *Ibid.*

24. *Ibid.*

25. *Virgin Soldiers*, Dir. Dodge Billingsley, Combat Films, 2004.

26. War and War Crimes Project, FG3.

27. *Ibid.*

28. *Ibid.*

29. This is one of the more surprising elements among the research findings in my judgement (although perhaps I should not have been surprised).

30. *Daily Telegraph*, 21 July 2005.

31. The case resulted in the first conviction under the UK International Criminal Court Act, as discussed in Chapter 1. This would seem to confirm how misguided Collins was in making these comments.

32. War and War Crimes Project, FG3.

33. Lieutenant General Sir Rupert Smith, *The Utility of Force: the Art of War in the Modern World*, London: Allen Lane, 2005, p. 64.

34. War and War Crimes Project, FG2.

35. As one commentator on Nuremberg couched it: 'Total war, as we can now see more clearly, has a momentum of its own and what may appear as an atrocity by one side at the beginning of hostilities looks like civilised reticence when viewed from the crescendo of carnage that develops by the end'. Bradley F Smith, *Reaching Judgement at Nuremberg*, London: Andrew Deutsch, 1977, p. 301.

36. War and War Crimes Project, FG2.

37. War and War Crimes Project, FG5.

38. War and War Crimes Project, FG2.

39. Smith, *Utility of Force*, pp. 327–331.

40. War and War Crimes Project, FG1.

41. *Ibid.*

42. War and War Crimes Project, FG2.

43. *Cf.* Adam Roberts, 'Land Warfare: From The Hague to Nuremberg', in (M. Howard, M. et al., 1994, p.: 130).

44. War and War Crimes Project, FG2.

45. War and War Crimes Project, FG1.

46. *Ibid.*

47. War and War Crimes Project, FG3.

48. War and War Crimes Project, FG1.

49. War and War Crimes Project, FG2.

50. War and War Crimes Project, FG3.

51. The Scottish legal system is distinct from that of England and Wales (which have one joint legal system), and that of Northern Ireland—even though all four countries form the United Kingdom.

52. This is discussed in Chapter 3.

53. War and War Crimes Project, FG3.

54. Of course, this uninformed understanding was at odds with the detail of the case, as seen in Chapter 1.

55. War and War Crimes Project, FG3.

56. *Ibid.*

57. *Ibid.*

58. *Ibid.* Personal experience of jury service at a fraud trial confirms this point—so far as some members of the jury and I could follow the detail, there was a strong impression that other members of the jury struggled.

59. War and War Crimes Project, FG4.

60. Ludwig Wittgenstein, *The Blue and Brown Books: Preliminary Studies for the Philosophical Investigations*, 2nd edn, Oxford: Blackwell, 1969, p. 45.

61. War and War Crimes Project, FG4.

62. *Ibid.* This issue was also raised by a group of senior Serbian officers—see Chapter 5.

63. War and War Crimes Project, FG3.

64. War and War Crimes Project, FG4.

65. *Ibid.*

66. *Ibid.*

67. *Ibid.*

68. *Ibid.*

69. *Ibid.*

70. *Ibid.*

71. War and War Crimes Project, FG2.

72. War and War Crimes Project, FG1.

73. One view expressed leaned in this direction, when cautioning against an approach to prosecution that rested entirely with the military itself: 'We try to be tried by people who understand our system. But if you have Courts-Martial, you separate responsibility from the politicians. It all has to be in the military circle. But the military execute political decisions'. (War and War Crimes Project, FG3).

74. War and War Crimes Project, FG2.

75. War and War Crimes Project, FG4.

76. *Ibid.*

5. CONDUCT AND CASES

1. There is an important body of literature on civil-military relations. Classic and key elements include: Samuel P. Huntington, *The Soldier and the State: the Theory and Politics of Civil-Military Relations*, Cambridge, Mass.: The Belknap Press,

1957; Samuel E. Finer, *The Man on Horseback: the Role of the Military in Politics*, Harmondsworth: Penguin, 1968; Morris Janowitz, *The Professional Soldier: a Social and Political Portrait*, Glencoe: The Free Press, 1960 and *The Military in the Political Development of New Nations*, Chicago: University of Chicago Press, 1964; Amos Perlmutter, *The Military and Politics in Modern Times*, New Haven: Yale University Press, 1977; Martin Edmonds, *The Armed Services and Society*, Leicester: University of Leicester Press, 1988; Peter D. Feaver, 'The Civil-Military Problematique: Huntington, Janowitz and the Question of Civilian Control', *Armed Forces and Society*, Vol. 23, No. 2, 1996; Elliott A. Cohen, *Supreme Command: Soldiers Statesmen and Leadership in Wartime*, Glencoe: The Free Press, 2002.

2. Michael Bothe, 'The Protection of the Civilian Population and NATO Bombing on of Yugoslavia: Comments on a Report to the Prosecutor of the ICTY', *European Journal of International Law*, Vol. 12, No. 3, 2001, p. 531.

3. *Prosecutor v. Tihomir Blaskic, Judgement*, IT-95–14-A, 27 January 2005; *Prosecutor v. Staislav Galic, Judgement*, IT-98–29-A, 30 November 2006; see William J. Fenrick, 'A First Attempt to Adjudicate Conduct of Hostilities Offences: Comments on Aspects of the ICTY Trial Decision in the Prosecutor v. Blaskic', *Leiden Journal of International Law*, Vol. 13, No. 4, 2000; see also Fenrick, 'The Prosecution of Unlawful Attack Cases Before the ICTY', *Yearbook of International Humanitarian Law*, Vol. 7, 2004—this last contribution is a deeply informed and major wide survey of the state of the law on unlawful attacks in light of cases at the ICTY.

4. *Prosecutor v. Staislav Galic, Judgement*, IT-98-29 *Judgement*, 30 November 2006.

5. Although this statement was made with reference to another category of crime—where direct targeting had been alleged and found—the statement, reflecting the defence against that charge, captured the situation overall and the essence also of Blaškić's defence against charges of disproportionate bombardment. *Prosecutor v. Tihomir Blaskic, Judgement*, IT-95–14-A, Para. 103.

6. Fenrick, 'A First Attempt', p. 931.

7. *Prosecutor v. Dario Kordic, Tihofil (also known as Tihomir) Blaskic et al., Indictment*, IT-94–14, November 1995.

8. Milena Michalski and James Gow, *War, Image and Legitimacy: Viewing Contemporary Conflict*, London: Routledge, 2007, pp. 157–63 and 215.

9. *RFE/RL*, 2 April 2007, http://www.rferl.org/content/article/1075637.html, accessed 6 July 2011.

10. Philip Bobbitt, *Terror and Consent*, New York: Knopff, 2009, pp. 250–85. John Yoo, Deputy Assistant Attorney General in the Office of Legal Counsel at the U.S. Department of Justice 2001–3, was intimately involved in, and responsible for, much of the legal advice involved and his *War by Other Means* sets out the justification for various legal interpretations and policies adopted: *War by*

Other Means: An Insider's Account of the War on Terror, New York: Atlantic Monthly Press, 2006; *Crisis and Command: the History of Executive Power from George Washington to George W. Bush*, New York: Kaplan, 2009. The official perspective of the administration on the detentions and the legal issues surrounding them was offered by John B. Bellinger, III, 'Legal Issues in the War on Terrorism', London School of Economics, 31 October 2006.

11. *The Washington Post*, 2 November 2005.

12. Telford Taylor, *The Anatomy of the Nuremberg Trials: a Personal Memoir*, New York: Bloomsbury, 1993, p. 253.

13. David Chuter, *War Crimes: Confronting Atrocity in the Modern World*, London: Lynne Rienner, 2003, p. 11.

14. *Convention (III) Relative to the Treatment of Prisoners of War*, Geneva, 12 August 1949 (hereafter Geneva III).

15. This was the view of a British military legal advisor, in discussion with the author.

16. *Geneva III*, Article 13.

17. *Ibid.*

18. All quotation and reference in the present this section is from War and War Crimes Project, FG3, unless otherwise stated.

19. William Shakespeare, *King Henry V*, ed., J.H. Walter, The Arden Edition of the Works of William Shakespeare, London: Methuen, 1954, Act IV, Scs. vi–vii. See also the discussion in Theodor Meron, *War Crimes Law Comes of Age: Essays*, Oxford: Oxford University Press, pp. 118–20. Meron notes that the action attributed to Henry would have been contested in medieval interpretations—and so arguably acceptable, and he very interestingly points out that the Lieber Code (see Chapter 3) otherwise much admired for its humanitarian qualities, left scope for showing 'no quarter' when it is 'impossible to cumber himself [the commander] with prisoners'.

20. I have not been able to identify a corroborating example from SOE operations in Yugoslavia. Yet, it seems likely that there would have been situations in which SOE officers, in Yugoslavia or elsewhere, would have needed to act this way—and the SOE training manual certainly encouraged them to think in this way. They were even trained to be efficient in performing such an act: 'A prisoner is generally a handicap and a source of danger, particularly if you are without weapons. So forget the Queensberry rules; forget the term "foul methods". That may sound cruel, but it is still more cruel to take longer than necessary to kill your opponent. "Foul methods", so-called, help you to kill more quickly'. Denis Rigden, 'Introduction', *SOE Syllabus, Lessons in Ungentlemanly Warfare World War II*, Introduction by Denis Rigden, London: Public Record Office, 2001.

21. Perhaps, in this sense, the US operation that killed Osama bin Ladin in Pakistan in 2011 avoided greater criticism for the killing of the al-Qa'ida leader than the operation would have garnered had it gone disastrously wrong.

22. It is not clear to what extent the later action that killed Osama bin Ladin might have altered this judgement, had it occurred a decade earlier.

23. See James Gow, *The Serbian Project and Its Adversaries: a Strategy of War Crimes*, London and Montreal: Hurst/McGill-Queen's University Press, 2003; Ivo Daalder and Michael O'Hanlon, *Winning Ugly: NATO's Kosovo War*, Washington DC: Brooking's Institution, 2000.

24. Dino Kritsiotis, 'The Kosovo Crisis and NATO's Application of Armed Force Against the Federal Republic of Yugoslavia', *The International and Comparative Law Quarterly*, Vol. 49, No. 2, 2000.

25. Marco Roscini, 'Targeting and Contemporary Aerial Bombardment', *International and Comparative Law Quarterly*, Vol. 54, No. 2, 2005, pp. 436–7.

26. Amnesty International, *NATO/Federal Republic Of Yugoslavia: 'Collateral Damage' or Unlawful Killings? Violations of the Laws of War by NATO During Operation Allied Force*, Amnesty International, AI Index: EUR 70/18/00, June 2000.

27. William M. Arkin, 'Operation Allied Force: "The Most Precise Application of Air Power in History"' in Andrew Bacevich and Elliott A. Cohen, eds, *War Over Kosovo: Politics and Strategy in a Global Age*, New York: Columbia University Press, 2001, pp. 1–37, provides extremely detailed figures on the air operations, as well as an excellent and fine-tuned account of the operational campaign from the U.S. military perspective in Washington, DC, based on extensive interaction with many of those involved. See also Gow, *The Serbian Project* and Bill Fenrick's extraordinarily careful assessment of the detail in the contexts of relevant—predominantly ICTY—jurisprudence and prosecutorial considerations (albeit from an 'outside' perspective)—William J. Fenrick, 'Targetting and Proportionality During the NATO Bombing Campaign Against Yugoslavia', *European Journal of International Law*, Vol. 12, No. 3, 2001, and its expanded version 'The Law Applicable to Targeting and Proportionality After Operation Allied Force: A View from the Outside', *Yearbook of International Law*, Vol. 3, 2000.

28. Human Rights Watch, *Ticking Time Bombs: NATO's Use of Cluster Munitions in Yugoslavia*, 11, 6(D), June 1999; Human Rights Watch, *Civilian Deaths in the NATO Air Campaign*, 12, 1(D), February 2000.

29. *Final Report to the Prosecutor by the Committee Established to Review the NATO Bombing Campaign Against the Federal Republic of Yugoslavia*, 13 June 2000, at http://www.un.org/icty/pressreal/nato061300.htm, accessed 5 September 2000.

30. *Final Report to the Prosecutor*, III.9.

31. For example, Paolo Benvenuti, 'The ICTY Prosecutor and the Review of the NATO Bombing Campaign Against the Federal Republic of Yugoslavia', *European Journal of International Law*, Vol. 12, No. 3, 2001.

32. Fenrick, 'Law Applicable'; Fenrick may be presumed to have been close to the Office of the Prosecutor (OTP) investigation—although the article is written from 'the outside', he had previously worked as a military lawyer in the OTP,

and at times betrays crucial nuggets from internal discussions—for example 'some persons involved with writing the OTP ICTY report were of the view that the aircrew [in the Grdelica railroad bridge action] might be criminally negligent in firing the second missile'. (p. 65) This is the kind of comment, as it is not footnoted, that must be presumed to reflect Fenrick's experience—and quite possibly, he was one of the 'persons' in question. It is comments and insights of this type that give credibility to Fenrick's assessment of the issues overall, broadly tallying as it does—though never explicitly—with the assessment in the OTP ICTY report. This indicates clearly that this incident, where the report was 'most critical' might, another time at least, have warranted further investigation, even if this was not the best use of resources when the report was made. However, Fenrick follows the OTP ICTY report in effectively skimming over the Niš incident—even reinforcing the decision not to develop that analysis and the arguably indiscriminate use of cluster munitions adjacent to civilian population centres, in effect. He does so by pointing out that only the US stopped using cluster munitions after the incident (and the Human Rights Watch report) and that changes in the rules of engagement 'need not be regarded as evidence of culpability', but might 'reflect a continuing good faith endeavour to make practical changes to comply with legal obligations'. (p. 77).

33. For example, Bonnie Docherty, 'Legal Analysis of Cluster Munitions', Cluster Munition Coalition, 14 February 2005, http://www.stopclustermunitions.org/the-problem/history-harm/?id=108 accessed 6 July 2011.

34. *The Fall of Milosevic*, Dir. Dai Richards, Brook-Lapping, 2001, Part 2.

35. Human Rights Watch, *Civilian Deaths*; it is notable that the Human Rights Watch report was the basis of questioning by the UK House of Commons Foreign Affairs Select Committee, which quoted from it directly in posing questions. House of Commons, *Foreign Affairs—Minutes of Evidence*, Q. 341, 8 February 2000, http://www.publications.parliament.uk/pa/cm199900/cmselect/cmfaff/28/0020801.htm at accessed 7 July 2011. This ratio shift contrasts with the general pattern in operations, which tends to move more towards precision munitions over time.

36. This raises notable issues that would have to be part of any genuine criminal investigation about events in Niš, as the airfield was known to be located—and would have been known to be—in at the edge of the town.

37. I am grateful to Gordon Burck for informing me that a Chechen group was advised at the Centre for Strategic and International Studies in Washington DC to try to find unexploded Russian cluster devices as a way of providing evidence of Russia's alleged crimes.

38. In the research, the NATO-Kosovo case was identified as a prompt for the scenario, however, it was not stipulated which country had decided to halt use of cluster munitions, and which had continued to operate with them.

39. All quotations and references in the present section are from War and War Crimes Project FG5, unless otherwise stated.

40. War and War Crimes Project, FG1.

41. *Cf.* Shifting Securities Project FGs 9 and 10, where the process of targeting was explored.

42. It was pointed out that similar questions arise with artillery-fired cluster munitions, meaning that this is not purely an issue of air warfare.

43. It should be noted that there were no American participants in this particular focus group specifically discussing the Kosovo-inspired scenario. It can only be presumed that the presence of an American participant would have given an extra dimension to this part of the research. The absence of an American voice is a potential limit on the research findings reflecting on the US.

44. Pictures of Peace and Justice Project, FG11.

45. This comment should probably be understood in light of discussion at the time of the Kosovo operations and since then regarding NATO's bombing of the RTS (Radio Television Serbia) building in Belgrade, which was controversial because it was a civilian broadcaster—even if it was involved very strongly in information support for the Belgrade authorities. More importantly, it was part of the Belgrade military communications hub. As Fenrick suggests, we should be 'extremely reluctant to classify a media outlet which is not also used as part of a military command, control and communications network as a military objective', and hence a legitimate target. ('Law Applicable', p. 71). He also indicates that the OTP ICTY view was that 'attacking RTS simply because it disseminated propaganda was probably unlawful but that it appeared RTS might also fulfil another function' (p. 66). As 'another function' was the reason for the attack, Marco Roscini's suggestion is probably wrong that the fairly swift return of RTS to broadcasting, combined with the fact that 'there was no military advantage gained', meant that the principle of proportionality could be 'seriously' questioned. (Roscini, 'Targeting', p. 424) It is not impossible that the Niš post office was, or could have been, part of a command and communications net—in the old Yugoslavia, almost everything was linked like this by dual roles. However, as noted in the main text here, it seems extremely improbable that NATO would use cluster weapons against a target of this kind—it would not make military sense and would risk strongly indiscriminate damage.

46. The empirical research presented here was carried out prior to 100 states agreeing a Draft Treaty to ban the use of cluster munitions, in Dublin, in May 2008. (*BBC News*, 28 May 2008; *Convention on Cluster Munitions*, CCM/77, 30 May 2008, available at http://www.clusterconvention.org/files/2011/01/Convention-ENG.pdf at accessed 7 July 2011). This demonstrates the insight and awareness that defence professionals have—and how their concerns and sensitivities might be ahead of those of activists, publics and governments.

47. In a later phase of the ICTY's work, three Croatian Generals faced trial in a case that also included issues of indiscriminate or disproportionate attack and bombardment. Two of them—Ante Gotovina and Mladen Markač—were convicted in April 2011 (the third, Ivan Čermak, was acquitted on all counts), with Markač directly responsible for the assaults in question. *Prosecutor v. Ante Gotovina, Ivan Cermak and Mladen Markac, Judgement*, Vols. I and II, IT-06–90-T, 15 April 2001.

48. In positing a scenario drawing on this situation, and in identifying that situation here, it should be made absolutely explicit that the aim is not to question the conviction of General Galić in The Hague, where, *inter alia*, there were a range of other issues and incidents forming the case, (*Prosecutor v. Stanislav Galic, Judgement*, Case IT-98–29, 30 November 2006) and where Galić was convicted and sentenced to life imprisonment by the Appeals Chamber, an increase from the twenty years imprisonment initially sentenced by the original Trial Chamber (*Case Information Sheet, 'Stanislav Galic'*, IT-98–29, available at www.un.org/icty at accessed 1 July 2008). The case is only a departure point for intellectual interest, having identified it as what appears to be the first international trial ever conducted for what is, at first sight, purely a matter of military performance. This analysis is not meant to suggest that the General or others should be acquitted and released—a point that, despite her own generally strong intellectual curiosity, Sabrina Ramet appears to have missed in her reading of my identifying the novelty of the Galić case and the *prima facie* elements to consider mitigation, while noting the other issues involved, which prompted the broad enquiry undertaken in the present volume. See Gow, *The Serbian Project*, pp. 304–5; and Sabrina Ramet: *Thinking About Yugoslavia: Scholarly Debates About the Yugoslav Breakup and the Wars in Bosnia and Kosovo*, Cambridge: Cambridge University, 2005, pp. 100–1.

49. William J. Fenrick, 'The Targeted Killings Judgment and the Scope of Direct Participation in Hostilities', *Journal of International Criminal Justice*, Vol. 5, No. 2, 2007, p. 334.

50. It is astonishing to me that some readers of my earlier work on the Serbian strategy of war crimes during the 1990s have considered my intellectual reflection about, and empirical consideration of, the factors affecting Serbian strategy as somehow seeking to justify the Serbian action. This is all the more astonishing, given that the very title of the book indicates not only the judgement of the criminal record at the ICTY (to which I made some footnote contributions as an expert witness for the Office of the Prosecutor), but also the personal perspective that informed all my academic work on this matter and my assistance to the court. At least, Sabrina Ramet, in this selection, has stated that she finds it 'hard to imagine' that I am suggesting that criminal action is somehow 'justifiable'. Evidently, I had a need to be clearer, in this context—and I hope that

similar misunderstandings will not emerge in response to the present analysis. Gow, *The Serbian Project*; James Sadkovich, 'Balkan Battlegrounds', *Journal of Military History*, Vol. 70, No. 1, 2006, p. 191; Keith Doubt, '*The Serbian Project and Its Adversaries: a Strategy of War Crimes* by James Gow', Book Review, *Slavic Review*, Vol. 63, No. 4, 2004, p. 867; Ramet, *Thinking About Yugoslavia*, p. 101.

51. It should be self-evident that any worthwhile military will be a social organisation in which morale, *esprit de corps*, sacrifice and loyalty are among the factors that forge a strong bond, essential to the cohesion of an armed force. In moral—and legal—terms, military commanders 'have a duty to limit casualties in their own forces'. (Fenrick, 'Targeting and Proportionality'). Thus, commanders have always had a priority to protect their own force. Rupert Smith has suggested that social, political and financial concerns add to traditional questions of force protection in contemporary warfare—see Lt. Gen. Sir Rupert Smith, *The Utility of Force: the Art of War in the Modern World*, London: Allen Lane, 2005, pp. 292–7. Fenrick, in 'Targeting and Proportionality', offers wise reflection on evaluating force protection concerns, as well as on weighing force protection questions against risks to civilians.

52. Of course, this is an over-simple approach. As Fenrick bluntly and correctly states: 'assessing proportionality is not a simple exercise in number crunching' (Fenrick, 'Prosecution of Unlawful Attack Cases', p. 177).

53. All quotations and references in the present section are from War and War Crimes Project FG4, unless otherwise stated.

54. 'Chemical Ali' was a cousin of Iraqi dictator Saddam Hussein and a senior military figure and former defence minister. He gained his nickname after employing chemical munitions against Kurdish civilians, an action that eventually resulted in his being convicted of genocide by the Iraqi High Tribunal and sentenced to death by hanging, which sentence was carried out in January 2010. *BBC News*, 25 January 2010.

55. Shifting Securities Project FGs 9 and 10.

56. Interview No. 9, Maj. Gen. (formerly Brig.) Graham Binns, Shifting Securities Project.

57. Marco Roscini argues that the 'US practice of prioritising the protection of its own combatants with respect to the enemy's civilians in order not to lose the support of public opinion also erodes the principle of proportionality'. (Roscini, 'Targeting', p. 416). This 'risk averse' mode of warfare was the target of sociologist Martin Shaw's major critique of the 'Western' way of warfare, where the risk is seen as being transferred away from professional Western militaries to civilians in the areas of operations. (Martin Shaw, *The New Western Way of War*, Cambridge: Polity, 2005). *Cf.* Fenrick, 'Targeting and Proportionality', discussed above in note 53.

58. In contrast, Fenrick quotes the Kordić Trial Judgement (reflecting broader jurisprudence at the ICTY and the view of most international legal commentators): 'the failure of a party to comply with its obligation to remove civilians, to the maximum extent feasible, from the vicinity of military objectives did not "relieve the attacking party of its duty to abide by the principles of distinction and proportionality when launching an attack"'. Fenrick, 'Prosecution of Unlawful Attack Cases', p. 169.

59. Concern about subterfuge and abuse of civilian or medical locations was also a concern in focus groups on the Basra attack, noted earlier. Shifting Securities Project FG10.

60. *Cf.* Fenrick, 'Prosecution of Unlawful Attack Cases', p. 169, on the ICTY Kordić judgement, discussed above in note 60.

61. The following paragraphs draw on Pictures of Peace and Justice FG11.

6. WAR AND WAR CRIMES

1. Many argued that the US, or Western, engagement with al-Qa'ida should not be labelled 'war', but 'terrorism' (reflecting old understanding). But, the different character of this form of terrorism, compared with traditional, territorially focused action—such as that by the IRA, or ETA—in different global conditions, presents a new challenge that must be addressed. The response to al-Qa'ida and the nexus of associated actors and questions, including so-called 'rogue' and 'failing' states, as well as Islamist ideology and weapons of mass destruction or impact (WMD/I), was an important practical exercise in working out the boundaries of 'war' and 'non-war' in the early twenty-first century.

2. James Gow, *Defending the West*, Cambridge: Polity, 2005; *The National Security Strategy of the United States of America*, 2002, available at *http://usinfo.state.gov/topical/pol/terror/secstrat.htm*; Ivo Daalder, ed., *Beyond Preemption: Force and Legitimacy in a Changing World*, Washington, DC: The Brookings Institution Press, 2007; Lt. Gen. Sir Rupert Smith, *The Utility of Force: the Art of War in the Modern World*, London: Allen Lane, 2005.

3. Philip Bobbitt, *The Shield of Achilles* and *Terror and Consent: the Wars for the Twenty-First Century*, New York: Knopf, 2008.

4. Gow, *Defending the West*; *The National Security Strategy of the United States of America*, 2002; Daalder, *Legitimacy*; Michael Byers, *War Law*, London: Atlantic Books, 2005; Rein Müllerson, '*Jus ad Bellum*: Plus ça Change (le Monde) Plus C'est La Même Chose (Le Droit)?', *Journal of Conflict and Security Law*, Vol. 7, No. 2, 2002; Elizabeth Wilmshurst, *Principles of International Law on the Use of Force by States in Self-Defence*, ILP WP 05/01, Royal Institute of International Affairs, 2005 available at www.chathamhouse.org.uk/law.

5. Asaf Zussman and Noam Zussman, *Targeted Killings: Evaluating the Effectiveness*

of a Counterterrorism Policy, Discussion Paper 2005.02, Jerusalem: Bank of Israel, 2005; see also James Gow and Rachel Kerr, 'Law and War in the Global War on Terror', in Aidan Hehir, Natasha Kuhrt and Andrew Mumford eds, *International Law, Security and Ethics: Policy Challenges in the Post-9/11 World*, London: Routledge, 2011, which also covers material related to the present discussion.

6. For a discussion of some of the legal issues surrounding—and largely common to—the Global War on Terror and the case of Israeli-targeted killings, see Marko Milanovic, 'Lessons for Human Rights and Humanitarian Law in the War on Terror: Comparing *Hamdan* and the Israeli *Targeted Killings* Case', *International Review of the Red Cross*, Vol. 89, No. 866, June 2007.

7. It is notable, however, that those engaging in support of al-Qa'ida against the West regarded themselves as being soldiers, as the suicide video of Mohammed Siddique Khan, who led the attacks on the London transport system on 7 July 2005, made clear: 'We are at war and I am a soldier', he proclaims. A BBC television news report on 2 September 2005, including an extract from the farewell video, containing these words, is archived at news.bbc.co.uk/1/hi/uk/4206708.stm, accessed 11 August 2008.

8. It might be noted that, although al-Qa'ida's attacks had these characteristics, its capacity to conduct operations in this manner was severely circumscribed, once the controversial practice of targeted killings began to have an impact on its command structure.

9. International Committee of the Red Cross (ICRC), 'How is the Term Armed Conflict Defined in International Humanitarian Law?', Opinion Paper, March 2008. It should be noted that Common Article 3 states that it applies to 'armed conflicts not of an international character occurring on the territory of one of the High Contracting Parties'. While this means that any conflict must be on the territory of one of the states in the world and might be applicable, it is also clear that the transnational character of al-Qa'ida, its aims and operations does not fit the assumption of action contained, more or less, within the boundaries of a state party to the Conventions. This is made more problematic by Additional Protocol II to the Conventions, which specifies that a group must 'exercise such control over a part of its [the state's] territory' as to be able to carry out operations, and exercise the provisions and protections of the Conventions. Clearly, this does not apply to al-Qa'ida.

10. Müllerson, '*Plus ca Change*'.

11. Detaining civilians is allowed under the Fourth Geneva Convention, as a security provision. This even includes those who might be labelled 'illegal belligerents', as they have been extensively discussed in relation to the Geneva Convention, and what the US named as 'unlawful combatants'. This possibility applied to civilians in the context of armed conflict, or as aliens on territory under the control and (possibly) occupation of the forces of a protecting

power—that is, a state party to the Geneva Conventions. Detention was allowed, as a security provision, under Geneva Convention IV (Arts. 41, 42, 43, 68, 78 and Section IV), even though the terms on which it was drafted did not foresee the circumstances of transnational and international insurgency in which the US found itself. Thus, technically, those detained were quasi-prisoners of war, but were not prisoners of war, as such, under the conventions. The US conceded, in time, that, seeking to work in the spirit of the Geneva Conventions, as far as possible, it had to extend protection in accordance with Convention III to former members of the Taliban in Afghanistan.

12. See, for example, *NOW: Guantanamo Justice?* (dir. Not Known, 2006) available at www.pbs.org/now/shows/331/index.html, accessed at 30 August 2008.

13. Presidential candidate Barack Obama, a lawyer by profession, described the SMCs as a 'dangerously flawed legal approach'. (*The Wall Street Journal*, 18 May 2009). This was a view he perhaps regretted expressing after he came to office as President and sought to end the trial program and move it to normal civilian courts, an initiative that failed because of the security obstacles it would present, in terms of security, and the difficulty of the trials themselves. Obama subsequently managed only marginally to reform the SMCs, which were to continue, recognising that, for the most part, they had been designed to take account of the concerns in trying individuals such as Sheik Khalid Mohammed, and were an uncomfortable effort to address the difficult balance of justice and other factors. Even after the Obama reforms, the SMCs would not have satisfied the legal standards expected by such close allies as Australia and the United Kingdom, both of which had quietly negotiated the transfer of their citizens set to face the SMCs, even though each would have preferred to see these men remain at Guantanamo. However, concerns such as the death penalty, rights to access defence lawyers (improved by Obama), the types of evidence admissible and, above all, the absence of a proper right of appeal meant that London, for instance, preferred reluctantly to bring individuals to the UK, where there was no prospect that they could face trial, rather than allow its citizens to face the relative injustice of the SMCs. (Gow and Kerr, 'Law and War').

14. John B. Bellinger, III, 'Legal Issues in the War on Terrorism', London School of Economics, 31 October 2006.

15. Gow and Kerr, 'Law and War'.

16. Bobbitt, *Terror and Consent*, offers, as might be expected, an insightful exposition of the issues in relation to US and international law (pp. 250–85). John Yoo's books are particularly important in this context. Yoo was Deputy Assistant Attorney General in the Office of Legal Counsel at the US Department of Justice from 2001 to 2003. He was intimately involved in, and responsible for, much of the legal advice to President Bush, which proved to be controversial as both the 'grey area' and the Administration's preferences were negotiated. His

War by Other Means sets out the justification for various legal interpretations and policies that were adopted, while the later *Crisis and Command* offers commentary on how the Obama Administration failed to find alternatives on some issues, and made mistakes in its attempt to change others. Yoo, *The Powers of War and Peace: the Constitution and Foreign Affairs After 9/11*, Chicago: University of Chicago Press, 2005; *War by Other Means: an Insider's Account of the War on Terror*, New York: Atlantic Monthly Press, 2006; *Crisis and Command: the History of Executive Power from George Washington to George W. Bush*, New York: Kaplan, 2009.

17. It is noticeable, in this context, that the US approach—which privileged US citizens and territory, in terms of protection, while allowing almost unrestrained scope of official action, subject to legal sanction, regarding aliens—contrasts sharply with the situation in the European Union. In the UK, anti-terrorist provisions passed by Parliament, which meant the detention as a security provision (not as criminal suspects) of ten non-citizens at the Belmarsh high security prison, was ruled to be contrary to the European Convention on Human Rights on the grounds that such discrimination in terms of human rights between citizens and non-citizens was not tenable. As a result, the ten were released, then immediately detained once more under a new law that affected both citizens and non-citizens equally, but could not result in incarceration, merely restrictions on movement and monitoring—including the application of electronic tagging.

18. *The Washington Post*, 30 June 2006; *Hamdan v. Rumsfeld, Secretary of Defense* et al., Supreme Court of the United States, No. 05–184, argued 28 March 2006, decided 29 June 2006.

19. Again, the transnational, non-territorial aspect of the Global War on Terror, or, at least, of al-Qa'ida as an actor in it, generated problems. Its 'soldiers' did not fit the understandings that underpinned the Conventions, even Common Article 3, with its territorial references. None the less, there could be a case for applying its very limited terms, in principle, absent anything more specific. However, this would be to give al-Qa'ida personnel a degree of legitimacy that would be hard for many, especially in the US, to accept politically.

20. *Hamdan v. Rumsfeld*.

21. William J. Fenrick, 'The Targeted Killings Judgment and the Scope of Direct Participation in Hostilities', *Journal of International Criminal Justice*, Vol. 5, No. 2, 2007, p. 337.

22. *Ibid*.

23. Human Rights Watch, *Getting Away with Torture?*, Washington, D.C: Human Rights Watch, 2005.

24. It should be noted that the type of visit, reporting and reaction in question here all related to the International Committee of the Red Cross, not to any activi-

ties by domestic Red Cross organisations, which, even though they might be members of the International Federation of the Red Cross, can, inevitably, be subject to local political values, power and manipulation. This was the case, for example, in the Bosnian Serb entity Republika Srpska, where, from 1993, in the middle of the years of war in Bosnia and Hercegovina, the local Red Cross was headed by Ljilijana Karadžić, wife of Radovan Karadžić, the Bosnian Serb leader who was charged, *inter alia*, with genocide at the ICTY.

25. ICRC, 'Guantanamo Bay: Overview of the ICRC's Work for Internees', 30 January 2004, available at www.icrc.org/web/eng/siteeng0.nsf/htmlall/5qrc5v?opendocument, accessed 30 August 2008.

26. The difficulties of engaging with the changing character of war and law were compounded by the apparent tendency in the George W. Bush Administration to see the law as an instrument of political power. This was exemplified, in the case of federal prosecutors sacked, it seemed, according to an email, for failing to be 'loyal Bushies', to be replaced by prosecutors who would be more pliable—a matter that precipitated considerable concern on Capitol Hill, where the President's long-time legal advisor, Attorney General Alberto Gonzales, was repeatedly questioned. (*CBS Evening News*, 8 March 2006). As Senator Lindsay Graham (Republican), South Carolina, made clear, the Administration's character raised questions about its attempt to deal with the challenges of a new legal and strategic environment: 'I think that the Administration has looked at the legitimate power of the executive in time of war and taken it to extremes, to the point that you would lose constitutional balance'.

26. This new kind of war required new legal approaches, but there would still be limits and restraints on the conduct of that war.

27. The neologism 'unlawful combatant' mapped on to 'unprivileged combatant', a term of long heritage. That heritage and problems with the 'unlawful combatant' notion are treated in Milanovic, 'Lessons', pp. 386–7.

28. Jean-Marie Henckaerts and Louise Doswald-Beck, *Customary International Humanitarian Law*, Vol. 1, Rules, Cambridge: Cambridge University Press for the ICRC, 2005, reprinted with corrections, 2009, p. *xxxiv*.

29. Jessica Lincoln, *Transitional Justice, Peace and Accountability Outreach and the Role of International Courts After Conflict*, London: Routledge, 2011.

30. The limited scholarly research to underpin what remain largely impressionistic views—though not necessarily misplaced ones—has mostly concentrated on the former Yugoslavia, particularly Bosnia and Hercegovina. By focusing on wider developments, such as institutional development, rather than merely popular values and attitudes, Lara Nettlefield has offered a more nuanced view of the Hague Tribunal's impact on Bosnia and Hercegovina; based on strong research, she concludes that judging the Tribunal's effects in the country as 'at best ineffective' is not supported by her rich, mixed-methodology research,

which finds that 'the court's work has indeed aided processes of democratisation in numerous ways'. Lara J. Nettlefield, *Courting Democracy in Bosnia and Herzegovina: the Hague Tribunal's Impact in Postwar State*, New York: Cambridge University Press, 2010, p. 273. See also: Eric Stover, *The Witnesses: War Crimes and The Promise of Justice in The Hague*, Philadelphia: University of Pennsylvania Press, 2005; Stover, and Harvey M. Weinstein, eds, *My Neighbor, My Enemy: Justice and Community in the Aftermath of Mass Atrocity*, Cambridge: Cambridge University Press, 2205.

31. An anonymous ICC official, quoted in *The New York Times*, 21 March 2012; *Situation in the Democratic Republic of the Congo in the Case of the Prosecutor v. Thomas Lubanga Dyilo, Public, Judgment pursuant to Article 74 of the Statute* ICC-01/04–01/06, 14 March 2012.

32. *The Daily Telegraph*, 14 March 2012.

33. Guglielmo Verdirame, 'Human Rights in Wartime: A Framework for Analysis', *European Human Rights Law Review*, No. 6, 2008, p. 689.

34. *Ibid.*, p. 690.

35. *Ibid.*, p. 694.

36. *Ibid.*, p. 693.

37. *Ibid.*, p. 703.

38. Quoted in *The Herald*, 19 May 2011, as reprinted in *The Scottish Law Reporter*, 19 May 2011, p. 2.

39. *ITN*, 18 May 2009; *The Daily Telegraph*, 19 May 2009.

40. The Appeals Court ruling compounded other recent problems for the British defence establishment. On 13 May 2009, the National Audit Office (NAO) issued a report stating that no more than 57 per cent of equipment supplied for troops in Iraq was getting to them when scheduled, and that some items acquired under the Urgent Operations Requirements provision, such as the Vector armoured vehicle, were inadequate. The Vector had been withdrawn from service in April because of mechanical inadequacies, despite its having been purchased as an urgent replacement for lightly armoured Snatch Land Rovers, which had proved particularly vulnerable to roadside explosive attacks. In addition to the negative operational consequences, the inadequacy of both these vehicles could be the basis for future claims under the HRA. (*The Daily Telegraph* 13 May 2009). On 15 May 2009, the Army Chief of Staff, General Sir Richard Dannatt, who had been outspoken in the past and was blocked from promotion by Prime Minster Gordon Brown because of this, gave a speech vehemently criticising the government for squandering the defence budget on buying the wrong equipment, thus leaving the armed forces to 'muddle through'. This was exactly the kind of situation that might lead to future HRA legal cases based on 'inadequate' provision. (*The Times*, 15 May 2009).

41. As noted in Chapter 4, respondents identified this issue already, raising con-

cerns that coalition action might be significantly impaired as different legal questions, including those of human rights, are raised.

42. *The Times*, 19 May 2009.

43. See, for example, Michael J. Dennis and André M. Surena, 'Application of the International Covenant on Civil and Political Rights in Times of Armed Conflict and Military Occupation: the Gap Between Legal Theory and State Practice', *European Human Rights Law Review*, No. 6, 2008.

44. I am grateful to Vesko Popovski, who brought this development to my attention at a very early stage and later wrote a significant article detailing the cases. Vesselin Popovski, 'Terrorizing Civilians as a "Counter-terrorist Operation": Crimes and Impunity in Chechnya', *Journal of Southeast European and Black Sea Studies*, Vol. 7, No. 3, 2007. See also Philip Leach 'The Chechen Conflict: Analyzing the Oversight of the European Court of Human Rights', *European Human Rights Law Review*, No. 6, 2008.

45. Elspeth Guild, ed., *War or Crime? National Legal Challenges in Europe to the War in Iraq*, Nijmegen: Wolf Legal Publishers, 2009.

46. André Nollkaemper, 'Dual Attribution: Liability of the Netherlands for Removal of Individuals from the Compound of Dutchbat', 8 July 2011, http://www. sharesproject.nl/dual-attribution-liability-of-the-netherlands-for-removal-of-individuals-from-the-compound-of-dutchbat/, accessed at 3 September 2011.

47. *Hamdan v. Rumsfeld* was a key example of this trend. There were two reasons for the relative absence of 'international' language in the US context. One was an American tendency only to consider things 'American' as legitimate and to be sceptical of 'foreign' or 'international' interference, or law. The other, more important—and particularly notable, given the often unfair barbs directed at the US regarding international law—is that the spread of human rights politically and legally, in the twentieth century and beyond, was always driven by powerful US motors. There can be no doubt, for example, that there would be no International Criminal Court had Washington not been the mainspring for it, even if the US had problems once the Treaty had been agreed.

48. James Gow, 'The ICTY, War Crimes Enforcement and Dayton: The Ghost in the Machine', *Ethnopolitics*, Vol. 5, No. 1, 2006.

49. Michael Howard, *War and the Liberal Conscience*, (Oxford: Clarendon, 1979; and *War and the Liberal Conscience*, With a New Introduction, London: Hurst and Co., 2008. It is my conviction that this concise, elegant book should be mandatory reading for everyone.

INDEX

3-block warfare 25, 72, 186
9/11 – see September 11
Abu Ghraib 3, 41, 42, 94, 161
Abuse 3, 4, 7, 8, 10, 14, 16, 41, 42,
 68, 79, 83, 87, 94, 109, 122, 166,
 196
Accountability 89, 90, 139, 162, 165,
 180, 181, 200
Afghanistan 16, 38, 94, 117, 118, 198
Africa 4, 19, 70, 93
Agincourt, Battle of 96
Al-Qa'ida 16, 36, 94, 117, 118, 119,
 120, 121, 122, 133, 135, 190, 196,
 197, 199
Albanians (Kosovo) 82, 98
Alić, Fikret 40
Americas, the 19, 70, 93
Amnesty International 4, 162, 169,
 183, 191
Aquinas, Thomas 15, 161
Armed forces vii, 1, 2
Artillery 4, 16, 86, 87, 92, 93, 97, 99,
 104, 105, 108, 109, 111, 112, 169,
 193
Arts and Humanities Research Coun-
 cil vii, 2, 19
Arusha 84
Asia 19, 70, 93

Attorney General, UK 82, 83
Australasia 19, 93
Australia 56, 181, 198
Axis, the 15

Baghdad 3, 94, 182
Bagram 94
Balkans, the 78, 79
Basra 7, 9, 107, 131, 169, 196
Belgrade vii, 6, 19, 69, 93, 98, 110,
 169, 174, 193
Belligerent reprisal 79, 80, 98
Bible, the 46, 175
Blaškić, Tihomir (Tihofil) 92–3, 104,
 164, 189
Bobbitt, Philip 15, 36, 198
Bosnia and Hercegovina 4, 16, 33,
 39, 40, 41, 56, 62, 63, 104, 105,
 112, 118, 135, 136, 165, 167, 194,
 200, 201
Bosnia War Crimes Court 56, 126, 127
Bosnian Muslims 4
Bosnian Serb Army 63, 98, 110
Bothe, Michael 18
Boyce, Sir Michael 54, 55, 82, 180
Breisach 50, 178
British Army 68, 76, 95, 131, 163,
 164, 169, 185, 201

Brown, Prime Minister Gordon 132, 201

Browne, Des 132

Burck, Gordon viii, 192

Bush, President George W. 27, 116, 117, 123, 171, 210

Center for Interdisciplinary Postgraduate Studies, University of Sarajevo vii, 69, 93

Changing character of warfare – see warfare

Chemical Ali – see Majid, Ali al-'Chemical Ali'

Chemical weapons 80, 139, 195

Chief of the Defence Staff 54, 82, 132, 161

Child soldiers/prisoners 123, 129, 159, 169

China 117

Chisnall, Steve ix

CIA 136

Civil justice 4, 8, 59, 116, 129–33, 139

Civilians vii, 7, 10–12, 16, 68, 85, 91, 93, 95, 99–104, 109, 110, 120–22, 129, 139, 145, 156, 157, 159, 160, 164, 186, 195, 196, 197

Clausewitz, Carl von 1, 20, 23, 26, 28, 29, 32, 36, 37, 115, 134, 136, 137, 171, 174

Cluster munitions 4, 21, 93, 98–104, 113, 138, 139, 192, 193

Cluster Munitions Treaty – see Convention on Cluster Munitions

Coalition 7, 35, 36, 38, 74, 107, 117, 182

Cockburn, Jocelyn 130, 132

Cold War 2, 25, 26, 27, 54, 56, 57, 60, 94, 116, 124, 125, 127, 128

Collins, Tim 76, 187

Combatants 119, 121–2, 195, 197

Commanding Officer – CO 64, 75, 81, 88, 106, 112

Common Article 3 – see Geneva Conventions Common Article 3

Conduct of warfare – see warfare

Contemporary warfare – see warfare

Convention on Cluster Munitions 139, 193

Conventional warfare – see warfare

Court of Appeal, UK 131, 132, 201

Crane, David 128

Creveld, Martin van 26

Crimes Against Humanity 4, 10, 11, 16, 42, 49, 51–3, 61, 63–4, 104, 127, 178, 184, 185, 186

Croatia 92, 104, 111, 112, 194

Croatian Army 111

Cuba 118

Cumberland 51

Customary international law 46, 48, 49, 50, 51, 60, 61, 66, 120, 123, 139, 177, 183, 184

Daily Telegraph, The 76

Dandeker, Christopher ix, 174

Danspeckgrüber, Wolfgang ix

Democratic Republic of Congo (DRC) 129

Detainees 7, 8, 118, 121–2

Deuteronomy 46, 175

Diana, Princess of Wales 80

Dijxhoorn, Ernst ix, 170

Disproportionate 4, 16, 65, 92, 93, 104, 106–7, 112, 189, 194

Dixon, Rodney ix

Doenitz, Karl 53

Donne, John 117

DRC – see Democratic Republic of Congo

Dresden 11–12

Drone attacks 41

East Timor 126

East Timor Serious Crimes Unit 126
Eastern Front (Second World War) 79
Economic and Social Research Council viii, 2, 19
Edmonds, Martin ix, 1
England 5, 51, 187
English and Welsh law 82, 187
Eritrea 117
Ethics viii, 3–5, 9, 11, 12, 14, 15, 16, 18, 30, 40, 42–3, 45, 48, 53, 65–7, 69–71, 74–81, 89–90, 91–2, 95–6, 97, 101, 103, 104, 105, 116, 117, 124, 133–7, 140–1, 161, 179
Ethiopia 117
Europe 51, 82, 133, 199
European Convention on Human Rights 64, 65, 199, 121; Article 2 65, 121
European Court of Human Rights 64, 65, 133
European Union (EU) 127, 199
Extraordinary Chambers in the Courts of Cambodia 56, 58, 126

Fallujah 17–18
Fenrick, William vii, ix, 122, 164, 191, 192, 193, 195, 196
Film – see visual material and war crimes
First Queen's Lancashire Regiment (1st QLR) 7–8, 163
First World War 51
Force Protection 95–101, 105–108, 195
Fourth Generation Warfare 25
France 51, 52
Freedman, Sir Lawrence ix, 1, 25–6
Frost, Mervyn ix

Galić, Stanislav 104–6, 110, 112, 169, 194
Gas, use of 10, 80

Geneva Convention of 1864 47, 48
Geneva Convention of 1929 48
Geneva Conventions of 1949 47–9, 61, 66, 89, 95, 97, 99, 119–23, 185, 197–8; Common Article 3 48, 49, 61, 193, 195; Geneva Convention of 1949 III 95, 119, 121, 198; Geneva Convention of 1949 IV 109, 121, 197, 198; Additional Protocols 48–9, 61, 66, 197; Additional Protocol II 1977 48–9, 61, 197
Genocide 4, 16, 47, 48, 51, 52, 73, 74, 125, 177, 185, 195, 200
Genocide Convention, 1948 47, 48
Germany 10, 14, 51–4, 128
German troops 78
Gillespie, Marie ix, 2
Global War on Terror 3, 26, 36, 116, 117, 119–21, 197, 199
Goebels, Joseph 168
Goerring, Hermann 53
Gonzales, Alberto 200
Goražde 39
Gotovina, Ante 111–12, 194
Gowan, David ix
Grayling, A.C. 10–14, 167
Guantanamo 3, 82, 94, 118, 120, 123, 128, 198; Camp Delta 122; Camp X-ray 122

Hagenbach, Peter von 50
Hague Conventions, the 47, 49, 52, 95; 1899 47, 49, 129; 1907 10, 47, 95
Hague, The vii, 7, 59, 60, 62, 84, 129, 194, 200
Hamburg 20–1
Hammes, Thomas G. 25
Harris, Arthur 'Bomber' 13
Hearts and minds 5, 17, 36, 175, 186
High Court, UK 131

INDEX

Hiroshima 13, 167

Hizbollah 118

Holocaust, the 10, 51

Holy Roman Empire 50

Honig, Jan Willem ix, 1

Hoskins, Andrew ix, 2

House of Lords 131

Howard, Sir Michael ix, 1, 2, 138

Human Rights Act (2000), UK 131, 132

Human rights vii, 4, 16, 18, 47, 57, 58, 59, 64, 65, 67, 72, 89, 95, 98, 100, 111, 122, 128, 130, 131, 132, 133, 134, 137, 139, 140, 166, 192, 198, 199, 202

Human Rights Watch 4, 98, 100, 122, 192

Humanitarian Law Center, Belgrade vii, 6, 69, 93

Humanitarian Law Center, Pristina vii

Hussein, Saddam 125, 135, 195

Hutton, John 133

Hybrid courts 56, 126, 136, 170, 182

Hybrid war 25

Images – see visual material and war crimes

Indiscriminate 14, 92–3, 99, 101, 103, 104, 111–2, 192, 193, 194

Inge, (Peter) Lord 15, 17, 167

Intelligence 30–1, 111, 129

International Committee of the Red Cross/the Red Crescent 47, 122–3, 176–7, 197, 199–200

International Criminal Court 3, 7, 9, 46, 50, 54, 56, 58, 60–1, 63, 67, 82, 125, 126, 128, 129, 180, 183, 184, 185; Rome Statute of 3, 7, 50, 55, 58, 61–3, 125, 126, 180, 183, 184, 185

International Criminal Court Act, UK 7, 8, 54–5, 67, 82, 185, 187

International Criminal Law 54–66

International Criminal Tribunal for Rwanda – ICTR 46, 55, 58, 60, 61–3, 125–6, 181, 184, 185; Statute 61–3, 184; Statute Article 4 61

International Criminal Tribunal for the former Yugoslavia – ICTY vii, 4, 6, 16, 46, 55, 56, 57, 58, 59–61, 63, 92, 99, 125, 126, 127, 128, 139, 165, 167, 168, 169, 181, 183, 184, 189, 191, 192, 193–4, 196, 200; Appeals Chamber, ICTY 61, 62, 92, 128, 194; Statute 56, 61, 62, 63, 125; Article 2 61; Article 3 61; Article 5 63

International Military Tribunal, Nuremberg 10–13, 51–54, 59, 63, 95, 127, 166, 169, 180, 187

International Military Tribunal, Tokyo 51, 52, 54, 58, 59, 169

IRA – Irish Republican Army 119

Iran 94, 118

Iranian Revolutionary Guard 94

Iraq 2, 3, 4, 7–8, 14, 16, 26, 27, 38, 41, 48, 56, 58, 71, 73, 75, 78, 82–3, 87, 94, 103, 126, 127, 131, 132, 133, 163, 164, 167, 168, 171, 180, 182, 195, 201

Iraqi High Tribunal 56, 58, 126, 127

Jackson, Sir Michael 132

Japan 11, 54

Jews 53

Joint Services Command and Staff College viii, 19, 68, 69, 93

Jomini, Antoine-Henri 32

Judge Advocate 8

Just war theory 2, 15, 17–18, 45, 48, 65, 69, 71, 80, 98, 136, 161, 167; *jus ad bellum* 3, 17–18, 48, 51, 98, 136, 161; *jus in bello* 3, 17–18, 48, 71, 98, 136, 161

INDEX

Kaldor, Mary 26
Kampala Review Conference on the Rome Statute of the International Criminal Court 2010 50, 180
Kandić, Nataša 6
Karadžić, Ljiljana 200
Karadžić, Radovan 200
Kellog-Briand Pact, 1928 52
Kerr, Rachel ix, 2, 170
KFOR 82, 99
Khan, Inara ix, 160
Khmer Rouge 127
Kinetic force 25, 27, 29, 31, 35
King Edward I 50–1, 178
King Henry V 5, 96, 200
King Henry V 5, 96, 200
Knin 112
Kopf, David 10–11
Kosovo 4, 16, 58, 71, 82, 98–102, 103–4, 132, 136, 139, 167, 182, 193
Krstić, Radislav 62, 63, 169
Krulak, Charles 38, 186
Kuwait 14, 48

Land mines 80
Lane, Ann ix, 170
Leadership 87, 134
Legitimacy 2, 3, 15–17, 20, 21, 23, 24, 26, 29, 33–43, 71–4, 85, 113, 116, 118, 123, 134–7, 138, 140, 174, 175, 199
Leipzig 51
Liberia 4, 60, 181, 183
Libya 6, 68, 103, 129, 186
Liddell-Hart, Basil 32
Lieber Code, the 47, 176, 190
Lind, William S. 25
Ljutić, Gojko 111–12
London Charter of the International Military Tribunal 49, 51–2
London Conference, 1944 51

London Submarine Protocol, 1936 53
Lubanga, Thomas 129

MacArthur, Douglas 54
MacKinnon, Justice 8
Majid, Ali al- – 'Chemical Ali' 107, 195
Marines 8, 75, 94
Markusen, Eric 10–11
Massacre 4, 5, 10, 12, 13, 16, 41, 46, 47, 53, 62, 91, 92, 125, 127, 166
Mauritania 129
Media (news) 4, 5, 16, 59, 67, 73, 76, 86, 89, 109, 137, 178, 193
Michalski, Milena ix, 170
Middle East 70, 93
Military ethos 73, 89, 102, 105, 140
Military professionalism vii, 8, 18, 21, 25, 66, 68, 69, 71, 73, 76, 80, 89, 92, 96, 100, 110, 113, 116, 132, 135, 138–40, 169, 178, 193, 195
Milošević, Slobodan 6, 62, 99, 125, 127, 163, 167
Ministry of Defence, UK – MoD 131–2, 161
Mladić, Ratko 4, 124–5, 127
Mohammed, Sheik Khalid 121, 198
Mousa, Baha 7–9, 55, 163
Müllerson, Rein ix
Multidimensional Trinity Cubed (Plus) – see *Trinity³(+)*
Multiple launch rocket system – MLRS 86

Nagasaki 13, 167
Napoleon 25, 27, 32, 171
NATO 4, 71, 82, 98–9, 103, 129, 139, 167, 186, 192, 193
Naumann, Klaus 15, 167
Naval warfare 86, 139
Nazis 10–12, 14, 47, 51, 54, 60, 125, 127, 166, 168

INDEX

NBC 8
Netherlands Court of Appeal, the 4
Netherlands, the 4, 75, 133
Newton, Paul ix
Nice, Sir Geoffrey ix, 6
Niš 99–100, 103–4, 192
Non-international armed conflict 47–9, 58, 61, 121
Non-war, definition 65, 118, 120, 124, 196
Northern Ireland 82, 119, 187
Northern Irish law 82, 187
Northumberland 51
Nuhanović and Mustafić v. The Netherlands 75, 133
Nuhanović, Hasan 75, 133
Nullum crimen sine lege 52–3, 166
Nuremberg 10, 11, 12, 13, 47, 49, 51–4, 58, 59, 63, 95, 127, 166, 180, 187
Nye, Joseph P. 26

O'Loughlin, Ben ix, 170
Obama, President Barrack 117, 123, 198, 199
Old Testament, the 46
Oluja, Operation 111–12
Operational logs 85, 96, 110, 111

Pajić, Zoran ix, 170
Pakistan 125
Payne, Donald 7–9, 55, 163
Peace Support Operations, PSO 33–4, 72, 78, 174
Persecution 63, 64
Poland 14
Post-Clausewitzian warfare 26
Post-Cold War 60, 127, 128
Prisoners of war 5, 21, 41, 92–98, 118, 119, 121–3, 139, 190, 198; quasi-prisoners of war 119, 122, 198; see also 'non-war'

Pristina viii, 19
Project Clarion 11
Proportionality 4, 16, 18, 45, 64, 65, 68–9, 73, 81, 87, 92–3, 95–6, 104–7, 112, 123, 130, 134, 139, 189, 193, 194, 195
Protected persons 61, 109, 120–1, 123, 131

Qadaffi, Muammar 103, 129, 186
Qadaffi, Saif 129

R. v. Payne and others 7–9, 55, 163
Raeder, Eric 53
Red cross 47, 109, 110, 197, 199–200 (see also International Committee of the Red Cross/Red Crescent – ICRC)
Rome 3, 7, 50, 55, 61, 62, 63, 125, 126, 183
Roscini, Marco 17, 166, 193, 195
Royal Air Force 13, 68, 194
Royal College of Defence Studies viii, 19, 69, 193
Royal Marines 194
Royal Navy 194
Rules of engagement, ROE 74–6, 78, 87, 164. 180, 192
Ruxton, Gavin ix, 178, 181
Rwanda 46, 55, 58, 60–3, 125–6, 181

Sands, Bobby 119
Sanussi, Abdullah al 129
Sarajevo viii, 39, 69, 93, 104, 105, 112, 169
Schrag, Minna ix, 183
Scorpions (Serbian Security Service Unit) 6, 163
Scotland 40, 131, 132, 178
Scottish law 82, 187
Second World War 10, 14, 46, 47, 49, 51, 53, 59, 60, 66, 74, 79, 95, 97,

127, 128, 168; Allies 12, 51, 53, 54, 60, 167, 168

Secretary of State for Defence 131–2, 163

Secretary of State for Scotland 132

Self-defence 34, 48, 72, 82, 118, 166

September 11 82, 163, 197, 199

Serbia 4, 6, 7, 62, 92, 98, 103, 104, 105, 110–12, 118, 135, 139, 163

Serbian military 4, 6, 92, 98, 103, 104, 105, 110–12, 163, 184

Serbian MUP 6

Shakespeare, William 5, 190

Shepherd, Robert ix

Siege 93, 104–13

Sierra Leone 4, 46, 56, 58, 60, 126, 128, 136, 181, 182, 183

Sites, Kevin 8

Smith, Bradley F., 11–13, 179, 187

Smith, Catherine 131–2

Smith, Jason 131–2

Smith, Sir Rupert 15, 17, 35, 37, 77, 173, 195

Socialist Federative Republic of Yugo-slavia – see Yugoslavia

Soviet Union, the 51, 52, 79, 166

Special Court for Sierra Leone 46, 56, 58, 60, 126, 128, 136, 181, 182, 183; Appeals Chamber, SCSL 181

Special Military Commissions 121, 128, 198

Special Operations Executive SOE 97, 190

Special Tribunal for Lebanon 56, 126

Spence, Jack ix

Srebrenica 4, 6, 9, 39, 41, 42, 52, 62, 75

St. Augustine 15, 161

Stevanović, Obrad 6

Strategic coherence 32–3, 39, 40

Strategic initiative 33–4, 39

Strategy 1–43, 66, 67–90, 109, 112,

113, 120, 124, 134, 136, 137, 138, 140, 171, 172, 173, 194

Submarine warfare 53, 139

Success (strategic) 5, 16, 20–24, 27, 29, 30, 31, 32, 33–43 *passim.*, 47, 76, 97, 111, 113, 116, 129, 132, 134–7, 138, 168, 172

Sun Tzu 31, 175

Šušak, Gojko 111

Syria 118

Taliban 118, 122, 198

Targeted killings 94, 118, 197

Targeting 11, 13, 17, 71, 86–7, 92–3, 99, 100, 102–4, 107–8, 110–2, 115, 119, 122, 189, 193, 195

Taylor, Charles 60, 136, 181, 183

Taylor, Telford 10, 95

Terrorism 82, 116–19, 196

Total war – see war

Transnational communities 3, 35, 36, 38, 118–20, 134, 178, 197–8, 199

Treaty law 48, 49, 52, 54, 55, 58, 104, 123, 126, 176, 193, 202

Trinity (Clausewitz) 20, 23–7, 36–9, 136, 171

Trinity³(+) viii, 20, 21, 23–43, 66, 68, 116, 132, 134–6, 138

Trnopolje 40

Tudjman, Franjo 111

Twin Towers, the – see World Trade Center

UK Defence Academy ix

United Kingdom 7, 19, 42, 51, 54–6, 64, 66, 67, 69, 82, 93, 94, 95, 100, 101, 102–3, 119, 130, 131–3, 163, 169, 180, 182, 184, 187, 192, 197, 198, 199

United Kingdom Government 3, 169, 201

United Kingdom Parliament 68, 119, 132, 199

United Nations vii, 4, 33, 47, 48, 55, 56, 58, 59, 125, 126, 127, 130, 135, 166, 181, 182

United Nations Charter 48, 55, 57, 126, 130, 181, 182; Article 2(7) 57, 182; Article 51 48; Chapter VII 33, 48, 55–7, 126, 181

United Nations General Assembly 59

United Nations Security Council 33, 48, 55, 56, 57, 58, 59, 125, 126, 181, 182

United Nations Security Council Resolution 827 56

United Nations Security Council Summit of Heads of State and Government, January 1992 57

United States 3, 8, 11, 27, 38, 41, 47, 51, 53, 54, 60, 75, 82, 94, 100, 102, 108, 112, 116, 117, 118–22, 133, 136, 161, 176, 182, 186, 190, 191, 192, 193, 195, 196, 197, 198, 199, 202

United States Administration 117, 123, 198–9, 200

United States Constitution 121

United States Department of Justice 189, 198

United States Supreme Court 121

Unites States Air Force 11, 191

Unites States Marines 8, 38, 75, 186

Universal jurisdiction 50, 56

Unlawful attack vii, 92–3, 100, 104, 109, 112, 122, 124, 130, 189, 193

Unlawful combatant 121, 123, 197, 200

Unprivileged belligerent 123, 200

Use of force 1–3, 14, 15, 17, 25–43 passim., 45, 48, 64, 65, 75, 85, 109, 113, 134–5, 136, 137

USS Abraham Lincoln 27, 171

Verdirame, Guglielmo 65, 130

Victor's justice 53, 60, 180

Victory 2, 25–7, 31, 36, 37, 51, 111, 134, 168, 171

Visual material and war crimes 6, 8, 9, 15, 37, 40, 41–2, 75, 163, 164, 168, 183

Vukušić, Iva ix

Wales 178–9, 197

Walker, Andrew 131

Wallace, William 50–1, 178

Walzer, Michael 13, 161, 167

War – definition 1–2, 17, 137–8; total war 12–4, 25, 187 – see also non-war, defintion

War Crimes – definition in relation to war 3, 17, 137–8

War Crimes Act, 1990, UK 56

War Crimes Act, Australia 56

War Crimes Research Group, King's College London ix, 19, 93

War criminals 8, 11, 50, 51, 52, 55, 62, 63, 104, 106, 112, 123, 124, 127, 197, 194, 195

Warfare 2–4, 12–18 passim., 20–28 passim., 29, 32, 33–43, 54, 46, 51, 53, 64–6, 67, 69, 73, 78, 80, 85, 89–90, 91, 93, 94, 106, 112–113, 115–120 passim., 123, 124, 129, 133, 134, 137–141, 161, 162, 166, 168, 171, 175, 193, 195; Changing character of war 2–4, 6, 14, 16–19, 23–8, 37–42, 66, 70–74, 76, 78–9, 81, 83, 89, 98, 103, 116–20, 123, 129–30, 134, 137, 162, 184, 197, 200; Conduct of warfare vii, 2–4, 10, 13, 15–17, 23, 30–1, 37, 40, 42–3, 46, 47–51, 54, 59, 70–3, 77, 89, 91–113 passim, 117, 120, 122, 124, 129–30, 133, 135, 136, 137, 139, 140, 161, 186, 197, 210; contemporary warfare 2, 3, 5, 9, 15,

17, 18, 20, 21, 23, 24–8, 29, 30,
33–6, 38, 40, 42, 43, 47, 48, 64,
66, 73, 74, 77, 78 85, 87, 88, 91,
93, 94, 96, 97, 98, 100, 113, 115,
116, 117, 121, 134, 137, 138, 139,
140, 168, 175, 195; conventional
warfare 3, 4, 6, 29, 37, 38, 67, 119
– see also 3-block war
Washington 3, 191, 192, 202
West, the 4, 14, 15, 16, 28, 46, 47,
53, 54, 60, 68, 71, 74, 94, 113,
116, 123, 133, 161, 167, 195, 197

Westmorland 51
Whetham, David ix
Wittgenstein, Ludwig 84
World Trade Center, the 41

Yoo, John 189, 198–9
Yugoslav war, the 4, 57, 125, 167, 173
Yugoslavia vii, 55, 97, 190, 193, 200

Živković, Zoran 99
Zrnić, Bojan ix
Zveržhanovski, Ivan ix, 170